"Dr. Collins has presented a careful defense of Adam and Eve. This methodologically rigorous st of contemporary discussions on both biblical a further contributes to the wider discussion on science and religion. Perhaps more importantly, he has successfully demonstrated the theological significance of this traditional reading, all the while using language that an informed layperson can digest and engage. This work deserves to be widely circulated."

David W. Pao, Chair of the New Testament Department, Trinity Evangelical Divinity School

"Working through questions of myth and history, Bible and science, harmonization and complementarity, Collins brings fresh arguments to stimulate wide-ranging thought and improved appreciation of the way the first chapters of the Bible affect the whole."

Alan Millard, Emeritus Rankin Professor of Hebrew and Ancient Semitic Languages, The University of Liverpool

"I could hardly imagine a more *honest* book on this controversial topic. Its openness (in a user-friendly format) is no naivety—it is combined with undeniable *competence* on the ancient Near East, recent literature, and methodological discussions. Standing firm on vital issues, accepting diversity on others, the reader meets in C. John Collins a sensitive and *godly* guide."

Henri A. Blocher, formerly Gunther Knoedler Professor of Systematic Theology, Wheaton College Graduate School

"Few scholars are better equipped than Professor C. John Collins to provide a well-informed, up-to-date assessment of what may and may not be known about Adam and Eve. With clarity, Collins offers a balanced discussion of the relationship between Genesis 2–3 and current theories on the origins of the human race. Recognizing the limitations of human knowledge, he highlights the vital contribution made by the Genesis account for understanding the human predicament. Marked by both erudition and sanity, here is a book worth reading."

T. Desmond Alexander, Senior Lecturer in Biblical Studies and Director of Postgraduate Studies, Union Theological College, Belfast

"Collins has done a great service to the church by providing us with this crucial volume. It will quickly prove to be a vital resource for pastors, students, and laypeople around the world. With careful scientific analysis and convincing biblical exegesis, Collins graciously answers the skeptics and thoroughly reinforces the historic Judeo-Christian position."

Burk Parsons, Associate Pastor, Saint Andrew's Chapel, Sanford, Florida; editor, *Tabletalk* magazine

"In a sense, the way one reads the first few chapters of Genesis will determine his or her way of reading the whole Bible. Dr. Collins has expounded in a lucid manner how the original narrator intended this vital part of the Bible to be read. Cogency combines with erudition to make this book worthy of appreciation by those who do not espouse his general stance, as well as by readers who may be unaware of their own premises."

Nobuyoshi Kiuchi, Professor of Old Testament, Tokyo Christian University

"This book will boost your confidence in the Bible, especially in its capacity to address a common experience of all peoples. By treating the Bible as Scripture, Collins has modeled for us how Christians should approach the faith-science questions. The Bible has answers to the human predicaments and needs. Only if what it says is true can we truly make sense and move forward in this sinful world. The real payoff of this book goes beyond the unequivocal biblical witness of Adam and Eve's historical existence. For it is the human dignity based on our common ancestry and a shared perception of sensing the abnormality of this world that open a way for the redemption and restoration of all peoples through the *real* life and works of the second Adam."

Natee Tanchanpongs, Academic Dean, Bangkok Bible Seminary

"I commend this book merely for the courage of taking the adventure in addressing this debated issue both biblically and scientifically. Even if the reader does not fully agree with Collins's conclusions he/she is compelled to listen carefully to his arguments."

Riad A. Kassis, Regional Director, Overseas Council for Middle East, North Africa, and Central Europe; adjunct professor of Old Testament, Arab Baptist Theological Seminary, Lebanon

"It is not often that a book in this controversial field of human origins takes seriously both the Bible (in terms of textual exegesis, literary form, and theological coherence) and science (in terms of its findings and its theoretical possibilities). Jack Collins does both with graciously applied scholarship, conviction, and humility, making very clear where biblical faithfulness requires us to be uncompromisingly affirmative, and where there is room for varying opinion over possible scenarios that could be consistent with such biblical conviction."

Christopher J. H. Wright, International Director, Langham Partnership International; author, *The Mission of God*

Did Adam and Eve really exist?

C. John Collins

Did Adam and Eve really exist?

Who they were and why it matters

ivp

INTER-VARSITY PRESS
Norton Street, Nottingham NG7 3HR, England
Email: ivp@ivpbooks.com
Website: www.ivpbooks.com

Published by Crossway Books, a publishing ministry of Good News Publishers,
Wheaton, Illinois 60187, USA. This edition published by arrangement with
Good News Publishers. All rights reserved.

First published 2011

British Library Cataloguing in Publication Data
A catalogue record for this book is available from the British Library.

ISBN: 978-1-84474-525-8

Typeset in the United States of America
Printed and bound in Great Britain by Ashford Colour Press Ltd, Gosport,
Hampshire

Inter-Varsity Press publishes Christian books that are true to the Bible and that
communicate the gospel, develop discipleship and strengthen the church for its
mission in the world.

Inter-Varsity Press is closely linked with the Universities and Colleges Christian
Fellowship, a student movement connecting Christian Unions in universities and
colleges throughout Great Britain, and a member movement of the International
Fellowship of Evangelical Students. Website: www.uccf.org.uk

CONTENTS

ACKNOWLEDGMENTS 9

1. INTRODUCTION 11

2. THE SHAPE OF THE BIBLICAL STORY 23
2.a Story and Worldview 23
2.b History, Myth, and Worldview Story 28
2.c Features of the Biblical Story 41

3. PARTICULAR TEXTS THAT SPEAK OF ADAM AND EVE 51
3.a Genesis 1–5 52
3.b Adam, Eve, Eden, and the Fall in the Rest of the Old
Testament 66
3.c Second Temple Jewish Literature 72
3.d The Gospels 76
3.e The Pauline Writings 78
3.f Elsewhere in the New Testament 90

4. HUMAN UNIQUENESS AND DIGNITY 93
4.a The Image of God 93
4.b Universal Human Experiences: Yearning for Justice,
Need for God 100

5. Can Science Help Us Pinpoint "Adam and Eve"?   105

   5.a   *Does the Bible Connect to History and Science?*

        The Problem of "Concordism"   106

   5.b   *Making Sure We Read the Bible Well*   111

   5.c   *Criteria for Good Scenarios*   116

   5.d   *A Sampling of Scenarios Examined*   121

6. Conclusions   133

   6.a   *What I Think I Have Shown*   133

   6.b   *Why I Think It Matters*   133

   6.c   *A Concluding (and Unacademic) Anecdote:*

        How to Grieve   135

Appendices

   1.   *Ancient Near Eastern Texts and Genesis 1–11*   137

   2.   *Review of James Barr,* The Garden of Eden

       and the Hope of Immortality   161

   3.   *The Date of Genesis*   167

Bibliography   171

General Index   183

Scripture and Apocrypha Index   189

ACKNOWLEDGMENTS

This is not a book I ever took it upon myself to write. The way this project developed is evidence to me of how God shows his providential care by way of the people he brings across our paths.

The project began as an invited paper for the American Scientific Affiliation, of which I am a member. In its August 2009 meeting, the society had a forum on human origins. I thank Walter Bradley of Baylor University for inviting me, and Loren Haarsma of Calvin College for moderating. My conversation partners, Daniel Harlow and John Schneider, also of Calvin College, each provided a thought-provoking case for the "other side." Many who attended the forum offered helpful questions, critique, and advice; if I single out Dennis Venema, Denis Lamoureux, Terry Gray, and Arie Leegwater, I mean no dishonor to anyone else.

I have benefited from suggestions and help from a number of friends and colleagues, including John Bloom, Fazale Rana, Vern Poythress, John West, and Dick Fischer. And then I think of the people who actually read this manuscript at various stages and commented on it: Dr. Hans Madueme, Dr. Arend Poelarends, Diane Collins, Joy Collins, Ransom Poythress, and Cheryl Eaton. My goodness, how thankful I am that I do not have to go it alone!

The faculty and administration of Covenant Theological Seminary, where I have taught since 1993, constantly make it a privilege to work here. The President, Bryan Chapell, is steadfast in his friendship and advice, and the Dean of Faculty, Mark Dalbey, has always been supportive—even when this became my unplanned "sabbatical project"! Among my faculty colleagues, I especially thank Mike Williams, Jerram Barrs, Greg Perry, Jay Sklar, Nelson Jennings, Jimmy Agan, Dan Zink, and Dan Kim, who have always given me help and encouragement when I needed it.

Of course I don't imply for a second that all (or even *any*!) of these people agree with everything I have written here! Often their help has come in the form of "iron sharpening iron" (Prov. 27:17), what the late Derek Kidner calls "the healthy clash of personalities or views." I know the blessing of which he speaks: "A true friendship should have both elements, the reassuring and the bracing."[1]

And I have other friends who have chipped in, in so many different ways: Ed and Jenny Savage, Sarah (Savage) Joseph, Susan Thomas, and Vi Coulter come readily to mind. And I am especially grateful to Jim and Jackie Swinnie (and their son Jimmy), and to Josh and Bryonie Moon, for making me and my family part of very personal things.

Clarence Oddbody once reminded George Bailey, "No man is a failure who has friends." I have those, and much more. God said about Adam, "it is not good that the man should be alone," and went on to make him just the right helper. So too he has given me just the right companion, and I am "the happy husband of a good wife," the woman who makes my heart glad and keeps my face cheerful (Sir. 26:1–4). And my "children are a heritage from the LORD," and I am blessed indeed (Ps. 127:3; 128:4). The Maker of heaven and earth is good beyond measure!

<hr>

[1] Derek Kidner, *Proverbs*, Tyndale Old Testament Commentary (Leicester, U.K.: Inter-Varsity Press, 1964), 45.

1

INTRODUCTION

Through most of the church's history Christians, like the Jews from whom they sprang, have believed that the Biblical Adam and Eve were actual persons, from whom all other human beings are descended, and whose disobedience to God brought sin into human experience. Educated Western Christians today probably do not grant much weight to this historical consensus: after all, they may reason, for much of the church's history most Christians thought that creation took place in the recent past over the course of six calendar days, and even that the earth was the physical center of the universe. I agree with those who argue that we do not change the basic content of Christianity if we revise these views, even when the revisions are drastic. As I see it, effective revisions are the ones that result from a closer reading of the Bible itself—that is, when after further review (as the football referees say) many scholars no longer think that the Bible "teaches" such things. Well, then: May we not study the Bible more closely and revise the traditional understanding of Adam and Eve as well, without threat to the faith?

What reasons might lead someone to abandon belief in a real Adam and Eve? Of course, different people will be moved by different factors. For example, some theologians and philosophers think it is impossible that you and I could be affected at our deepest level by anything done long ago. Or, there is the fact that the themes in Genesis parallel themes that we find in stories from other ancient Near Eastern cultures; this leads some theologians to conclude that Genesis is just as "mythical" in its intentions and meanings as these other stories are. Recent advances in biology seem to push us further away from any idea of an original human couple through whom sin and death came into the world. The evolutionary history of mankind shows us that death and struggle have been part of existence on earth from the earliest moments. Most recently, discoveries about the features of human DNA seem to require that the human population has always had at least as many as a thousand members.

One factor that allows these appeals to the biological sciences to get serious attention from traditionally minded theologians is the work of Francis Collins, the Christian biologist who led the Human Genome Project to a successful conclusion. Collins has written about how his faith relates to his scientific discipline, advocating a kind of theistic evolution that he calls the "Biologos" perspective.[1] Collins agrees with those biologists who contend that traditional beliefs about Adam and Eve are no longer viable.

A colleague of mine, a specialist in studying world mission, assures me that most contemporary Christians around the world still hold to the traditional perspective on Adam and Eve. They have this perspective in common, for all their disagreements on such questions as how long ago the first couple lived, or on how their sin and guilt are transmitted to us their children. Again, educated Westerners might not find this "consensus" particularly compelling; but the fact that there is a worldwide church, as I shall argue, should help to make the traditional position appealing to us.

---

[1]Francis Collins, *The Language of God: A Scientist Presents Evidence for Belief* (New York: Free Press, 2006). Collins and others have established the Biologos Foundation, with a Web site (biologos.org).

My goal in this study is to show why I believe we should retain a version of the traditional view, in spite of any pressures to abandon it. I intend to argue that the traditional position on Adam and Eve, or some variation of it, does the best job of accounting not only for the Biblical materials but also for our everyday experience as human beings—an experience that includes sin as something that must be forgiven (by God and our fellow human beings) and that must be struggled against as defiling and disrupting a good human life.

We will look first at the shape of the Biblical story—from creation to fall to redemption and final consummation—and the worldview that rides on that story, and see whether it requires an historical Adam and Eve and an historical fall. Second, we will examine the main Biblical and Second Temple Jewish texts that deal with the topic, to find out whether they really do support the traditional position. Third, we will consider the Biblical view of human uniqueness and dignity, and relate these to everyday moral and religious experience, asking whether these too are evidence for the traditional position.

Back in 1941, during the dark early days of the Second World War, C. S. Lewis began a series of broadcast talks aimed at defending Christian faith. He determined as much as possible to stay within the bounds of "mere Christianity"—a term he attributed to the great English Puritan pastor Richard Baxter (1615–1691).[2] His goal was to focus on the core of Christianity that was common to all traditional Christian denominations. In my admiration for Lewis's model, I both will make "mere Christianity" my stance throughout this book and will christen the position I am arguing for here "mere historical Adam-and-Eve-ism"—a much less elegant title than Lewis's, with no distinguished Englishman as its coiner. That is, I am not entering here into distinctions between various Christian positions on such topics as: the origin of the material for Adam's body, or how long ago he lived; the meaning of "the image of God"; how the sin of Adam and Eve comes to affect us; the process by which Genesis 1–2 came

---

[2] C. S. Lewis, in *Mere Christianity*, describes his approach in the preface. The book has been published in many editions; my copy is the 1952 edition published by Geoffrey Bles in London.

to be part of the same book.[3] In fact, even though I will give some critical examination to some of the specific views that Francis Collins presents, I am not at this point offering a critique of the Biologos perspective as a whole. Although all of these topics are indeed important matters, worthy of deep discussion, I do not consider agreement on them to be crucial for the traditional view I am advocating here. Keeping to this plan, I will finish my argument with a description of some sample scenarios for a scientific understanding of human origins; I will evaluate these scenarios for how true or untrue they are to "mere historical Adam-and-Eve-ism": I am not endorsing any one scenario, but seeking to explore how the traditional position might relate to questions of paleoanthropology.

I recognize that for some, simply establishing that Bible writers thought a certain way is enough to persuade them; that is how Biblical authority functions for them.[4] However, I do not assume that approach here: some may agree that a Bible writer "thought" a certain way, but disagree that the writer's way of thinking is crucial to the Bible's argument—in which case we need not follow that way of thinking. Others might even agree with me about the Bible writer's thoughts, and the place of those thoughts in the argument, but suggest that the writer speaks as a child of his time.[5] Therefore I need to examine the arguments of the Biblical writers, and to see whether their arguments do the best job of explaining the world we all encounter.

Obviously I am writing this book as a Christian: why else would I put any stress on what Biblical writers thought and how the Biblical

---

[3]Lewis made it clear that his own views were those of a faithful member of the Church of England, and he professed general adherence to the *39 Articles*. Again in imitation of Lewis's model, I come clean: I am a minister in a conservative Presbyterian denomination, which practices what it calls "good faith subscription" to the *Westminster Confession of Faith*. Like Lewis, who explained that no one is actually supposed to live simply on "mere Christianity," but must instead associate himself or herself with a church, I readily acknowledge that "mere historical Adam-and-Eve-ism" is not intended to answer every question, and is not a suitable stopping point.

[4]I probably fit into this category myself, though I would say that things are more complicated than the simple statement I have given.

[5]This is how, e.g., Francis Collins et al. suggest handling the beliefs of the apostle Paul in "Question 16: Was there death before the Fall?" in *The Biologos Foundation: Questions* (biologos.org, accessed July 13, 2009).

story flows? If you are not a Christian believer, or if you have serious doubts about whether the Christian faith really holds any water, you might think that this approach is futile, or circular, or—even worse—boring. But think of the deepest intuitions you have about your own existence: that your life is real and meaningful, that you want others to treat you right, that there is something wrong at the heart of things, that there is still real beauty in the world, that sometimes people do really admirable things, and sometimes really abominable things (often enough it's the same people!), and that you hope there is some explanation for life's complexities. I am persuaded that the Christian faith, and especially the Biblical tale of Adam and Eve, actually helps us to make sense of these intuitions, by affirming them and by providing a big story that they fit into. I have a lot of respect for the work of science, and I hope you do too. At the same time, I will insist that for a scientific understanding to be good, it must account for the whole range of evidence, including these intuitions we share.

You will notice that I have said "a version of" and "some variation of" the traditional ideas. One of my themes throughout will be the importance of good critical thinking, and one of the basic principles of that thinking is expressed in Latin as *abusus usum non tollit*, "Abuse does not take away proper use." It is entirely possible that some killjoy has used a traditional view of the first sin of Adam and Eve to make all of life dour and mournful, to quell all delight in pleasure and beauty. But that would be a *mis*use, and the possibility of misuse is therefore not a logically valid argument against the traditional view. And supposing that we do find some difficulties: that may mean that we should try making some adjustments to the traditional view, but it does not of itself mean that we ought to junk the traditional view altogether.

Good critical thinking also requires us to be careful in how we approach some of the terms traditionally used, such as "the fall" and "original sin." When people deny historical Adam and Eve for theological and philosophical reasons, they are commonly objecting to these ideas. I cannot always tell, however, whether the objection is to *some* version of these ideas, or to *every one* of them. As I have just observed, though, even if we are right in rejecting one version, that does not mean we are right in rejecting all versions. Further, it simply will not do to argue that since the Bible does not use these terms, therefore they are "un-Biblical": most people have been well aware of the philological fact that these terms are absent from the Biblical text, and have used the terms as a theological shorthand. To the extent that I use the terms myself, I employ them as a shorthand as well: I am implying, not simply that humans are "sinful" (which is something we all can see), but that the sinfulness was not part of our original makeup; it derives from some primal rebellion on the part of our first ancestors. I am therefore not developing a "doctrine" of original sin, since I am not trying to explain *how* that primal rebellion comes to affect all of us.[6]

Whenever we read something, we ought to pay attention to what kind of literature it is. Certainly the book of Genesis includes Adam and Eve in its story, using a narrative, which is "history-like" in its form. But just identifying that form does not of itself settle anything; there are at least four possible ways of taking the material in Genesis:

(1) The author intended to relay "straight" history, with a minimum of figurative language.

(2) The author was talking about what he thought were actual events, using rhetorical and literary techniques to shape the readers' attitudes toward those events.

(3) The author intended to recount an imaginary history, using recognizable literary conventions to convey "timeless truths" about God and man.

(4) The author told a story without even caring whether the events were real or imagined; his main goal was to convey various theological and moral truths.

---

[6]Some recent efforts to defend ideas of original sin are worthy of note: Edward Oakes, "Original Sin: A Disputation," *First Things* 87 (November 1998): 16–24; Henri Blocher, *Original Sin: Illuminating the Riddle*, New Studies in Biblical Theology (Grand Rapids, MI: Eerdmans, 1997).

I am going to argue that option (2) best captures what we find in Genesis, and best explains how the Bible and human experience relate to Adam and Eve. There is an irony about option (1): it is held both by many traditional Christians, especially those who are called "young earth creationists," and by many Biblical scholars who endorse what is called "historical criticism" (an approach toward studying the Bible books oriented toward discerning how they came to be composed, which often assumes that the traditional view is over-simplified). The difference is that the young earth creationists think that Genesis was telling the truth, and the critical scholars think that Genesis is largely incorrect in its history. Mind you, this does not mean that critical scholars find no value in Genesis; they will commonly resort to something like option (4).

The critical Biblical scholars will often (though not always) deny that Adam and Eve were real people, though they agree that the author of Genesis *intended* to write of real people. Those who follow option (3) say that the author never intended for us to think of Adam and Eve as real, while those who follow option (4) say that it simply does not matter. When a particular scholar denies that Adam and Eve were historical, I cannot always tell which interpretive option he or she has followed; sometimes I wonder if the scholar himself knows! Of course, all of us, traditional and otherwise, run the danger of *starting* with the affirmation or denial of a real Adam and Eve, and then looking for a way of reading the Bible to support our starting point.

I have said that I will argue for option (2), which leads us to discuss whether rhetorical and literary techniques are even proper for the kind of narratives we find in the Bible. It is pretty plain that, overall, the Biblical writers, including the narrators, have used a great deal of pictorial and symbolic language, and that might strike us as a shortcoming on their part. How are we supposed to connect that kind of writing with history in the real world? We face the same kind of difficulty when we read Biblical descriptions of the future: they are heavily symbolic, and it is easy for us to conclude that they therefore have *no* connection to any experience that real people will ever have. As usual, C. S. Lewis has some helpful advice here:[7]

---

[7]Lewis, *Mere Christianity*, book 3, chapter 10 ("Hope"); italics added.

There is no need to be worried by facetious people who try to make the Christian hope of "Heaven" ridiculous by saying they do not want "to spend eternity playing harps." *The answer to such people is that if they cannot understand books written for grown-ups, they should not talk about them.* All the scriptural imagery (harps, crowns, gold, etc.) is, of course, a merely symbolical attempt to express the inexpressible. Musical instruments are mentioned because for many people (not all) music is the thing known in the present life which most strongly suggests ecstasy and infinity. Crowns are mentioned to suggest the fact that those who are united with God in eternity share His splendour and power and joy. Gold is mentioned to suggest the timelessness of Heaven (gold does not rust) and the preciousness of it. *People who take the symbols literally might as well think that when Christ told us to be like doves, He meant that we were to lay eggs.*

Well, I certainly want to be the kind of reader that Lewis would count as a "grown-up," which means that I will try to take the imagery for what it is—a tool that helps me to picture something—without doubting that the images are *about something real*. But of course this challenges us to ask what the imagery is actually about; how do we keep from making the mistake of concluding that the presence of symbolism means the story is *merely* symbolic?

All of us make judgments like this; they are part of being functional in a culture. After all, you probably do not run outside to catch yourself a new pet when it is "raining cats and dogs." And if your best friend tells you that "the whole world" knows about your bad temper, you probably should not spend any time discussing whether there are exceptions. Most of us have some rule-of-thumb criteria that we use for making these judgments; possibly if we put those criteria into words they would not stand up to cross-examination. That is fine for everyday communication, but if we want to say what makes a better or worse interpretation of a sacred text whose author is long dead, it is worth our while to see if we can explain what we are doing when we make sound judgments, making every effort to be true to what we know is good human behavior.

Working on this project has given me the chance to try to make formal some of my own rule-of-thumb criteria that I have learned to use for making this kind of judgment when I read the Bible. Three questions turn out to be helpful in this study (there might be others to add for some other study), and you will see how I apply them throughout my argument.

(1) *How does the person or event impact the basic story line?* My study of the Bible has convinced me that the authors were self-consciously interpreting their world in terms of an over-arching worldview story. Does making the persons or events "merely symbolic" distort the shape of the story?

(2) *How have other writers, especially Biblical ones, taken this person or event?* Any notion of Biblical authority requires me to respect what Biblical writers see; common sense requires me to check what I see against what others see, especially those who are closer to the original time and culture than I am. This is one reason I will not confine my conversation partners to people who already agree with me!

(3) *How does this person or event relate to ordinary human experience?* The Biblical writers, like the other authors from the ancient world that I will consider, were trying to enable their audience to live in the world as they found it. There are many intuitions we all share, such as our craving for God, our need for forgiveness, our yearning for human community governed by love and justice. Most cultures tell stories to give an historical reason for these needs, and some explanation for how they can be met, mollified, explained away, or denied. The Biblical approach to these rings true.

You will see from the bibliography that I have tried to consider as much as I can of other people's views, both in agreement and disagreement. My text interacts with these, and the footnotes take that further. Quite a lot has been written, and the issues sometimes get complicated, which means that we have to be careful and thorough. At the same time, I cannot see the point of documenting, even in the notes, *everything* I think about *everything* I have read. The bibliography will allow you to see what else I have read. In some cases I simply refer, without going into details, to arguments I have given in other places where I make fuller bibliography available.

My goal in this book is to help you think these matters through for yourself. I am not assuming that you are up to speed on all the arguments and on all the details of the Bible and theology. I will do my best to clarify the issues for you, using technical language only when I have to. One thing I will not do is dumb down the whole discussion for you; I hope you do not want that. So please be patient with the process as I try to help you do responsible critical thinking.

I admit it: I am a Westerner with a scientific education, easily smug in my imagined superiority to the less educated. People with my background might find the prevalence of pictorial language in the Bible a problem: why can't these authors just tell it to me straight? But when the Biblical authors describe people and events for us, they are aiming to give us more than simple facts; they want to capture our imaginations, to enable our whole person to lean into life with a vigorous faith and a zeal for goodness. The Christian philosopher Richard Purtill defended the way C. S. Lewis himself used imagery to help people imagine what eternal life with God might be like, saying, "Indeed, probably the major barrier to belief in life after death is more a matter of imagination than of argument."[8] There are, to be sure, arguments to be made; but sooner or later we have to act on what we conclude, and this requires a captivated imagination.

There is another advantage of the pictorial approach of the Bible: when it comes to living a faithful, fully human life, it puts a smug educated Westerner like me on the same footing with my children, and with my fellow human beings throughout the world, the ancient as well as the modern. Certainly I have access to tools for study that I need to share with them; but they have something to teach me too.

An important argument for any position is how well it actually explains ordinary human experience. This means that I will make our experience part of my discussion. This is unusual for a scholarly study today; and this work began its life as an invited paper for an

---

[8]Richard Purtill, *C. S. Lewis' Case for the Christian Faith* (San Francisco: Ignatius, 2004 [1981]), 170.

academic conference.[9] In the ancient world, and in classical Christianity, however, writers understood that theology and philosophy were about real life. If you read Aristotle, or Aquinas, or Calvin, you will find some pretty tough patches of dense thought, and some tedious passages as well, but you will usually know that the author was a human being with real feelings and needs.

In this book, then, I am trying to recapture a tradition for theological writing, insisting that it say something about everyday life. A number of things happened while I was working on this, which I cannot ignore and which have helped to shape my entire outlook. For example, my neighbors' severely handicapped son died suddenly and unexpectedly, and my family was heavily involved in their process of grieving and the funeral. A young couple that is dear to me had trouble conceiving, and then became pregnant with twins; but the woman went into premature labor, just a week or two before the babies might have been viable. The children survived only about an hour. A little later, this same couple thought they were pregnant again, only to have that pregnancy fail, too.

There is so much sadness in the world, and most of us feel that such sadness comes from things being *wrong*. I have found that a sound perspective on Adam and Eve helps us to come to grips with this wrongness, and to give full vent to our grief, in full faith toward God. I also listened to Haydn's oratorio *The Creation* for the first time, in a live performance. The poetry and the music combine to express unbounded delight in God's good work, and to help us to see more clearly the tragedy that has come into human experience, without diminishing the possibility of delight. More of that combination of tragedy and delight comes through in a recording I found as a gift for my wife, of Beethoven's Piano Concerto No. 5 ("Emperor"): the recording was first made in Berlin, on January 23, 1945, and during a part of it you can hear the boom of German anti-aircraft fire. The mixture of musical brilliance, excellent performance, and desperate setting shouts loudly of glory and shame. And when visiting my daughter at the university where she is a student in Ecology and

---

[9] All the papers for that session have now appeared in *Perspectives on Science and Christian Faith* 62:3 (September 2010).

Conservation Biology, I had an excellent conversation with her biology professor about what evolution does and does not say. He agreed emphatically that humans are distinct from all other animals! And finally, I also have to admit that I have far too much experience of expressing my own distinctness by doing what is wrong; I cannot write as a choir boy, still less as a saint.

2

THE SHAPE
OF THE BIBLICAL STORY

2.a Story and Worldview

A number of developments in Biblical studies over the last several decades have deeply enriched our ability to read the Bible well. In the nineteenth century, and through most of the twentieth, Bible scholars emphasized studying an ancient text to discover how it came into being. This kind of study focused on the sources that were supposedly brought together, and the editorial process by which the sources were reshaped into something new. Because these sources no longer exist (if they ever did), each scholar had his own opinion on what they looked like. Often enough, one discerned the boundaries between the sources by looking for differences in style and inconsistencies in outlook. In the late twentieth century, however, many Bible scholars came to a fresh appreciation of the literary qualities of the Biblical books; thus we have come to favor literary readings oriented toward the text as we have it, as opposed to reconstructing the presumed process by which the text came to its current form; this has focused attention on the means by which the Biblical authors communicate their point of view. In fact, it has now become respectable to explain what once appeared to be stylistic differences and ideological inconsistencies as literary devices of a coherent literary work.[1]

And what are some of the literary characteristics that the Biblical authors used? Now, since each one has his own style and preferences, generalizations are hazardous; but we can find some that are common to them all. The features that we will have to notice include:[2]

- The narrator is *reliable* and *omniscient*: that is, he serves as the voice and perspective of God.
- The narration is *scenic*: that is, the emphasis is on direct action and interaction of the characters rather than on descriptive detail of the environs.
- The narratives are *sparsely written*: that is, they focus on what is essential for the narrative.
- The author signals *heightened speech* using poetic diction: that is, elevated diction of a speech is evidence of its significance; often oracular, it may even be divine speech.

The result of these features is that, generally speaking, the author communicates his point of view by indirect and laconic means. The emphasis will be on *showing* (displaying the heart by action and speech) versus *telling* (the narrator telling us explicitly what kind of person the character is).

Hence if we want to be good readers of Old Testament narratives, we will pay attention to, for example, the way people speak: we will look for the relation between what they say and what they do, or between what the narrator has reported and what the character reports (if the character adds or deletes things, how does this reflect "spin"?), or between what someone says (or is told) he will say and what he does say. The Biblical narrators are fully aware that

---

[1] A highly regarded presentation of this approach is Meir Sternberg, *The Poetics of Biblical Narrative: Ideological Literature and the Drama of Reading* (Bloomington: Indiana University Press, 1985).

[2] These are drawn from V. Philips Long, *The Reign and Rejection of King Saul: A Case for Literary and Theological Coherence* (Atlanta: Scholars, 1989), especially from his section on "Selected Features of Hebrew Narrative Style" (21–41).

humans are sinful, and that even the best of us have mixed motives and imperfect morality.

Not everyone who is aware of these literary features will agree on just what they mean in a particular passage, and thus we cannot avoid the kind of discussion that evaluates proposed ways of reading. We must offer reasons for our preferences. Some help in navigating differences comes from developments in linguistics. For example, we now have a rigorous description of how Hebrew authors use verb tenses and word order to focus the readers' attention, in the discipline called "discourse grammar." One of the chief pioneers in this discipline is Robert Longacre, a linguist and Bible translation consultant who has drawn on experience with numerous non-Western languages (and Hebrew *is* a non-Western language). Since about the middle of the twentieth century, the discipline of lexical semantics—discerning the meanings of words in their contexts—has also become well developed.

Another area of linguistics that has made progress is called "sociolinguistics," which is the study of the way people use language in various social situations. The part of sociolinguistics called "speech act theory" focuses on how people *do things* with what they say. Some of the things they do include conveying information, but there is more: a speaker might be trying to shape an attitude, or he might be reminding his audience of what they already believe so that they will act upon it. Sometimes the speaker wants his audience to *infer* the right response. For example, by saying the sentence "there is a car coming down the street" you might be telling your son not to try crossing the street, or you might be telling your friend across the street to hold on to the Frisbee until the car passes. Usually if someone at a dinner table says, "Is there is any salt on the table?" he is not asking for information: he is making a polite request that someone bring the saltshaker to the table.

All of these factors will help us when we ask what a Biblical author is "saying" in his text: we are not limited to the actual words he uses. For example, we will note that Genesis 3 never uses any words for sin or disobedience; but it would be foolish indeed to conclude that what Eve and Adam did was not "sin." The author wants us to see that it was indeed, and to be horrified.

Another development in theological studies is that we pay more attention to the place of one's worldview, and we want to find a fully Biblical worldview.[3] I am using the term "worldview" in the way students of ideology use the term, to denote the basic stance toward God, others, and the world that persons and communities hold.[4] It has further become clear that a worldview is instilled by means of the grand story, which tells a community where we came from, what went wrong, what has been done about it (whether by gods or by man, or some combination), where we now are in the whole process, and where the whole world is headed. One student of world missions has suggested that tribal peoples learn their worldviews through the sacred stories their culture tells; my only correction is that this is true of *all* peoples, not just of tribal ones.[5]

A number of theologians have applied this perspective to the Bible: they have argued that the Bible presents us with an overarching worldview-shaping story, and not simply with a bunch of edifying stories.[6] We will take up the specific contours of this story shortly.

---

[3]See the helpful treatment in David K. Naugle, *Worldview: The History of a Concept* (Grand Rapids, MI: Eerdmans, 2002).

[4]Some writers use the term "worldview" to include such concepts as the shape of the world and the things in it: e.g., John H. Walton, *Ancient Near Eastern Thought and the Old Testament: Introducing the Conceptual World of the Hebrew Bible* (Grand Rapids, MI: Baker, 2006), cf. pages 165–78. Similarly, Peter Enns, *Inspiration and Incarnation: Evangelicals and the Problem of the Old Testament* (Grand Rapids, MI: Baker), 53–56. I find this confusing, and prefer to separate world*view* from world *picture*, as I discuss in *Genesis 1–4: A Linguistic, Literary, and Theological Commentary* (Phillipsburg, NJ: P&R, 2006), 260–62. Even more confusing is the way Francis Collins, *The Language of God* (New York: Free Press, 2006), describes the "scientific worldview" and the "spiritual worldview" as potentially complementary perspectives held by the same person.

[5]Don Pederson, "Biblical Narrative as an Agent for Worldview Change," *International Journal of Frontier Missions* 14:4 (1997): 163–66.

[6]These include N. T. Wright, *The New Testament and the People of God* (Minneapolis: Fortress, 1992); Craig G. Bartholomew and Michael Goheen, *The Drama of Scripture: Finding Our Place in the Biblical Story* (Grand Rapids, MI: Baker, 2004); Michael D. Williams, *Far as the Curse Is Found: The Covenant Story of Redemption* (Phillipsburg, NJ: P&R, 2005); Albert M. Wolters and Michael W. Goheen, *Creation Regained: Biblical Basics for a Reformational Worldview* 2nd ed. (Grand Rapids, MI: Eerdmans, 2005); Christopher J. H. Wright, *The Mission of God: Unlocking the Bible's Grand Narrative* (Downers Grove,

Albert Wolters and Michael Goheen have shown why this is a crucial insight:[7]

To miss the grand narrative of Scripture is a serious matter; it is not simply a matter of misinterpreting parts of Scripture. It is a matter of being oblivious to *which story is shaping our lives*. Some story will shape our lives. When the Bible is broken up into little bits and chunks—theological, devotional, spiritual, moral, or world-view bits and chunks—then these bits can be nicely fitted into the reigning story of our own culture with all its idols! One can be theologically orthodox, devotionally pious, morally upright, or maybe even have one's worldview categories straight, and yet be shaped by the idolatrous Western story. The Bible loses its forceful and formative power by being absorbed into a more encompassing secular story.

People who write about the relationship between worldview and overarching story do not always use the same verbs for the relation between the story and the worldview: does the story *carry* the world-view, *equate to* it, *communicate* it, or something else? However one might wish to articulate this, there is one common affirmation: the worldview is not an abstraction derived from the story; that is, one cannot treat the story simply as the husk, which we can then discard once we have discovered the (perhaps timeless) concepts. This is not to deny that there may well be such things as transcendent truths (such as moral norms); but they gain their power from their place in the story—that is, they equip the members of a community to play their parts in the story meaningfully.[8] It is the worldview story that, if well told, captures the imaginations of those who own it, thereby driving them on and holding their loyalty.

IL: InterVarsity Press, 2006). For a brief (and, one hopes, accessible) summary of this approach, see C. John Collins, "The Theology of the Old Testament," in Lane T. Dennis et al., eds., *The ESV Study Bible* (Wheaton, IL: Crossway, 2008), 29–31 (which includes applications to reading the New Testament as well).
[7]Wolters and Goheen, *Creation Regained*, 125.
[8]In "Theology of the Old Testament," 30b–31a, I explain why we should be careful not to say that we read the whole Bible *as* a story, but rather *in relation to* the story. In "Proverbs and the Levitical System," *Presbyterion* 35:1 (2009): 9–34, at 30–32, I show how wisdom equips the faithful for their little stories in relation to God's overarching Big Story.

2.b History, Myth, and Worldview Story

This notion of a worldview story ties in with the sense of "myth" in C. S. Lewis's essay, "The Funeral of a Great Myth."[9] Here Lewis is describing the story of "developmentalism," a purely naturalistic evolutionary tale of how we got here and where we are going. He distinguishes this story from the theories of the particular sciences: the story uses the theories to the extent that these theories support the story.[10] What makes this "myth" attractive is its imaginative appeal; as Lewis said, "I grew up believing in this myth and I have felt—I still feel—its almost perfect grandeur." Could it be that "myth" is the right category for the kind of stories we find in the ancient world, whether from the Egyptians, Mesopotamians, or even the Hebrews?

The difficulty is that in popular usage the term "myth" implies a judgment that the story is not true.[11] The word can have a range of other meanings, but untrue (or at least unhistorical) usually attaches to it, whatever we may intend.[12] For example, consider how the Old Testament scholar Peter Enns defines "myth":[13]

---

[9]C. S. Lewis, "The Funeral of a Great Myth," in *Christian Reflections* (Grand Rapids, MI: Eerdmans, 1967), 82–89.

[10]Lewis rightly says that the sciences are logically separable from the mythic tale; at the same time, there seems to be something about the human mind that cannot rest content with an account of origins until it is given a "mythic" or "poetic" (i.e., imagination-capturing) quality. The last paragraph of Charles Darwin's *Origin of Species* (my copy is the sixth edition of 1872, and was published in the Harvard Classics series by P. F. Collier and Sons of New York, 1909) has us contemplating a "tangled bank" as the product of the laws Darwin has described in his book. He tells us in words approaching poetry, "There is grandeur in this view of life, with its several powers, having been originally breathed by the Creator into a few forms or into one; and that, whilst this planet has gone cycling on according to the fixed law of gravity, from so simple a beginning endless forms most beautiful and most wonderful have been, and are being, evolved." I do not count this "poetic orientation" as a shortcoming, whether of Darwin or of anyone else; instead, it simply illustrates the general point that no one lives life in airtight compartments. As Lewis observed elsewhere, "All world views yield poetry to those who believe them by the mere fact of being believed"; see his "Is Theology Poetry?" in *The Weight of Glory and Other Addresses* (New York: Simon & Schuster, 1996 [1965]), 90–106, at 97.

[11]Lewis even falls into this when he writes, "Even to the present day, in certain moods, I could almost find it in my heart to wish that it was not *mythical*, but *true*" ("Funeral of a Great Myth," 88, italics added).

[12]See the fascinating discussion of the many meanings in G. B. Caird, *The Language and Imagery of the Bible* (Philadelphia: Westminster, 1980), 219–24; see also J. W. Rogerson, "Slippery Words, V: Myth," *Expository Times* 90 (1978), 10–14.

[13]Enns, *Inspiration and Incarnation*, 40.

It is an ancient, premodern, prescientific way of addressing questions of ultimate origins and meaning in the form of stories: Who are we? Where do we come from?

One difficulty in Enns's definition is its apparent triumphalism: it seems to imply that we in the modern scientific world are more sophisticated than the ancients. This overlooks the astounding achievements of ancient peoples in areas that we would call mathematics and engineering.[14] If we disagree with how they accounted for who we are and where we come from, let us do so without any patronizing nonsense about their naiveté. (Mind you, I do not deny that our culture enjoys enormous improvements over the ancient ones, only that theirs were any less the products of genius coupled with stupidity than ours.)

Another difficulty with Enns's definition, which should be obvious by now, is that the telling of stories to explain origins and meaning is by no means limited to "ancient, premodern, prescientific" cultures. Modern Western culture does exactly the same. For example, the biologist George Gaylord Simpson drew this conclusion from his study of evolution: "Man is the result of a purposeless and natural process that did not have him in mind."[15] This is in fact a story, albeit a bleak one, that puts our lives in perspective. Actually, if it is the true story of the world, it sounds like a heightened version of what Macbeth described in Shakespeare's play, once he discovered that Lady Macbeth had committed suicide:[16] "Life's . . . a tale told by an idiot, full of sound and fury, signifying nothing."

---

[14]For examples of the mathematical achievements of the ancients, see Lucas Bunt, Phillip Jones, and Jack Bedient, *The Historical Roots of Elementary Mathematics* (New York: Dover, 1988 [1976]), chapters 1–2. C. S. Lewis observed that the "idea [of developmentalism] is supported in [a modern person's] mind by a number of false analogies: the oak coming from the acorn, the man from the spermatozoon, the modern steamship from the primitive coracle. The supplemental truth that every acorn was dropped by an oak, every spermatozoon derived from a man, and the first boat by something so much more complex than itself as a man of genius, is simply ignored." See Lewis, "Modern Man and His Categories of Thought," in *Present Concerns* (London: Collins, 1986), 61–66, at 63–64.
[15]George Gaylord Simpson, *The Meaning of Evolution* (New Haven, CT: Yale University Press, 1967), 365.
[16]William Shakespeare, *Macbeth*, V.v.26–28.

29

Richard Purtill, a philosopher with a long-standing appreciation for C. S. Lewis and J. R. R. Tolkien (and who also writes science fiction and fantasy of his own), gave us the following definition of "myth":[17]

> Myths in the original, unstretched sense were stories of gods or heroes that usually had a religious or moral purpose. . . . When human beings begin to tell myths, they sometimes do so because they think, for whatever reason, that the stories are true. But the mythmaker need not think that every detail, or even every important element, of the story is true. . . .
>
> The original mythmakers did not aim only to tell an interesting story (though it is important to remember that they did intend at least that). They aimed to do something that they would probably have expressed as a desire to *honor* the gods and heroes and to *inspire* their listeners.

Purtill goes on to distinguish "myth" from what he calls "gospel":[18]

> Myth is related to what I call gospel, which includes but is not confined to the four New Testament accounts. In gospel we have stories of the acts of God and those close to God—saints rather than heroes. By the traditional believer (Tolkien himself, for instance), gospel is regarded as literally and historically true in all its important elements (and perhaps even in its details). It is specifically denied that human imagination or invention plays any part in gospel as I am using the term. . . .
>
> There is a human need that was once satisfied by original myth and is still satisfied for many by gospel, a need that can be damaging to the human personality if it goes unfulfilled. . . .
>
> What is this need that gospel and original myth seem to fulfill, whereas philosophical and literary myth do not? I think it might be called the need for *significant form* in our experience. We want to be able to relate the things that happen to us as parts of an understandable whole. . . .
>
> What does the job, I think, is the combination of truth and story.

---

[17]Richard Purtill, *J. R. R. Tolkien: Myth, Morality, and Religion* (San Francisco: Ignatius, 2003 [1984]), 1–2.
[18]Ibid., 3, 5–6.

I think I would restate the point Purtill makes about "gospel" being "literally and historically true in all its important elements (and perhaps even in its details)": I do not know what "literally" means here. I prefer to say that it is possible for "gospel" to come to us in different kinds of literary form, each having its own set of literary and rhetorical conventions, which we should not prejudge. I am sure, for example, that the four Gospels do fit reasonably well with his description, but am willing to allow that Genesis 1–11 uses a higher degree of pictorial language. However, we do not have to agree with every detail of Purtill's definitions to find this presentation extremely helpful. For example, even though Christians such as Purtill might judge the myths of pagan peoples to lack full historical truthfulness, nevertheless if we try to see those peoples from the inside, we can say that they thought they were telling the truth (of which history is a part).[19] The function of the stories is to set present life in terms of a coherent story; that is, the stories serve to convey a worldview and to equip the hearers to live in the world.[20]

Purtill is more comfortable applying the word "myth" to the stories from other ancient Near Eastern or Graeco-Roman peoples than to those from the Jews and Christians; but that is precisely because he does not accept them as factual. However (and consistently with Purtill's own acknowledgment), the evidence is that, at least in Mesopotamia (whose tales are the closest correlate to Genesis 1–11), the stories were felt to be true: true, that is, in the sense

[19]In other words, I think Purtill has shown a commendable sympathy toward the mythmakers. John Oswalt has recently written on the subject in *The Bible among the Myths* (Grand Rapids, MI: Zondervan, 2009), but rejects any attempt at such sympathy (cf. his pages 36–38), because that tends to reduce the Bible to the same level as other peoples' stories. While I agree with Oswalt's view of the Bible, I think Purtill, by recognizing a universal human need, has done a better job of allowing us to see what the Biblical authors were trying to accomplish.
[20]John Walton, *Ancient Near Eastern Thought*, puts it well: "Most peoples of the ancient world found the past interesting and found in it a key to social coherence lending meaning to life in the present" (223). Similarly, S. G. F. Brandon finds in a Sumerian origins story "a Sumerian aetiological myth designed to explain three things," among which is "the purpose of mankind, namely, to serve the gods." See Brandon, "The Origin of Death in Some Ancient Near Eastern Religions," *Religious Studies* 1 (1966), 217–28, at 222.

of talking about real events.[21] As Egyptologist Kenneth Kitchen has observed,[22]

> The ancient Near East did *not* historicize myth (i.e., read it as imaginary "history"). In fact, exactly the reverse is true—there was, rather, a trend to "mythologize" history, to celebrate actual historical events and people in mythological terms. . . . The ancients (Near Eastern and Hebrew alike) knew that propaganda based on real events was far more effective than that based on sheer invention.

Kitchen further argues,[23]

> As to definition [for the flood story], myth or "protohistory," it should be noted that the Sumerians and Babylonians had no doubts on that score. They included it squarely in the middle of their earliest historical tradition, with kings before it and kings after it.

With all this in view, I have argued in another book that Genesis 1–11, which bears so many points of contact with Mesopotamian stories of origins, ancient kings, the flood, and subsequent kings, is the beginning of an alternative worldview story to the Mesopotamian ones, whose "purpose is to shape Israel's view of God, the world, and mankind, and their place in it all."[24] Following Kitchen again,[25]

---

[21]My fuller discussion in appendix 1, "Ancient Near Eastern Texts and Genesis 1–11," justifies this evaluation of the Mesopotamian stories.

[22]Kenneth A. Kitchen, *On the Reliability of the Old Testament* (Grand Rapids, MI: Eerdmans, 2003), 262, 300. The same issue that applies to origin stories—that is, can miraculous and figurative accounts refer to actual events, whether in the past or in the future?—applies also to language we find in the Gospels and in apocalyptic literature; see N. T. Wright, *The New Testament and the People of God* (Minneapolis: Fortress, 1992), 424–27. As Wright observes, "the language of myth, and eschatological myths in particular (the sea, fabulous monsters, etc.), are used in the biblical literature as complex metaphor systems to denote historical events and to invest them with their theological significance. The Gospels, then, *are* 'myth' in the sense that they are foundational stories for the early Christian worldview."

[23]Kitchen, *On the Reliability of the Old Testament*, 425–26.

[24]Collins, *Genesis 1–4*, 242.

[25]Kitchen, *On the Reliability of the Old Testament*, 447. Cf. also Claus Westermann, *Genesis 1–11* (Minneapolis: Augsburg, 1984 [1974]), 65.

Gen. 1–11 is the Hebrew answer on how to present "prehistory/pro-tohistory" before the time of their first fully "historical" people, the patriarchs Abraham to Jacob. Again, the approach they adopted was common to their neighbors, using the same basic tools and concepts of that time: the succession of human generations, and how to span them. Mesopotamia chose to expand "heroically" the too-few reigns available. The Hebrew genealogies became telescoped through time, keeping a representative number. . . .

This leads us to the question of the relationship between "history" and the worldview story; but to address this question we must first decide what we mean by the word "history." The word "history" can be used in a variety of senses, and when writers are not clear on what sense they attach to the word, we can get confusion: a text might be "historical" in one writer's sense but not "historical" in another's. For example, some scholars use the word "historical" for an account that is told in proper chronological order, with few imaginative elements—or at least, that seems to be their meaning (though they often do not say it explicitly). Others restrict the word "history" to the kinds of accounts that trained historians write, or even to accounts that leave out all references to actions of God or the gods—and this could lead to the odd assertion, "This narrative is not *historical*, but that doesn't mean it didn't happen"![26]

Let me illustrate some of the confusions that come from using the word "history" without due caution. Some people draw a very tight connection between "historicity" and "literalism" in interpretation—that is, they assume that if a story is to qualify as "historical," it must not make much use of figurative elements. The strict young-earth creationist Douglas Kelly seems to have reasoned this way: since the creation story of Genesis is "historical," it therefore must be read in what he calls a "literal" fashion.[27] In my view this

[26]For more discussion, see V. Philips Long, *The Art of Biblical History* (Grand Rapids, MI: Zondervan, 1994), especially 58–87 (chapter 2).

[27]This notion of "history" serves as an unargued and therefore almost invisible premise of Douglas Kelly, *Creation and Change: Genesis 1.1–2.4 in the Light of Changing Scientific Paradigms* (Fearn, Ross-shire, U.K.: Christian Focus, 1997); e.g., see 41–42, 51 ("the text

leads to a very poor interpretation of the creation story, but that is not my point here. On the other hand, the "evolutionary creationist" Denis Lamoureux, operating with exactly the same tight connection, has come to very different conclusions: since the creation passage is not "true" when read in a literalistic fashion, therefore it is not historical.[28] Now, if I were to give a full reply to this assumption, I would have to talk at length about what is going on when people communicate, a discussion that draws on ideas from speech act theory and rhetorical criticism. God willing, I will take that up in more detail in a future book. All I need to say for now is that there is nothing in the meaning of the word "history," nor in common human behavior, that requires this equation.

There is a simple, ordinary language sense of the word "history," and this will be my meaning: I will take the term "historical account" to mean that the author wanted his audience to believe that the events recorded really happened. This definition is not intended to settle every question of how we should correlate the literary statements with the way *we* would describe things, since we have to take into account the communicative purpose of the text we are considering. In particular,[29]

(1) "historical" in this sense is not the same as "prose," and certainly does not imply that our account has no figurative or imaginative elements;

---

of Genesis is clearly meant to be taken in a literal, historical sense"). This is apparently also a premise for Kelly's fellow young-earth creationist Kurt Wise, in his *Faith, Form, and Time* (Nashville: Broadman & Holman, 2002): e.g., on page 44 he equates "taken at face value" with "intended to convey history."

[28]Denis Lamoureux, *Evolutionary Creation: A Christian Approach to Evolution* (Eugene, OR: Wipf & Stock, 2008), cf. page 150: "Therefore, since the heavens are not structured in this way [i.e., according to a literalistic reading of Genesis 1], Gen 1 cannot be a historical account of the actual events that created the heavens."

[29]See Collins, *Genesis 1–4*, 249–51. There I use the example of Psalm 105:26–38, which "retells the story of the plagues in Egypt, but it tells them in a different order from that in Exodus, and it does not tell about all of the plagues. Is the psalm—a poem—thereby unhistorical? Or should we set it against Exodus, and maybe declare Exodus the product of a different tradition? Neither: they are two different types of writing, with different communicative purposes."

(2) "historical" is not the same as "complete in detail" or "free from ideological bias," neither of which is possible or desirable anyhow;

(3) "historical" is not necessarily the same as "told in exact chronological sequence" unless the text claims that for itself.

This means that we might do best if we think of "history" less as a literary *genre* (another word that has multiple, and unregulated, meanings), and more as *a way of referring to events*. That is, if we say that something is (or is not) historical, we are not so much describing the kind of literature it is, as we are the way it talks about (or does not talk about) real events. Differing literary genres refer to events in different ways for different purposes—or make up fictitious events.

The conclusion to which this discussion leads us is this: If, as seems likely to me, the Mesopotamian origin and flood stories provide the context against which Genesis 1–11 are to be set, they also provide us with clues on how to read this kind of literature. These stories include divine action, symbolism, and imaginative elements; the purpose of the stories is to lay the foundation for a worldview, without being taken in a "literalistic" fashion. We should nevertheless see the story as having what we might call an "historical core," though we must be careful in discerning what that is. Genesis aims to tell the story of beginnings the right way.[30]

There is no telling what materials the author of Genesis used as he composed this story. We have reasons to suppose that he had access to some versions of the Mesopotamian stories; but beyond that, God alone knows what else he might have had. Maybe there were Hebrew stories of the patriarchs, beginning with Abraham;

---

[30]Martin Emmrich (whose conclusions about authorship are to the "left" of mine) puts the matter well in "The Temptation Narrative of Genesis 3:1–6: A Prelude to the Pentateuch and the History of Israel," *Evangelical Quarterly* 73:1 (2001): 3–20: "I think that the text demands the acknowledgement of at least a core of historical referentiality." Within that core he includes "an actual garden (the location of which we cannot be sure about) with two occupants, despite the mythical character of much of the J source [i.e., of the putative source of Genesis 2–3]. In all likelihood, this is the way the original audience would have taken the story" (p. 4, and note 6). To support this last assertion, he calls in Gerhard von Rad, *Genesis* (London: SCM, 1961 [1956]), 73.

some of them might even have been written. Perhaps Henri Blocher's suggestion has merit, that the author of Genesis "reconstructed" the past, working backwards from ordinary human experience to what must have caused it, giving us a tale that provided a contrast to the other stories:[31]

> Genesis aims to supply the true reconstruction, guided and guaranteed by divine inspiration, over against the fantasies and errors reconstructed by the others. There is nothing in that which allows us to take the event as a symbol.

As Blocher also points out, "The presence of symbolic elements in the text in no way contradicts the historicity of its central meaning."[32]

If we recognize this, we can see that authors who say things like, "Genesis 1–11 aims to tell us, not history or science, but theology,"[33] are trying to say something worth saying about the nature of Genesis 1–11, but they are indulging in a disjunction that is problematic. The theology is not separable from the story, as we can see from the fact that one of those "theological truths" is that the one who created the world is the good God who revealed himself to Israel, and not the capricious gods of the other peoples—an historical assertion!

Some authors go even further, and propose that the main goal of the early part of Genesis is to convey "timeless truths."[34] It is unclear, however, whether these truths are really as "timeless" as supposed.

---

[31] Henri Blocher, *In the Beginning* (Downers Grove, IL: InterVarsity Press, 1984), 159.
[32] Ibid., 155.
[33] E.g., John Stek, "What Says the Scripture?" in Howard J. Van Till, Robert E. Snow, John H. Stek, Davis A. Young, *Portraits of Creation* (Grand Rapids, MI: Eerdmans, 1990), 203–265, at 242, cf. at 263. Gordon Wenham is far more careful when he writes, "Though historical and scientific questions may be uppermost in our minds as we approach the text, it is doubtful whether they were in the writer's mind, and we should therefore be cautious about looking for answers to questions he was not concerned with." Gordon Wenham, *Genesis 1–15*, Word Biblical Commentary (Milton Keynes, U.K.: Word, 1991), liii. See also Bruce Waltke with Cathy J. Fredericks, *Genesis* (Grand Rapids, MI: Zondervan, 2001), 75–78.
[34] For example, see Daniel Harlow, "Creation according to Genesis: Literary Genre, Cultural Context, Theological Truth," *Christian Scholars Review* 37.2 (2008), 163–98, at 198: one of his "timeless theological truths" is that "God created." Actually, in light of his entire presentation, one wonders how the empirical sinfulness of human beings is a "timeless truth":

Besides the "timeless theological truth" that "God created," which is actually historical (and therefore *not* "timeless"), scholars thinking along these lines might suppose that Genesis 3 teaches that "humans are sinful." But this is not a timeless truth on its own: sooner or later someone will want to know, did God create humans with a tendency (or at least an openness) toward sinning, or did he make them good, only for humans to *become* sinful? If they became sinful, how did that happen? Do not our innermost intuitions favor the explanation that humans have somehow declined from a prior state of goodness and health? In other words, the supposed timeless truth, once it interacts with actual human experience, demands answers to historical questions.

Perhaps another observation from Blocher might be helpful here:[35]

> The real issue when we try to interpret Genesis 2–3 is not whether we have a historical account of the fall, but whether or not we may read it as the account of a historical fall. The problem is not historiography as a genre narrowly defined—in annals, chronicles, or even saga— but correspondence with discrete realities in our ordinary space and sequential time.

If we recognize that these stories serve to convey a worldview, then that also guides us in how to receive these stories as Scripture: the stories tell us what combination of choices and actions, on the part of God and man, have led up to where we are now. They call on us to learn from those choices, and they enlist the faithful to play their part in the ongoing story.

Now, this has not always been the way that Christian and Jewish preachers and devotional writers have approached the stories;

---

it seems to become "God created mankind with a tendency (or at least openness) toward sinning"—an historical statement with much to argue about!

[35]Henri Blocher, *Original Sin: Illuminating the Riddle*, New Studies in Biblical Theology (Grand Rapids, MI: Eerdmans, 1997), 50. Blocher has reaffirmed his views in the recent article, "The Theology of the Fall and the Origins of Evil," in R. J. Berry and T. A. Noble, eds., *Darwin, Creation and the Fall: Theological Challenges* (Leicester, U.K.: Apollos, 2009), 149–72. Throughout this article Blocher also indicates his agreement with the relevant points in my *Genesis 1–4*.

generally these preachers and writers have treated the tales as instantiations of some "timeless" moral or spiritual truth. For example, David facing Goliath (1 Samuel 17) becomes pretty much an instance of great faith confronting a daunting circumstance, and the historical event fades from view. The message becomes, "identify the Goliaths that you face, and let your faith make you brave like David was." The text of Samuel, however, shows that its concern is with the historical event, in which David served as a "champion" who fought the Philistine champion *on behalf of* the whole people (1 Sam. 17:4, 8–10), and thereby proved himself truer to the ideal of kingship than Saul was. The actual event sets a pattern for all kings in David's line, and even enables Christians to appreciate what it means to have David's heir, Jesus, as their king.

I do not say that there is no place for an approach that looks for moral or spiritual "lessons" in Biblical stories; we find something like it, for example, in Hebrews 11. Besides, one job of the faithful king is to be an example of faithfulness for all the people. But the historical element is always there. The devotional approach that is more common among Christians and Jews, however, usually loses the historical element altogether, in favor of the "timeless." As a matter of fact, this approach has a theorist, Aristotle, who wrote (in his *Poetics*, 9.1–3) about his preference for what he called "poetry" (by which he means fictional narrative) over "history" (by which he means a tale of things that actually happened, even if told in verse). For Aristotle, "poetry" deals with the universal and is therefore more "philosophical," while "history" is too particular.

The fact that this preference was well established in Christian devotions made it easy for someone like S. R. Driver, who rejected much historical reliability for the stories in Genesis, to preserve a form of piety by treating the narratives as giving us "immortal types of weakness yielding to temptation."[36] It made it easy, in my judgment, because people were accustomed to nonhistorical, moralizing approaches to the Bible already, and thus the historical doubts did not seem to undermine piety.

---

[36]S. R. Driver, *The Book of Genesis*, Westminster Commentary (London: Methuen, 1904), lxviii–lxix.

Many people today are deeply doubtful that something someone else did, long ago, can have any serious impact on our lives right now. This attitude shows itself in the way that much of twentieth-century theology assumes that historical events are irrelevant to contemporary personal experience, following the German Gotthold Lessing (1729–81). For these theologians, theology must be based on timeless truths, and "the accidental truths of history can never become the proof of the necessary truths of reason."[37] Something like this seems to lie behind Karl Barth's (1886–1968) interpretation of Romans 5 as referring to a nonhistorical fall: "The sin which entered the world through Adam is like the righteousness manifested to the world, timeless and eternal."[38]

The recent Genesis commentary of Leon Kass regularly advocates that we read Genesis "anthropologically" and "philosophically" (terms that strike me as intentional echoes of Aristotle), rather than "historically": that is, as a record, not of what *did* happen, but what *might* happen, and what *always* happens.[39] This, he contends, gives us a much richer way of reading. But literary scholar Alan Jacobs sees clearly that Genesis itself does not invite this kind of reading, since its audience are heirs of its events. Jacobs, in his review of Kass's book, observed:[40]

> Philosophical reading strives to locate in the text whatever is universal to human experience, and to find ways of describing the particular experiences of particular people in the most broadly relevant terms possible. . . .
>
> From one who belongs to a covenant community, then, the appropriation of the biblical narrative must be done by *historical* rather than what Kass would call philosophical means. Our task is not to find a conceptual vocabulary that will allow us to build analogical bridges

---

[37]See the discussion in Long, *Art of Biblical History*, 102–103.
[38]Karl Barth, *Romans* (Oxford: Oxford University Press, 1933 [1921]), 170–72 (on Rom. 5:12).
[39]Leon Kass, *The Beginning of Wisdom: Reading Genesis* (New York: Free Press, 2003), e.g., pages 9–11.
[40]Alan Jacobs, "Leon Kass and the Genesis of Wisdom," *First Things* 134 (June/July 2003): 30–35, at 32ab. I find that I share Jacobs's admiration for Kass personally. With Jacobs, I came to pray that the inquiring Kass will "hold fast to the book until it blesses him" (Jacobs, "Leon Kass," 35b).

between the biblical text and our experience; rather, we must understand that we dwell in the same history that the people of Israel relate in the Pentateuch. . . . Genesis is not *analogous* to our experience, it *is* our experience, in its historical aspect.

Against Kass's claim that Genesis is primarily about whether it is "possible to find, institute, and preserve a way of life that accords with man's true standing in the world and that serves to perfect his godlike possibilities," Jacobs replies,[41]

Genesis, and the culture from which it emerges, doesn't seem to give a damn about our "true standing in the world" and our "godlike possibilities"; rather, as far as I can tell, it is about God and what he has done, and is doing, to repair what his rebellious and arrogant creatures have broken: our relations with ourselves, with one another, with the creation, and with God Himself.

This discomfort with history has become especially pronounced as a result of the Enlightenment, with its preference for the timeless (probably influencing Kass). And existentialism reduces meaning to individual experience (influencing Barth). The New Testament scholar George E. Ladd countered these trends:[42]

It is clear that the presence of the Kingdom in Jesus' mission has inescapable existential, that is, personal consequences. The Kingdom of God is concerned with my existence, my personal response and responsibility, my freedom from bondage to the past, to sin, to pride, to the world. It demands openness to God's future. But all of this is true because first of all something happened *in history*. Jesus was a historical person. His words were historical events. His deeds involved other people; but they were far larger than the boundaries of personal existence. His deeds included interpersonal fellowship, healings of bodies as well as minds. His mission created a new fellowship of men; and this fellowship after the resurrection became the Christian church, which has become one of the most influential

---

[41]Jacobs, "Leon Kass," 34b (citing Kass, *Beginning of Wisdom*, 661).
[42]George E. Ladd, *The Pattern of New Testament Truth* (Grand Rapids, MI: Eerdmans, 1968), 63–64.

institutions in Western culture. All of this happened in history; and it is only because certain events first happened in history that other results were experienced in the existential dimension. Existential import results only from historical event.

To lay a stress on the particularity of an historical event takes nothing away from the personal and experiential side; rather, the historical guarantees that our experience is in touch with reality. Relating the Biblical narratives to the overarching worldview story, therefore, treats those narratives as they deserve to be treated.

2.c Features of the Biblical Story

Now let us turn to some of the specifics of the Biblical story line. Here is a simple summary of the Biblical story, including its function as Scripture:[43]

> The OT is thus the story of the one true Creator God, who called the family of Abraham to be his remedy for the defilement that came into the world through the sin of Adam and Eve. God rescued Israel from slavery in Egypt in fulfillment of this plan, and established them as a theocracy for the sake of displaying his existence and character to the rest of the world. God sent his blessings and curses upon Israel in order to pursue that purpose. God never desisted from that purpose, even in the face of the most grievous unfaithfulness in Israel.
>
> This overarching story serves as a grand narrative or worldview story for Israel: each member of the people was to see himself or herself as an *heir* of this story, with all its glory and shame; as a *steward* of the story, responsible to pass it on to the next generation; and as a *participant*, whose faithfulness could play a role, in God's mysterious wisdom, in the story's progress. . . .
>
> The NT authors, most of whom were *Jewish* Christians, saw themselves as heirs of the OT story, and as authorized to describe its proper completion in the death and resurrection of Jesus and the Messianic era that this ushered in. These authors appropriated the OT as Christian Scripture, and they urged their audiences (many of whom were

---

[43]Collins, "Theology of the Old Testament," 30b. See further how I apply this perspective to a disputed interpretive issue in Proverbs in my essay "Proverbs and the Levitical system."

Gentile Christians) to do the same. There is debate over just how the NT authors used the OT as Scripture . . . , but the simplest summary of the NT authors' stance would be to say that they saw the OT as constituting the earlier chapters of the story in which Christians are now participating.

Any telling of the Biblical story must include the notion of *sin*: human beings are estranged from God, and Israel is God's means of bringing light to the world. The theologian Cornelius Plantinga describes sin as "culpable disturbance of shalom," and though this will not work as actual definitions of the Hebrew and Greek words we find in the Bible, it nevertheless captures one of the ruling ideas in the Biblical worldview.[44] We see this idea of sin as an intrusive element, a disturbance, in the way that Israel's ritual system includes among its several functions provisions for dealing with personal and corporate sin. Some of the sacrifices (namely, the burnt offering, the sin offering, and the guilt offering) are said to "work atonement" (e.g., Lev. 1:4; 4:20; 5:16) and though there is some debate among scholars of Leviticus over just what this expression means, we can say at least that it tells us that the sacrifices deal with sin as a defiling element that ruins human existence and renders people unworthy to be in God's presence.[45] The New Testament authors use these atoning sacrifices to explain the benefits of Jesus' death in dealing with the sins of believers: for example, when Peter tells Christians that they were ransomed "with the precious blood of Christ, like that of a lamb without blemish or spot" (1 Pet. 1:19), he is using the burnt offering— one of the atoning sacrifices—to explain what Jesus achieved.[46] (Of course there are more aspects to what Jesus accomplished with his death. I am not arguing here that we must make this the only, nor even necessarily primary, model for understanding the cross, only that it be included.)

---

[44]Cornelius Plantinga, Jr., *Not the Way It's Supposed to Be: A Breviary of Sin* (Grand Rapids, MI: Eerdmans, 1995), 16.

[45]For a fine recent discussion see Jay Sklar, *Sin, Impurity, Sacrifice, Atonement: The Priestly Conceptions* (Sheffield, U.K.: Sheffield Phoenix Press, 2005).

[46]For a brief survey of these usages, see C. John Collins, "The Eucharist as Christian Sacrifice," *Westminster Theological Journal* 66 (2004): 1–23, especially 21–23.

Further, the Biblical authors show a keen interest in seeing moral improvement in the faithful. Moral formation in the Bible is seen, fundamentally, as restoring the creation pattern that has been damaged. As Christopher Wright observes, the two crucial aspects of proper moral conduct are imitating "the character and ways of God" and returning to the good pattern of creation.[47] Wright goes on to say,

> The purpose of the ethical provisions given in the context of redemp-
> tion, which include both the covenant law of the Old Testament and
> the ethics of the kingdom of God in the New, is to restore to humans
> the desire and the ability to conform to the creational pattern—God's
> original purpose for them.

The apostle Paul displays this same picture of moral renovation when he describes Jesus as "the image of the invisible God" (Col. 1:15). Paul speaks this way, probably both because Jesus is the "new Adam" (that is, as Adam was to do, Jesus is or bears God's image) and because his character is the norm and goal toward which God is molding the Christian believer, restoring the damaged image (Col. 3:10; Eph. 4:24; Rom. 8:29; 1 Cor. 15:49).

The way that Genesis presents the call of Abraham (Gen. 12:1–3) indicates that God's intention was that through this man and his family the rest of mankind was to find blessing. As I will argue in chapter 3, the very way in which Genesis presents the call of Abram indicates that he is a kind of new Adam, whose task is to undo what Adam did.[48] This presupposes that all human beings have some things in common: a need to know God, a distance from him due to sin, and the possibility of their moral transformation as they receive

---

[47]Christopher Wright, *Walking in the Ways of the Lord: The Ethical Authority of the Old Testament* (Downers Grove, IL: InterVarsity, 1995), 13–45. See also Wright's *Old Testament Ethics for the People of God* (Downers Grove, IL: InterVarsity Press, 2004); and Gordon Wenham, *Story as Torah: Reading Old Testament Narratives Ethically* (Grand Rapids, MI: Baker, 2000). My discussion of creation ordinances, and of the reflections on marriage based on Gen. 2:24, in *Genesis 1–4*, 129–32, 142–45, applies these ideas.
[48]See the discussion in section 3.b below. See also my *Genesis 1–4*, 87–88.

the message.[49] This commonality has traditionally been held to stem from their common origin.

Even though the Bible presents God as aiming to expand his influence among all kinds of people, there is of course much resistance to God's light. Nevertheless, the Biblical story is headed to a glorious conclusion, the final defeat and banishment of sin from human experience; those who cling to their sins will not be allowed a place in such glory (cf. Rev. 21:1–8). I agree with those who see the original task of man to have been to work outward from Eden, spreading Edenic blessings throughout the earth, turning the whole world into a sanctuary. Human sin interfered with man's ability to carry this out, but did not deter God from holding fast to this plan. The book of Revelation portrays the final victory of God's purposes, using Edenic and sanctuary imagery to describe glorified human life—for believing Jews and Gentiles.[50]

On the other hand, a trend among some contemporary philosophers and theologians is to see "evil" as something inherent in the very idea of a creation in which rational beings can exercise free will. For example, W. Sibley Towner surveyed trends in twentieth-century interpretation of Genesis 3, and the impact of those trends in contemporary formulations of "original sin."[51] After describing formulations of "original sin" in Roman Catholicism and in traditional Presbyterianism, he asserts,

---

[49]Another aspect of the Bible's presentation is that it recognizes moral achievement among "even" the Gentiles—an achievement that can serve, not only as a rebuke to faithless Israel, but even at times as a model for God's own people (as in Prov. 31:1–9). On this point, see my study, "Echoes of Aristotle in Romans 2:14–15: Or, Maybe Abimelech Was Not So Bad After All," *Journal of Markets and Morality* 13:1 (2010): 123–73.

[50]This is the main theme of Gregory Beale, *The Temple and the Church's Mission: A Biblical Theology of the Dwelling Place of God*, New Studies in Biblical Theology (Downers Grove, IL: InterVarsity Press, 2004); and though I might prefer to put many of Beale's detailed results differently from how he has done, I still think he sustains his thesis. I have supported this idea independently, e.g., Collins, *Genesis 1–4*, 69, 185–86; *NIDOTTE* 2:582–83 (on Hebrew √k-b-d).

[51]W. Sibley Towner, "Interpretations and Reinterpretations of the Fall," in Francis A. Eigo, ed., *Modern Biblical Scholarship: Its Impact on Theology and Proclamation* (Villanova, PA: Villanova University Press, 1984), 53–85. Specific quotations come from 57–58, 76.

Modern believers and unbelievers alike tend to hold as patent non-sense the notion that all human sin and all death are generically descended from a single act by a single pair of human beings who lived at a single moment in time, or that the cause of their original transgression was Satan in the guise of a snake.

Towner quotes with approval the opinion of Bruce Vawter:

There was, therefore, no "fall" in the sense that men and women became something other than what they had been created. . . . The story of the 'Fall' is a paradigm of human conduct in the face of temptation, not a lesson in biology.

This pattern of conduct is, apparently, inherent in being human.

It would be possible to offer a critique of Towner's study on a number of levels. To begin with, he apparently wants to make his presentation more persuasive by his mention of the tendency of "modern believers and unbelievers alike." But of course, this raises all manner of questions: Who are these modern people, and why should we follow them? What does it mean that they "tend" to think a certain way: can Towner cite a survey, or does he simply mean the modern people he knows? Have these modern people given reasons for their tendency, and do those reasons account for other deep instincts these people doubtless share (see chapter 4 below)? And if they now represent a majority, what of it? By Towner's own admission, a majority once held the view he rejects: in other words, majorities can be wrong.

Towner claims that Irenaeus is a forerunner to this modern view, in seeing "the Fall as a movement from childish innocence toward adult maturity." If this is right, then it should give us pause; after all, Irenaeus, who lived from about A.D. 120 or 140 until about 200, was a leading Greek-speaking theologian of the early church. But as a matter of fact, Towner has distorted Irenaeus's actual view: according to Irenaeus, the first humans were created morally innocent, their innocence being more like that of a child than of a full adult. God's goal was for them to mature into moral

45

confirmation, but the fall interrupted the process (see more in section 3.a below).[52]

Further, Towner is selective in his presentation of the Biblical scholars, leaving out anyone who might have taken Genesis 3 otherwise—and these range from the moderately critical S. R. Driver to the fairly conservative Derek Kidner, not to mention Alexander Heidel, a highly respected Assyriologist who displayed a reasonable competence in handling Biblical material as well.[53] The fact that Heidel is an Assyriologist leads to another, and larger point: the Biblical scholars he cites respond to the perceived similarities between Genesis and other ancient Near Eastern stories by treating both kinds as equally unhistorical; but students of the other Near Eastern cultures often just as easily conclude that the Bible writers had a concern for actual events (see section 2.b above, as well as Appendix 1). Finally, Towner does not stop to analyze whether the trends in exegesis find their attractiveness more in the preferences of "modern believers and unbelievers," than in the features of the Bible itself.

A second example is James Barr, whose study of Genesis 3, *The Garden of Eden and the Hope of Immortality*, came out in 1993 (and cites Towner's study with approval).[54] He summarizes his findings:[55]

> What God pronounced to be 'good' was the created world as it still is, the humans being mortal as they still are. . . . That world contained elements, as we have seen, like the waters, the darkness, which he had not created, but the whole as it emerged was 'good'. . . . The fact is, it seems, that humanity was never 'perfect', and therefore the idea of a 'Fall' is otiose. More likely, we have to think, they were imperfect

---

[52]Towner, "Interpretations and Reinterpretations of the Fall," 60. For a careful study of Irenaeus, see Anders-Christian Jacobsen, "The Importance of Genesis 1–3 in the Theology of Irenaeus," *Zeitschrift für antikes Christentum* 8.2 (2005), 299–316.

[53]See S. R. Driver, *Genesis*, Westminster Commentary (London: Methuen, 1904); at 56–57 he accords a kind of historical core to the fall story (see chapter 5 below). Derek Kidner, *Genesis*, Tyndale Old Testament Commentary (Downers Grove, IL: InterVarsity Press, 1967); see pages 26–31. Alexander Heidel, *The Babylonian Genesis* (Chicago: University of Chicago Press, 1951); see pages 122–26 comparing the Mesopotamian Adapa story with Genesis 3.

[54]James Barr, *The Garden of Eden and the Hope of Immortality* (Minneapolis: Fortress, 1993). I have reviewed the book in appendix 2.

[55]Ibid., 92 (italics added).

from the start. . . . *Their imperfection makes it all the more natural that they disobeyed: everyone did.*

As with Towner, there are points here that I would find highly debatable: I do not, for example, think that Genesis presents any elements of the world that God had not created, nor do I find any traces of a primeval conflict there.[56] In any case, Barr makes it clear that he reads Genesis as implying man was "imperfect from the start"—and by this, he does not mean "immature and needing to grow" (which is not a problem) but prone to sin (which *is* a problem).

A last example is Keith Ward, whose book *Divine Action* laudably sets out to defend "a strongly supernaturalist idea of God as a purely spiritual creator of and personal agent in the cosmos, who was incarnate in the person of Jesus, who answers prayers and performs miracles." Nevertheless, he seems to agree with those modern theologians who no longer accept any account of the fall of mankind and of Satan, and suggests that "if suffering and destruction are ever possible in any world, they are necessarily included in God, not freely chosen by him. Thus God is not free to eliminate the possibility of suffering."[57]

A number of theological motivations lie behind these various efforts, and each scholar has his own subset of this group of motivations. One motive is to defend the reality of human freedom; another is to address the existence of pain and suffering in a world that God is supposed to have made.

No one can avoid these big questions, it is true, but we must judge these efforts a failure to do justice to those questions. Theologically, if we say that being prone to sin is inherent in being human with a free will, then we must say the Bible writers were wrong in describing atonement the way they did; and we must say that Jesus was wrong to describe his own death in these terms (e.g., Mark 10:45). Further, this approach makes nonsense of the joyful expectation of Christians that they will one day live in a glorified world from which sin and

---

[56]See my *Genesis 1–4*, 50–55 (cf. 45 n. 16).

[57]Keith Ward, *Divine Action: Examining God's Role in an Open and Emergent Universe* (Philadelphia: Templeton Foundation Press, 2007 [1990]); citations from pages vii, 40, 43.

death have been banished (Rev. 21:1–8). Do these modern authors mean to imply that those who dwell in a glorified world will be less human because they no longer sin?

These modern attempts do not let God off the hook for pain and suffering, either; or, if they succeed in doing so, the price is sickeningly high. Did God know about evil before he made the world? Most believers would say yes, and they trust that he had his reasons for "allowing" it. But these modern efforts seem to imply that somehow God just could not help himself; the only world he *could* make was one in which people commit evil. At least in the traditional understanding, *humans* are to blame for the evil they do and the pain they inflict; here, we can only blame God. This is not the Biblical view of God, whose very power and moral purity provoke such perplexity among his faithful (cf. Hab. 1:12–13). Neither does the modern approach give us any reason to hope that God will be able to succeed in achieving his final victory.

Another way to put my objections to these modern alternatives is to say that they end up telling a very different story from the one we find in the Bible. They also make God out to be a very different character from the One the Bible writers describe. Finally, they fail utterly to address one of our deepest intuitions, that there is something wrong with sin and death, and that we need God to help us and to heal us. This is exactly why Paul can describe the resurrection of Jesus as the firstfruits, the guarantee of our final healing (1 Cor. 15:23). In that same passage he describes sin and death as enemies (cf. 1 Cor. 15:26, 56) that God will finally and utterly defeat for the sake of his faithful. Jesus, in rising from the dead, set in motion the undoing of Adam's first sin (1 Cor. 15:21–22).

On the whole, then, the features of the Biblical story strongly support Plantinga's main point, that in "sin" we have something that is "not the way it's supposed to be." As he puts it,[58]

> "Culpable disturbance of shalom" suggests that sin is unoriginal, that it disrupts something good and harmonious, that (like a housebreaker) it is an intruder, and that those who sin deserve reproach. . . .

---

[58]Plantinga, *Not the Way It's Supposed to Be*, 16, 33.

A bad strain has gotten into the stock so that we now sin with the ease and readiness of people born to the task. . . . This fact, empirical as well as biblical, lies behind a broad consensus on original sin. Although, partly because of the silence of Scripture, Christians of various theological orientations differ on central issues in the doctrine of original sin—for example, how a child acquires the fateful disposition to sin, whether this disposition is itself sin, how to describe and assess the accompanying bondage of the will—they agree on the universality, solidarity, stubbornness, and historical momentum of sin.

The Biblical authors therefore portray sin as an alien intruder into God's good creation. The story of Adam and Eve, and their first disobedience, explains how this intruder first came into human experience, though it hardly pretends to explain how it is that rebellion against God—as expressed in the serpent's speech—came about in the first place.[59]

The best way to read the parts of the Bible, then, is in relation to the overarching story by which the individual Biblical authors deliberately interpreted their world. This story is focused on God's plan to use his human partners to bring blessing to the whole creation, a blessing that requires "redemption" for all people now that something has gone wrong at the headwaters of mankind. The Bible writers portray this as the true story for all people everywhere, and that "truth" involves events that really took place, or "history." If we are to indwell this story, we need to make every effort to hold on to its events and their meaning.

---

[59]For discussion of the literary portrayal of the serpent as Tempter, see Collins, *Genesis 1–4*, 170–72 (and see my summary in section 3.a below).

3

PARTICULAR TEXTS THAT
SPEAK OF ADAM AND EVE

The argument so far certainly favors the notion of an historical fall of the human race. It also supports a view of human unity, though one might wonder whether that unity depends on common descent from the first pair that sinned. Now we move on to examine specific Biblical texts about Adam and Eve, to see how they fit into this larger picture.

When we look at individual Bible texts, we encounter the "forest and trees problem": namely, how does our perception of the big picture (forest) interact with our interpretations of the texts (trees)? I do not propose a simple answer to that question—I only advocate that, in order to be responsible, we must ensure that they interact and mutually correct. Some people are by inclination big-picture thinkers, and they must discipline themselves to look at the fine details; others, like me, are detail people, who must make the effort to relate these details to the larger story. My own avenue to seeing the Biblical story as I have described it above is from the details; others will take a different route.

It is often said that references to Adam and Eve are infrequent in the Bible. It is not clear that this is strictly true, though some of the possible references are disputed. Hence it will be best to focus on the cake, those for which the disputes are of no concern, and only add in the more disputed ones as icing. Also, it will be helpful to include Jewish texts that are not in the (Protestant) canon, such as from the Apocrypha: these texts illustrate the world of Second Temple Judaism, which represents a way of reading the Old Testament, and which is the world into which the New Testament writers addressed their works.

3.a Genesis 1–5

As soon as we turn to Genesis, we face a number of questions before we can proceed. It is often said, for example, that we have in Genesis 1–2 two different creation accounts (1:1–2:3 and 2:4–25), which come from separate sources. We also hear frequently that the two accounts may even be difficult to reconcile with each other.[1]

As for the question of separate sources, the arguments for and against such sources will forever be indecisive, since none of these putative sources is actually known to exist. The only text that we have is the one that places these two passages together. Further, we have no reason to expect that whoever did put these passages together was a blockhead (or a committee of blockheads), who could not recognize contradictions every bit as well as we can. As James Barr—who accepted the common critical breakup of Genesis into putative sources, and a late date for its final composition—points out, it is reasonable to expect an editor to have smoothed out genuine contradictions between his sources, and tensions that remained would have invited ancient audiences to seek ways to "recognize the truthfulness of *both* narratives."[2] (Barr himself did not explain how

---

[1]From a scholarly source, see Daniel Harlow, "Creation according to Genesis: Literary Genre, Cultural Context, Theological Truth," *Christian Scholars Review* 37:2 (2008): 163–98. From a nonspecialist, see Francis Collins, *The Language of God: A Scientist Presents Evidence for Belief* (New York: Free Press, 2006), 150, presumably following someone else.
[2]James Barr, "One Man, or All Humanity? A Question in the Anthropology of Genesis 1," in Athalya Brenner and Jan Willem van Henten, eds., *Recycling Biblical Figures: Papers Read at a NOSTER Colloquium in Amsterdam, 12–13 May 1997*, Studies in Theology and Religion (Leiden: Deo, 1999), 3–21, at 6. Speaking frankly, as a traditional Christian I am wary of any exegetical "gift" that Barr might offer; see my critical discussion of his famous 1984 letter to David Watson in Collins, *Science and Faith: Friends or Foes?* (Wheaton, IL:

he thought this smoothing actually worked.) Therefore, if literary and linguistic studies point to a way to read the whole production coherently, we do well to pay heed.

My own literary and linguistic studies have pointed to just such a coherence. I argue for a version of the traditional Rabbinic opinion, namely that, far from seeing two discordant accounts, we should see Genesis 1:1–2:3 as the overall account of the creation and preparation of the earth as a suitable place for humans to live, and Genesis 2:4–25 as an elaboration of the events of the sixth day of Genesis 1.[3] This traditional reading lies behind, say, the way Haydn's oratorio *Die Schöpfung (The Creation)* weaves the two narratives together: on the sixth day, God created man in his "own image" (Gen. 1:27), and breathed into his nostrils the breath of life (Gen. 2:7).[4] What I have done is to supply the grammatical justification for this traditional approach, by examining how Genesis 2:4–7 links the two stories. My argument is readily available in print, so I will just point out that its validity does not rest on any view of the authorship and date of Genesis.[5]

My grammatical conclusions, first fully published in 1999, are reflected in the English Standard Version of Genesis 2:4–7:[6]

> [4]These are the generations
> of the heavens and the earth when they were created,

Crossway, 2003), 364–66. See further my review of his book on Genesis 3 (appendix 2 below). At the same time, Barr's contributions to linguistic rigor in Biblical studies are substantial, and we ought to acknowledge his positions when he presents arguments to show their validity.

[3]C. John Collins, *Genesis 1–4: A Linguistic, Literary, and Theological Commentary* (Phillipsburg, NJ: P&R, 2006), 108–12, 121–22. For instances of the traditional Jewish opinion, see the Hebrew commentary of Yehudah Kiel, *Sefer Bereshit* (Genesis), Da'at Miqra' (Jerusalem: Mossad Harav Kook, 1997), page טז n. 7.

[4]Franz Joseph Haydn, *Die Schöpfung* (Hob. xxi:2), §§23–24.

[5]To some extent, however, the discussion of later "echoes" of these texts does require an opinion on the date of the Genesis materials: if they did not yet exist, a text could not be echoing them! One recourse would be to suppose that an earlier version of the current text did exist, and that the date of the final form is not the determining factor. However, I have added appendix 3 to give reasons for believing that Genesis came fairly early in Israel's life.

[6]Jack Collins, "Discourse Analysis and the Interpretation of Gen 2:4–7," *Westminster Theological Journal* 61 (1999): 269–76.

in the day that the LORD God made the earth and the heavens.

⁵When no bush of the field was yet in the land and no small plant of the field had yet sprung up—for the LORD God had not caused it to rain on the land, and there was no man to work the ground, ⁶and a mist was going up from the land and was watering the whole face of the ground—⁷then the LORD God formed the man of dust from the ground and breathed into his nostrils the breath of life, and the man became a living creature.

The purpose of Genesis 1:1–2:3, in my understanding, is almost "liturgical": that is, it celebrates as a great achievement God's work of fashioning the world as a suitable place for humans to live. "The exalted tone of the passage allows the reader to ponder this with a sense of awe, adoring the goodness, power, and creativity of the One who did all this."⁷ Possibly the best way to read the passage is in unison, in a service of worship. Then Genesis 2:4–25 focuses in on the making of the human couple that we know as Adam and Eve. The rendering of 2:4–7 given above enables us to see that in a particular region (called "the land" in verse 5), at a particular time of year (at the end of the dry season, before it had begun to rain, when the rain clouds ["mist"] were beginning to rise)—that is when God formed the man. In other words, we read Genesis 1 and 2 together when we take 2:4–25 as filling out details of the "sixth day," amplifying 1:24–31.⁸ Specifically, it explains how it was that God created mankind as male and female, and equipped them to be fruitful and multiply. We can see this further from the way "it is not good that the man should be alone" in 2:18 jars with the "very good" of 1:31: this shows us that chapter 2 has not reached the point of 1:31 until the man and the

---

⁷Collins, *Genesis 1–4*, 78–79. Moshe Weinfeld has declared that the passage is "liturgical" in its origin: see "Sabbath, Temple, and the Enthronement of the Lord—the Problem of the Sitz im Leben of Genesis 1:1–2:3," in A. Caquot and M. Delcor, eds., *Mélanges Bibliques et Orientaux en l'Honneur de M. Henri Cazelles* (AOAT 212; Neukirchen-Vluyn: Neukirchener, 1981), 501–12. I do not agree with all that lies behind such a statement, but I do think that it captures the celebratory tone of the passage.

⁸On the specific question of Gen. 2:19 and the order of events, see my discourse-oriented grammatical study, "The Wayyiqtol as 'Pluperfect': When and Why," *Tyndale Bulletin* 46: I (1995), 117–40, at 135–40.

woman have become one flesh. Once we get to 2:25, with the man and woman naked and not ashamed, we breathe a sigh of relief: we are now at the point where it is all "very good."

There are further features of Genesis 1–5 that display unity. It is not controversial to see Genesis 2–4 as a connected story, coming primarily from the same source (J, the "Yahwistic writer"). It is often said, however, that the genealogy of Genesis 5 comes from the same source as 1:1–2:3 (P, the "priestly writer").[9] Whatever we may think of these sources, we should see that the whole has been edited to produce a coherent narrative. For example, the shift in divine name from "God" (ch. 1) to "the LORD God" (chs. 2–3), and then simply to "the LORD" (ch. 4, except 4:25) has the rhetorical effect of identifying the LORD, the covenant God of Israel, with the universal and transcendent Creator: Israel's faith is intended to bring blessing to all mankind (cf. 12:1–3). Further, the "blessing" of Genesis 1:28 turns into a threefold "curse" in 3:14–19 (cf. 4:11); the hitherto joyful task of "multiplying" (1:28) becomes the arena of "multiplied" pain (3:16). In Genesis 4 we see the human family being fruitful and multiplying, in compliance with their commission (1:28). However, the sad and shameful outcomes of the descendants' behavior contrasts with the exuberant expectation of Genesis 1:26–31: the average Israelite's experience is probably more like Genesis 4 than it is like Genesis 1 or 2. This cries out for an explanation, and, as I will argue, we need some version of the traditional reading of Genesis 3 to make sense of these facts. Finally, I observe that Genesis 5:1–3 employs the personal names Adam and Seth, which come from Genesis 2–4.

In Genesis, the figure named "Adam" appears unambiguously in chapters 2–5. The proper name Adam transliterates the Hebrew word for "human being, mankind," 'adam.[10] In Genesis 2:20 (according to the

<hr/>

[9]See, e.g., the commentary of S. R. Driver, *The Book of Genesis*, Westminster Commentary (London: Methuen, 1904).

[10]It is common to see this as connecting "man" ('adām) with the "ground" ('adamâ, 2:7) from which he was formed. However, since the account goes on to say that the other animals were also formed from the ground (2:19), this wordplay seems less likely. The first-century Jewish writer Josephus (*Antiquities* 1.1.2, line 34) connected the word with the Hebrew for "red" ('adôm), which is as likely an explanation as any other (assuming that we have to find a wordplay).

received Hebrew text), "the man" is first called "Adam."[11] Genesis 2:5 says there was no *man* to work the ground, and thus in 2:7 the Lord God formed *the man* using dust from the ground. In 2:18 *the man* is alone, and the Lord God sets out to make a helper fit for him. Throughout 2:4–4:26, whether he is called *the man* or Adam, he is presented as one person. The man's one wife is simply called either "the woman" or "his wife" throughout—although when she receives her name Eve in 3:20, that name becomes another option (cf. 4:1, where both are used together). The name Adam appears also in the genealogy of 5:1–5.

The divine plan to "make *man* in our image, after our likeness" (1:26) may refer to mankind in general (as most commentators think),[12] or it may refer to the man in particular (as James Barr argued).[13] Whichever way we prefer, it is easy to read 2:4–25 as filling in the details of how mankind came to be composed of male and female members, both of whom are in God's image. Both the title "the Human," (ESV "the man") and the proper name Adam ("Human") are fitted to someone whose actions are in some sense representative of all mankind.[14]

But he might "represent" mankind either as a personification, or as a particular member, or perhaps as both. Which sense is fitted here? James Barr—rightly, it seems to me—argues the following in regard to 5:1–2:[15]

> This text, just here at the start of the genealogy, seems to me to make sense only if the writer intends one human pair, from whose descendants the world will gradually come to be populated.

---

[11]The usual rule is that the form with the definite article, *ha-'adam*, is "the man," the newly formed human being of 2:7. In the received Hebrew text the form in 2:20 lacks the article, so it is rendered "Adam." Some prefer to insert the article at 2:20 (which would only be the change of a vowel, from *lᵉ'adam* to *la'adam*), thus deferring the first instance of the proper name to 3:17 (or even to 4:25).

[12]See Richard Hess, "Splitting the Adam," in J. A. Emerton, ed., *Studies in the Pentateuch*, SVT (Leiden: Brill, 1991), 1–15, at 1.

[13]Barr, "One Man, or All Humanity?" 9, based on the wording of 5:1–2.

[14]See Hess, "Splitting the Adam," 12; cf. also Kiel, *Sefer Bereshit*, קב (at Gen. 4:1). See also Dexter E. Callender, Jr., *Adam in Myth and History: Ancient Israelite Perspectives on the Primal Human*, Harvard Semitic Studies (Winona Lake, IN: Eisenbrauns, 2000), 32: "There is an obvious and understandable awareness that Adam stands between God and humanity."

[15]Barr, "One Man, or All humanity?" 9.

This reading, that Adam and Eve are presented as a particular pair, the first parents of all humanity, is pretty widespread in the exegetical literature, both from writers who have some kind of traditionalist commitment to the Bible's truthfulness, and from those who do not (such as Barr).[16] At the same time, this does not exclude Adam from being a representative in the sense of being a kind of paradigm through which we learn something about how temptation works.

At any rate, the man who was once "alone" (2:18), now has a wife; these two disobey God and leave the garden of Eden. They have children, who also have children (chapter 4). The genealogy of Genesis 5 links this pair to subsequent people, leading up to Noah (5:32), from whom came Abraham (11:10–26), the forefather of Israel. It makes no difference for our purposes whether the flood is thought to have killed *all* mankind (outside of Noah and his family); nor does it matter how many generations the genealogies may or may not have skipped. The genealogies of Genesis 1–11 link Father Abraham, whom the people of Israel took to be historical, with Adam, who is otherwise hidden from the Israelites in the mists of antiquity.

I say "the mists of antiquity" to remind us that we are dealing with the kind of literature that deals with "prehistory" and "protohistory." The Assyriologist William Hallo uses the term "prehistory" for the period of human existence before there are any secure written records, and "protohistory" for the earliest stages for which there are records.[17] And, as Kenneth Kitchen argues, in the nineteenth century B.C., people "*knew already* that their world was old, very old."[18] Therefore the phrase "mists of antiquity" represents the perspective the ancients themselves would have held. I see no reason to dispute the view that Israel's narrative of prehistory bears a relationship with the narratives of prehistory found in Mesopotamia,

---

[16]Cf. Barr, "One Man, or All Humanity?" 5: "We no longer believe that all humanity originated in one single human pair. In respect of our beliefs about humanity the narrative of chapter 1 is closer to what we actually believe"—i.e., under the reading that "man" is just a collective for all humanity, which Barr proceeds to reject.

[17]William W. Hallo, "Part 1: Mesopotamia and the Asiatic Near East," in William W. Hallo and William K. Simpson, eds., *The Ancient Near East: A History* (Fort Worth, TX: Harcourt Brace College Publishers, 1998), 3–181, at 25.

[18]Kenneth A. Kitchen, *On the Reliability of the Old Testament* (Grand Rapids, MI: Eerdmans, 2003), 439.

already mentioned above (and discussed in more detail in appendix 1). This implies that, like those other stories, Genesis aims to tell the true story of origins; but it also implies that there are likely to be figurative elements and literary conventions that should make us very wary of being too literalistic in our reading.[19] That is, the genre identification for Genesis 1–11, prehistory and protohistory, does *not* mean that the author had no concern for real events; far from it, it implies that real events form the backbone of his story.

At the same time, as is widely known, there are important differences between Genesis 1–11 and the Mesopotamian prehistories. The way the stories are told conveys very different stances toward the divine, the world, and man's calling. The Mesopotamian prehistories do in places suggest that the gods created a *group* of first humans. Barr mentions this feature of the Mesopotamian stories but then shows that it does not of itself entail that Genesis does likewise:[20]

> The creation of humans should be [so the argument goes] analogical [with the origin of the other animal kinds as a whole in Genesis 1]: therefore he creates the human beings as a whole, all humanity. Some support for this view may come from Mesopotamian parallels: in important examples the gods do not create individual humans, but the human race. And this is a good argument, but it is not fully coercive. Perhaps the Hebrew writer had reasons that persuaded him just at this point *not* to continue with large categories but to consider humanity on a more individual basis. . . . Moreover, even if Mesopotamian sources think of humanity as a class, we have certain proof that the individual view of human creation was deeply embedded in

---

[19]Cf. the remark of A. R. Millard on the topic of excessive literalism in general: "The writers were describing unusual riches in phrases that convey the thought clearly enough, *without demanding a literal interpretation*": Millard, "Story, History, and Theology," in A. R. Millard, James K. Hoffmeier and David W. Baker, eds., *Faith, Tradition, and History: Old Testament Historiography in Its Near Eastern Context* (Winona Lake, IN: Eisenbrauns, 1994), 37–64, at 49 (italics added).

[20]Barr, "One Man, or All Humanity?" 10. As John Walton observed, in the other ancient Near Eastern accounts "there is no indication of an original human pair that became the progenitors of the entire human race (monogenesis). This is one of the distinctives of the Genesis account" (John H. Walton, *Ancient Near Eastern Thought and the Old Testament: Introducing the Conceptual World of the Hebrew Bible* [Grand Rapids, MI: Baker, 2006], 205).

Hebrew culture: namely the narrative of Genesis 2–3 itself, the story of Adam and Eve.

Barr mentions "reasons" that persuaded the Hebrew author of Genesis to tell a story different from those the Mesopotamians told; these reasons have to do with the radically differing ideologies of these prehistories, as we will see (and consult appendix 1 below).

Umberto Cassuto saw this clearly. After describing the similarities and differences between the other stories and those of Genesis, he observes:[21]

> In another respect, too, the Pentateuchal account differs from those given in the aforementioned texts, namely, in that it speaks of the creation of only one human pair, a fact that implies the brotherhood and equality of man, whereas the pagan texts refer to the mass creation of mankind as a whole.

The ideology of the Genesis prehistory-protohistory is clear from its own literary context as the front end of the book of Genesis: that is, Genesis 1–11 is the backcloth of the Abraham-Isaac-Jacob story, which is the backcloth of the Exodus story. This prehistory grounds the call of Abraham by showing how all human beings are related, and therefore equally in need of God's blessing, and equally reachable with that blessing. Abraham is God's answer to this universal need (Gen. 12:1–3): he is to be the vehicle of blessing to "all the families of the earth," starting the family through which all mankind, which is now estranged from God, will come to know the true God.

Once we recognize this, we might also recognize that the telling of Genesis 1–11 is deliberately shaped with this purpose in mind. Many, for example, have noticed the way in which the garden of Eden becomes a pattern for describing the Israelite sanctuary, and even

---

[21]Umberto Cassuto, *From Adam to Noah: Genesis I–VI.8* (Jerusalem: Magnes, 1961 [1944]), 71–83, at 83. This remark has an extra poignancy when we recall that Cassuto was an Italian-born Jew who emigrated to Israel and wrote this commentary in Hebrew during the Holocaust. It is not entirely clear how Cassuto wanted to reconcile this insight with his general demurral from historical reading, except that he appears to have been looking for timeless lessons.

the land of Israel.[22] That is to say, the Old Testament views Eden as the first sanctuary, where God is present with his covenant partners (Adam and Eve); the tabernacle, and later the temple, reinstate this Edenic blessing. What makes the Promised Land special is that it too is to be like a reconstituted Eden, whose fruitfulness displays for all the world the presence of God.[23] There is every reason to expect that Genesis portrays Adam with goals like this in mind: that is, he is "like" an Israelite, so that each member of God's people will see himself or herself as God's "new Adam" in the world. These considerations help us to see that the author may well use such devices as anachronism if it serves his purpose; "historical verisimilitude" (aiming to get all the details of life exactly as the characters would have known them, even if the audience did not live that way) is not strongly claimed by the text itself.[24]

The marriage of Adam and Eve (Gen. 2:23–25) is taken as the paradigm for any sound future marriage of human beings. The comment makes clear that this is programmatic for human life: "Therefore [because of the events of verses 21–23] a man [Hebrew 'ish, any male human being] shall leave his father and his mother and hold fast to his wife, and they shall become one flesh" (2:24).[25]

The disobedience of Adam and Eve also has historical import, as seen from its consequences. The hiding from God in Genesis 3:8; the fear and blame game of 3:10–13; the solemn sentences of 3:14–19; the evil deeds of chapter 4: all of these are in jarring discord with

[22]This is the thesis of, e.g., Martin Emmrich, "The Temptation Narrative of Genesis 3:1–6: A Prelude to the Pentateuch and the History of Israel," *Evangelical Quarterly* 73:1 (2001), 3–20. Not all of his points are persuasive, but his suggestion that "the garden of Genesis 2–3 wants to be viewed as the archetype of the land of Israel" (5) is sound.
[23]See, e.g., Christopher Wright, *The Mission of God: Unlocking the Bible's Grand Narrative* (Downers Grove, IL: InterVarsity Press, 2006), 334.
[24]Indeed, historical verisimilitude in literary compositions did not arise, at least in the West, until the modern period. This, by the way, is one of the arguments in favor of seeing ancient tradition, rather than free composition, behind the stories of the patriarchs (Genesis 12–50): their manners and customs reflect accurate recollections of the time in which the events occurred, not simply the time of whoever wrote the stories down. On this last point, see A. R. Millard, "Methods of Studying the Patriarchal Narratives as Ancient Texts," in A. R. Millard and Donald J. Wiseman, eds., *Essays on the Patriarchal Narratives* (Leicester, U.K.: Inter-Varsity Press, 1980), 43–58.
[25]This probably lies behind the wording of Mal. 2:15 (ESV), "Did he not make them one?"

the idyllic scene of blessing and benevolent dominion (1:28–29) and innocent enjoyment (2:8–9, 18–25). Some have suggested that, because there are no words for "sin" or "rebellion" in Genesis 3, therefore the text does not "teach" that Adam and Eve "sinned."[26] Of course this is absurd: the question of 3:11 (have you done what I told you not to do?) is as good a paraphrase of disobedience as we can ask for. Some have also suggested that, since the text of Genesis does not *say* that humans "fell" by this disobedience, therefore Genesis does not "teach" such a thing.[27] But the jarring discord we have just noticed is instruction enough on that point. These objections stem from a failure to appreciate that Biblical narrators tend to prefer the laconic "showing" to the more explicit "telling," leaving the readers to draw the right inferences from the words and actions recorded.[28]

I have also heard the objection that the disobedience of Genesis 3 is pretty tame in comparison with the violence of Genesis 4: therefore how can the one be the cause of the other? I would not quite put the relationship between the two sins that way, as "cause" and "effect": I would rather say that the sin of Genesis 3, under the influence of a Dark Power that has the goal of ruining human life, has opened the door to all manner of evil in the world. I might further query whether the disobedience of Genesis 3 is really all that "small": after all, it came after God had loaded the human beings with blessings and delights, and it resulted from yielding to a subtle and despi-

---

[26]E.g., James Barr, *The Garden of Eden and the Hope of Immortality*, 6. For more on this matter, see Collins, *Genesis 1–4*, 155.

[27]See, e.g., Harlow, "Creation according to Genesis: Literary Genre, Cultural Context, Theological Truth": "Genesis itself, however, does not propound a doctrine of the fall or original sin" (189). See also Towner, "Interpretations and Reinterpretations of the Fall," e.g., 59: "Nowhere is it said [in Genesis] that human nature was irrevocably altered in a fundamental way that afternoon in the garden. . . . That is all that the Biblical account says—it has never said any more than that."

[28]The ideas of "showing" and "telling" were established concepts in literary studies by 1981, well before Towner's 1984 article; see V. P. Long, *The Reign and Rejection of King Saul: A Case for Literary and Theological Coherence*, SBL Dissertation Series (Atlanta: Scholars, 1989), 31–34. But in light of subsequent developments in literary readings of the Bible, the remarks in the previous note sound very clumsy. See Collins, *Genesis 1–4*, 173 n. 66 for another example of a leading commentator's (Westermann) failure to account for showing over telling.

cable assault on the character of the God who had shown himself so overflowing with goodness. Let Israel, and all who read this, take warning, and never underestimate the power of even the apparently smallest sins.

Does Genesis give us any clues—showing, if not telling—as to *how* sin was transmitted to Cain, to Lamech, and on to others? The details are sketchy; it is probably not enough to say that Adam and Eve set a bad example for their children. Probably the best answer is that of Paul, who uses the expression "in Adam," implying some way in which human beings are "included" in Adam; we will come back to that in our discussion of texts from Paul.

And what shall we make of the "death" that God threatens in Genesis 2:17? I have argued that the primary reference is "spiritual death," as exhibited in Genesis 3:8–13. But that is not all: it would appear (to me at least) that this is followed by their physical death as well (v. 19). We will take this up in more detail a little later, in section 5.b. At this point I will simply observe that we should be careful about letting the *distinction* between spiritual and physical death, which is proper, lead us to drive a wedge of *separation* between the two kinds of death: it looks like the author presents them as two aspects of one experience. In other words, physical death is not any more "natural" for human experience than spiritual death is.

In Genesis 3:20 the woman receives a name, "Eve." This is connected in some way to the Hebrew word for "live," and the Septuagint renders it as *Zoe* "Life." The form of the Hebrew name, however—*Khawwâ*, from the root *kh-w-h*, "to live"—probably indicates a causative significance, i.e., "she who gives life," "Life-Giver" (see ESV footnote).[29] This supports the interpretation found in the ancient Jewish Aramaic translation called Targum Onkelos (no later than fourth century A.D.): "the mother of all the children of man."[30]

We sometimes encounter scholars who refer to "folkloristic" elements in Genesis 2–3, such as the etiological purpose (e.g., the origin of marriage), a talking snake, and the "magic trees." I would reply

---

[29]See Collins, *Genesis 1–4*, 154 n. 22, drawing on Scott C. Layton, "Remarks on the Canaanite Origin of Eve," *Catholic Biblical Quarterly* 59:1 (1997): 22–32.
[30]See Kiel, *Sefer Bereshit*, חוה (on Gen. 3:20).

that calling these elements "folkloristic" stems from a number of mistakes. I have discussed these points at length in a number of places, so I will only summarize my arguments here; the footnotes will show where I have dealt with the issues in greater length.

I begin by noting that an etiological narrative might actually give the *true* origin of some feature of contemporary life; simply calling it "etiological" settles no questions at all.[31] I have a large scar on my left knee, and I can tell you a true story of how it got there. The story is interesting to me, and to my children, because it involves a dangerous situation that I got into through a lack of foresight, and a dramatic deliverance. That true story is an etiology.

Further, the fact that the snake talks is a clue to its function in the narrative. The commentator Hermann Gunkel finds this to be a feature of fairy tales and legends, where you expect to read of talking animals; oddly enough, he actually refers to Balaam's donkey in Numbers 22: "Hebrew legends also know of the talking donkey."[32] I call this odd, because the narrator in Num. 22:28 says that the LORD "opened the mouth of the donkey," which is what enabled it to speak. In other words, the writer of this passage did not portray a world in which donkeys speak; he instead recounted what he thought was a *miracle*.[33] That is to say, the only other example of a talking animal in a Biblical narrative attributes that speech to some kind of interference with the animal's proper "nature." Besides, when we observe the serpent's knowledge of what God said in Genesis 2:17 (in 3:4 the serpent echoes the divine "surely die"), in addition to the evil that the serpent speaks (he urges disobedience to God's solemn command, calls God a liar, and insinuates that God's motives cannot be trusted), we see that the Jewish and New Testament interpretive tradition (e.g., Wisdom 1:13; 2:24; John 8:44; Rev. 12:9; 20:2) that sees the Evil One ("Satan" or "the devil") as using this serpent as its mouthpiece is on a firm footing. In fact, to deny this by insisting that Genesis never mentions the Evil One is actually a bad reading, because it requires

---

[31]On this point see Millard, "Story, History, and Theology," at 40–42.
[32]Hermann Gunkel, *Genesis* (Macon, GA: Mercer University Press, 1997 [1910]), 15.
[33]On this point see my discussion in *The God of Miracles: An Exegetical Examination of God's Action in the World* (Wheaton, IL: Crossway, 2000), 96–97.

telling and does not account for *showing*. If we read the story badly like this, we will miss a crucial part of the story.[34]

Gunkel makes another mistake when he interprets Genesis 3 as giving a lesson in natural history, to the effect that the curse of v. 14 ("on your belly you shall go, and dust you shall eat all the days of your life") explains why all serpents travel as they do and why they eat soil.[35] I recall hearing this when I was young; it was probably not in church, for I was not well churched as a youth. I still remember my delight in learning, as a teenaged herpetologist, that boa constrictors have vestigial legs (just like Genesis said!). But this is a failure to read the text well: the curses of Genesis 3:14–19 are rhetorically high (set as poetry in modern Bibles), which leads us to expect vivid figurative language. And an expression close to "eat dust" is used elsewhere as a figure for humiliation and defeat (e.g., Isa. 49:23; Mic. 7:17; Ps. 72:9). I suspect that most Israelites would have known that serpents do not "literally" eat dust anyhow; it does not take much time in the desert to discover that they eat mice, lizards, other snakes, and so on (cf. Ex. 7:10–12).[36] Besides, a good reader already knows that the serpent is not acting for itself; it is a tool of a Dark Power that intends harm for man. Therefore it makes for better reading to take "dust you shall eat" as describing the humiliation the Dark Power will undergo, and "on your belly you shall go" as a similar figure for how that Power will always cringe before the mighty God.

There is no reason to describe the two trees, the "tree of the knowledge of good and evil" and the "tree of life," as "magic" without any nuance.[37] The nature of the "knowledge of good and evil" has given rise to many competing interpretations; I agree with those who think that the tree of the knowledge of good and evil is the tree by which the humans were intended to acquire a knowledge of good and evil—if they stood the test, they would know good and evil from above, as

---

[34]See further my *Genesis 1–4*, 171–72.

[35]So Gunkel, *Genesis*, 20.

[36]The Hebrew word for "serpent" here is *tannîn*, while Gen. 3:1 uses *nakhash*. Nevertheless, since Ex. 4:3, the precedent of Ex. 7:10–12, uses *nakhash*, the point I am making stands. On this matter, see further United Bible Societies, *Fauna and Flora of the Bible* (London: United Bible Societies, 1980), 73.

[37]See further my *Genesis 1–4*, 115–16.

those who have mastered temptation; sadly, they came to know good and evil from below, as those who have been mastered by temptation. This explanation fits well with the fact that God acknowledges that the humans have actually gained some knowledge (3:22); it also fits with the other uses of the expression, "to know good and evil" (and phrases like it), in the rest of the Hebrew Bible, to express the idea of discernment (which is often gained through maturation).

In fact, this interpretation also helps us to appreciate what is going on in the temptation. In my own work I have argued that the humans were created morally innocent, but not necessarily "perfect" (so long as "innocence" does not mean naiveté or moral neutrality). Their task was to mature through the exercise of their obedience, to become confirmed in moral goodness. We cannot say that they were *at this point* necessarily "immortal"; but the narrative does not dwell on what might have been. This, as it turns out, has some interesting similarities to Irenaeus's reading of Genesis 1–3. By his understanding, the innocence of Genesis 2 was more like that of a child than of a full adult; God's goal for them was their maturity (a possible sense of "knowing good and evil," see Deut. 1:39). Their fall broke the process of growth.[38]

But what of the "tree of life"? Does it work "automatically," which is what most mean by calling it magical? Genesis says very little about it. What it does say (3:22, where God fears that the man might live forever if he takes of it) should be put together with the other passages that use the same idea. In Proverbs 3:18; 11:30; 13:12; 15:4, various blessings are likened to a tree of life: all of these blessings, according to Proverbs, are means to keep the faithful on the path to everlasting happiness. In Revelation 2:7; 22:2, 14, 19, the tree is a symbol of confirmation in holiness for the faithful. This warrants us in finding this tree to be some kind of "sacrament" that sustains or confirms someone in his moral condition: that is why God finds it so horrifying to think of the man eating of the tree in his current state. I call it a "sacrament," because I do not know how it is supposed to convey its effects, any more than I know how the Biblical sacrifices,

---

[38]See Anders-Christian Jacobsen, "The Importance of Genesis 1–3 in the Theology of Irenaeus," *Zeitschrift für antikes Christentum* 8.2 (2005), 299–316, at 302–303.

or the washing ceremonies, or baptism, or the Lord's Supper work. But they *do* work.[39] Only in this sense may the tree be called "magic," but this sense has moved us away from folklore.[40]

In sum then, we have plenty of reasons from the text itself to be careful about reading it too literalistically; and at the same time we have reasons to accept an historical core. The historicity of Adam is assumed in the genealogies of 1 Chronicles 1:1 and Luke 3:38. Similarly, although the style of telling the story may leave us uncertain on the exact details of the process by which Adam's body was formed, and whether the two trees were actual trees, and whether the Evil One's actual mouthpiece was a talking snake, we nevertheless can discern that the author intends us to see the disobedience of this couple as the reason for sin in the world. It explains why the Mosaic covenant will include provisions for the sins of the people: Mosaic religion, and Christianity its proper offspring, is about redemption for sinners, enabling their forgiveness and moral transformation to restore the image of God in them. This story also explains why all mankind, and not just Israelites, need this redemptive, healing touch from God.

3.b Adam, Eve, Eden, and the Fall in the Rest of the Old Testament

For an interpretation of Genesis 1–5 to be adequate, it must account for the details of the Hebrew narrative, the similarities and differences between that narrative and its possible parallels from elsewhere in the ancient Near East, and the location of that narrative as the front end of the whole book of Genesis—indeed, of the whole Pentateuch, which therefore means of the whole Old Testament.[41]

---

[39]In a forthcoming book, I will take up the question of "sacramental realism" in the Biblical ceremonial system.

[40]See C. S. Lewis, *Prayer: Letters to Malcolm* (London: Collins, 1966), 105: he describes the sacrament of communion as "big medicine and strong magic," and then defines his term: "I should define 'magic' in this sense as 'objective efficacy which cannot be further analysed.'"

[41]In light of this, there are numerous proposed readings of this story, or parts of it, that I will not spend time assessing: for example, Lyn M. Bechtel, "Genesis 2.4b–3.24: A Myth about Human Maturation," *Journal for the Study of the Old Testament* 67 (1995): 3–26, finds here a myth about the process of growing up; but she has not taken account of the story's

In this section I will show how the themes of Genesis 1–5 are played out in the rest of the Hebrew Old Testament.

It is often said that references to the fall story are rare, or even nonexistent, in the rest of the Old Testament. Consider, for example, the way that Claus Westermann put it:[42]

> First of all, it must be stated that in the Old Testament the text did not have [an] all-embracing meaning. It is nowhere cited or presumed in the Old Testament; its significance is limited to primeval events.

There are several difficulties with this claim: the first is, what exactly constitutes a "citation," presumption, or echo? A related difficulty is, does an allusion to any part of Genesis 1–5 count as one of these echoes? And there is still more: has this perceived rarity of allusion become part of a circular argument—that is, once we think that there are no allusions, do we then dismiss possible allusions because we "know" that such an allusion is unlikely since it is so rare? Finally, does not the presence or absence of allusions depend on the communicative intentions of the Biblical writers and their perceptions of the needs of their audiences? That is, a later writer may or may not find an echo of this passage useful to what he is trying to do with his later text—which means that the (perceived) rarity of citation hardly implies that this story has no bearing on the rest of the Hebrew Bible.

I will try to be mindful of all these factors in this section. However, the literary unity of the current text of these chapters (as already described) gives us a warrant for qualifying the claim of rarity: after all, there are numerous references to creation (e.g., Psalms 8, 104) and to marriage (e.g., Mal. 2:15, using Gen. 2:24). Human rest on the Israelite Sabbath imitates God's rest after his work of creation (Ex. 20:11, echoing Gen. 2:2–3).[43]

---

themes of obedience and disobedience, the meaning of the "curses," or of the sequel in Genesis 4, which depicts the increase of sin. Further, her reading does not fit into the rest of Genesis, nor does it explain what later Biblical authors have found in the story.

[42]Claus Westermann, *Creation* (London: SPCK, 1974), 89, as cited with approval in Towner, "Interpretations and Reinterpretations of the Fall," 72.

[43]I discuss many such "reverberations" in my *Genesis 1–4*.

We begin by noting that Genesis 1–5 is well integrated into the whole flow of Genesis 1–11, and into the whole of Genesis. I have already mentioned how the genealogies of Genesis 5 and 11 connect the primal pair to subsequent generations, particularly to Abraham. Further, the connection with Mesopotamian stories of prehistory and protohistory comes from the pattern of creation, early generations of people, flood, further generations of people, leading to "modern times"; this makes the first five chapters an inherent part of this pattern, which includes *all* of Genesis 1–11.

Genesis presents Noah to us as a kind of new Adam: he is the representative who receives God's covenant on behalf of his descendants and also of the animals (6:18–19; 9:8–17); God "blesses" him and tells him to "be fruitful and multiply and fill the earth" (9:1).

The call of Abraham is another fresh start on God's plan to bring his blessing to the human race. The "blessing" idea is explicit in 12:2–3 and is combined with being fruitful and multiplying in 17:20; 22:17–18; 26:3–4, 24; 28:3, 14: these echo God's blessing on the original human pair (1:28). Another theme that ties Genesis 1–5 with the rest of Genesis is the repeated word "seed" (best translated "offspring," as in the ESV): cf. 3:15; 4:25 with 12:7; 13:15–16; 15:3, 5; 17:7–9, 19; 22:17–18; 26:3–4; 48:4. Especially pertinent is the apparent individual offspring referred to in 3:15; 22:17–18; 24:60—who, by the time of Psalm 72, is identified as the ultimate heir of David through whom God's blessing will finally come to the whole earth (Ps. 72:17, echoing Gen. 22:17–18).[44]

I have already indicated that the call of Abraham to be the vehicle of blessing to the rest of the world presupposes that the other nations need the blessing of God's light. The story of Genesis 3, and the pro-

---

[44] On the matter of the "offspring" in Genesis, see T. Desmond Alexander, "From Adam to Judah: The Significance of the Family Tree in Genesis," *Evangelical Quarterly* 61:1 (1989): 5–19; "Genealogies, Seed and the Compositional Unity of Genesis," *Tyndale Bulletin* 44:2 (1993): 255–70. On the individual offspring, see J. Collins, "A Syntactical Note on Genesis 3:15: Is the Woman's Seed Singular or Plural?" *Tyndale Bulletin* 48:1 (1997): 141–48, with Alexander's development in "Further Observations on the Term 'Seed' in Genesis," *Tyndale Bulletin* 48:2 (1997): 363–67, with further development from Collins in "Galatians 3:16: What Kind of Exegete Was Paul?" *Tyndale Bulletin* 54:1 (2003): 75–86.

gression into further moral and spiritual darkness in Genesis 4–11, explains *why* the other nations are so needy.

I have also already mentioned the way in which the garden of Eden is the pattern for the Israelite sanctuary, Gregory Beale has a book-length treatment of the overall theme that this sanctuary in Genesis was intended to be the pattern for the whole earth as a sanctuary.[45] The expulsion of Adam and Eve from the garden interrupted the plan but did not deter God from carrying it out eventually. Israel's sanctuaries, the tabernacle and then the temple, were God's down payment on the accomplishment of his plan; the Christian church furthers it, and the description of the final state of the world (Revelation 21–22) is the completion. There are plenty of details in Beale's development that I might prefer to say another way; but his overall case is sound and persuasive. This means that the image of the sanctuary from Genesis 2–3, from which humans are exiled and to which they need to return—a return that God provides purely by his grace—is a controlling image for the entire Bible story.

Outside of Genesis 1–5, explicit references to Eden as a prototypical place of fruitfulness occur in Genesis 13:10; Isaiah 51:3; Joel 2:3; and Ezekiel 28:13; 31:8–9, 16, 18; 36:35. In particular, Ezekiel 28:11–19 portrays the king of Tyre as having once been in Eden, blameless, who nevertheless became proud and violent. That is, Ezekiel has a "fall story" based on Genesis 3. I think it is a mistake to think of this as another version of the Eden story; rather, we should think of it as a rhetorically powerful application of that story to the Phoenician king, or, better, to the city that he represented. That we are dealing here with personification becomes clear when we read the prophet's mention of "your trade" and "your midst" (Ezek. 28:16): "you," the king, personifies the city. And when the prophet says that his addressee was "an anointed guardian cherub," we can recognize that we are reading imagery here, not a literal description. The point is that "the extravagant pretensions of Tyre are graphically and poetically portrayed . . . , along with the utter devastation inflicted

[45]Gregory Beale, *The Temple and the Church's Mission: A Biblical Theology of the Dwelling Place of God*, New Studies in Biblical Theology (Downers Grove, IL: InterVarsity Press, 2004).

upon Tyre as a consequence."[46] The rhetorical power derives from reading Genesis 3 as a fall story; there would be no such power in another reading.

Another passage that is likely to be an echo of Genesis 3 read as a fall story is Ecclesiastes 7:29:

> See, this alone I found, that God made man (Hebrew *ha-'adam*, mankind) upright, but they have sought out many schemes.

As the Israeli commentator Yehudah Kiel suggests, this is best taken as a description of the "fall of man."[47] It is well to stop and appreciate what this says: it gives an historical sequence, in which mankind was once (namely, at the time that God made them) "upright" (which need not be the same as "perfect in every way," though it does describe moral innocence), but, through their own "seeking out of many schemes" became other than upright—probably, in context, came to have the character described in verse 20: "Surely there is not a righteous man on earth who does good and never sins" (cf. 1 Kings 8:46; Prov. 20:9). It also makes good sense to read the phrase "return to the dust" (Eccles. 3:20; 12:7) as a deliberate echo of Genesis 3:19 ("for you are dust, and to dust you shall return").

There are two other passages that are worth our attention, but they are both highly disputed. The first is Hosea 6:7, which the ESV renders,[48]

> But *like Adam* they transgressed the covenant;
> there they dealt faithlessly with me.

Others prefer to interpret the words rendered *like Adam* in the ESV as "like any human beings," or even "at (the place called) Adam." The

---

[46]David J. Reimer, note on Ezek. 28:11–19 in Lane Dennis et al., eds., *The ESV Study Bible* (Wheaton, IL: Crossway, 2008), 1542.

[47]Kiel, *Sefer Bereshit,* יב (commenting on Gen. 3:10).

[48]My former student Brian Habig has promised a full discussion of this passage defending this interpretation; but as his work has not yet appeared in print, I will say enough here to show why I think it is correct.

ESV is the simplest interpretation of the Hebrew words, k^e'*adam*, as Vasholz summarizes:[49]

> The hard issue is: to whom or to what does "Adam" refer? Many commentators suggest a geographical locality. The difficulty is that there is no record of covenant breaking at a place called Adam (Josh. 3:16), and it requires a questionable taking of the preposition "like" (Hb. *ke-*) to mean "at" or "in." "There" represents the act wherein Israel was unfaithful to the covenant (cf. Hos. 5:7; 6:10). "Mankind" is another suggestion for "Adam," but that would be a vague statement with no known event indicated, and therefore it would not clarify the sentence. It is best to understand "Adam" as the name of the first man; thus Israel is like Adam, who forgot his covenant obligation to love the Lord, breaking the covenant God made with him (Gen. 2:16–17; 3:17). This also implies that there was a "covenant" relationship between God and Adam, the terms of which were defined in God's words to Adam, though the actual word "covenant" is not used in Genesis 1–3.

This reading makes sense in light of the way that Hosea stresses the abundant generosity of God, who had loaded Israel down with all manner of good things—and Israel had simply repudiated the Giver (cf. Hos. 2:8–13; 7:15; 11:1–4; 13:4–6).

Another possible allusion to Adam as transgressor is Job 31:33, which reads in the ESV:

> if I have concealed my transgression as others do [margin: as Adam did]

There is no really good way to decide, one way or the other, between the interpretation of the text ("as others do") or the margin ("as Adam did"); the Hebrew, k^e'*adam*, can go either way. What we must not do is enforce circular reasoning, to the effect that since references to Adam are so rare, therefore one is unlikely here. We will instead leave this one as an open question.

---

[49]Robert I. Vasholz, note on Hosea 6:7 in Dennis et al., eds., *The ESV Study Bible*, 1631.

Finally, I have already shown (section 3.a) that the tree of life receives further mention in the rest of Bible (Prov. 3:18; 11:30; 13:12; 15:4; Rev. 2:7; 22:2, 14, 19).

3.c Second Temple Jewish Literature

The Second Temple period, which technically began with the Jews' building of a new temple after their exile to Babylon (c. 516 B.C.) and ended when the Romans destroyed that temple (A.D. 70), was one of severe foment among Jews, as they sought to explain their situation in light of their understanding of the covenants with Abraham, Moses, and David. There were still parts of the Hebrew Bible to be produced (such as Ezra and Nehemiah), and many other writings as well (some Christian churches include some of this other material in their canon, though no one includes it all). One must use great discretion in reading this other material, since there is no single form of Judaism, and many of these writings are from very sectarian groups (such as the Qumran community, who produced what we call the Dead Sea Scrolls). At the same time, if there is widespread consistency among these various writings, that will give us some idea, both of how people read the Old Testament material they had, and of what features of the Jewish world the New Testament writers faced.

What we know as Judaism today is dominated by the influence of the Pharisees, who survived the Roman suppression of the Jewish revolt (A.D. 66–70), and became the leaders of Judaism afterwards. As a matter of fact, the Pharisees were already more or less the "mainstream" of Judaism before then, at least if we are to believe the Jewish historian Josephus (A.D. 37 to some time after 100), who tells us that the Pharisees were the "sect" with the most influence on the people at large (*Antiquities*, 13:10.5 [13, 288]; 18.1.3 [18, 12]). Although the New Testament authors could be very critical of some of the Pharisees' attitudes, they generally sided with them in matters of doctrinal dispute, as we can see in Acts 23:6–9 (see also Mark 12:18–34)—except, of course, on the question of whether Jesus was indeed the Messiah. When Jesus asks his Jewish audience whether, if one of their sheep fell into a pit on the Sabbath, they would rescue it (Matt. 12:11), he is assuming that they would rescue the animal.

But he is commending them for that, as over against the regulation of the Qumran community that forbade such a rescue, instructing their followers to keep the animal safe until the next day,[50]

Of the Second Temple material available to us, the books we call the Apocrypha, together with the writings of Josephus, come the closest to being in the Jewish mainstream. It is therefore worthwhile to give them most of our attention.

The clearest and most complete statement about Adam and Eve from the Apocrypha comes in the book of Tobit (from somewhere between 250 and 175 B.C.).[51] The character Tobias is taking Sarah to be his wife, and the angel Raphael had instructed him on how to protect himself and his wife from a demon that threatened harm. Following the angel's instructions, Tobias says these words as part of his prayer (Tob. 8:6):

> [O God of our fathers,] You made Adam and gave him Eve his
> wife
> as a helper and support.
> From them the race of mankind has sprung.
> You said, "It is not good that the man should be alone;
> let us make a helper for him like himself."

As was common in Jewish prayers, Tobias begins with an historical recital of God's good deeds in the past as the basis for hope. This recital agrees with what I have argued is present in Genesis itself.

Other books in the Apocrypha also refer to the creation and fall of Adam and Eve. For example, consider the book called Wisdom of Solomon (from some time after 200 B.C. and before the New Testament), whose aim seems to be to relate Jewish faith to the higher elements of Hellenistic culture in Alexandria, Egypt. Alexandria was one of the most highly cultured cities in the Graeco-Roman

---

[50]*Damascus Document*, xi, 10–15. See Geza Vermes, *The Dead Sea Scrolls in English*, 4th ed. (London: Penguin, 1995), 109.
[51]Ordinarily I will use the dates suggested in David A. deSilva, *Introducing the Apocrypha: Message, Context, and Significance* (Grand Rapids, MI: Baker, 2002). I cannot say that I agree with all of his assessments, but this will do for our purposes. Ordinarily I will cite the English of the Apocrypha from *The English Standard Version Bible with Apocrypha* (Oxford: Oxford University Press, 2009), though I have checked the original.

world, and it looks like the writer wanted to fortify Jews against assimilating, and perhaps also to draw cultured Gentiles to Jewish faith. After describing the schemes of wicked people against the "righteous" (presumably faithful Jews), he tells us that the wicked are ignorant of God's secret purposes, and do not discern the prize blameless souls receive; in 2:23–24 he says,

> [23]for God created mankind for incorruption
> and made him in the image of his own character,
> [24]but through the devil's envy death entered the world,
> and those who belong to his party experience it.

Most people suppose that the author is recounting the story of Genesis 3, seeing the serpent as "the devil's" mouthpiece. He takes it as an historical event that shapes contemporary life (cf. 1:13–14; 7:1; 10:1).

Jesus Ben Sira was a scribe and wisdom teacher in Jerusalem, who finished his book in Hebrew somewhere between 196 and 175 B.C., and whose grandson translated the book into Greek around 132 B.C. (as the grandson explains in his translator's prologue to the Greek), giving us the book called Ecclesiasticus (or Sirach, or Ben Sira). Parts of the Hebrew text have been discovered, but there still remain textual difficulties. This author mentions the creation of man, and the fall with its consequences, mostly in passing (Sir. 14:17; 15:14; 17:1; 33:10 [Hebrew 36:10]; 40:1). In one passage (25:16–26) he makes use of the "fall story" to explain a current malaise, namely the situation in which one's wife is evil. In 25:24 he says,

> From a woman sin had its beginning,
> and because of her we all die.

This sounds misogynistic, and it may be; but Ben Sira does go on to allow that a woman can be virtuous, and a blessing to her husband (26:1–4, 13–18), so we should take his words as portraying evil women as followers of Eve at her worst.[52] The simplest reading of

---

[52]Stanley Porter, "The Pauline Concept of Original Sin, in Light of Rabbinic Background," *Tyndale Bulletin* 41:1 (1990): 3–30, denies that Ben Sira is referring to Eve. But his reading

this is that he took the event as historical, although one cannot be absolutely certain.

However, the citation in Sirach 49:16 makes it clear that he did take Adam to be an historical person. He is recalling worthies from the history of Israel in chapters 44–49 ("let us now praise famous men," 44:1), leading up to his contemporary Simon (II), son of Onias (high priest ca. 219–196 B.C.). He begins with Enoch and Noah as the first named "famous men," then goes on to Abraham and so forth through Biblical history. Just prior to his extended praise of Simon, he finishes with Nehemiah (49:13), and then returns to Genesis, naming Enoch and Joseph (49:14–15). He completes the run-up to Simon in 49:16:

> Shem and Seth were honored among men,
> and Adam above every living being in the creation.

The way he mentions all these men in this context indicates that he took all of them as historical figures.

There are other references, in books called 2 (or 3 or 4!) Ezra and 2 Baruch, all of which follow the same lines.[53]

Two Jewish writers from the later part of this period, who are partly contemporary with the New Testament, are Philo of Alexandria (roughly 20 B.C.—A.D. 50) and Josephus. Philo, with his interest in philosophical allegory, does not say clearly whether he thought Adam to have been historical. In his discussion of Genesis 2:7, he seems to distinguish the man of Genesis 1 from the man of Genesis 2: the heavenly and the earthly man, he calls them (*Allegorical Interpretation*, 1.31).[54]

---

seems to me inadequate; cf. the Hebrew commentary of Moshe Segal, *Sefer Ben Sira Hashshalem* (Jerusalem: Mosad Bialik, 1958), קנב, for the connection.

[53] The book called 2 Esdras in the ESV is called 4 Ezra in the Latin Vulgate (where it is an appendix), and 3 Esdras in the Slavonic Bible. It is thought to have been written originally in Hebrew around the end of the first century A.D., then translated into Greek; but neither the Hebrew nor the Greek is extant. It has several passages about the fall of Adam as the means by which sin and suffering came into the world, e.g., 3:4–11, 21–22; it is hardly a treatise on "original sin," however. A translation and commentary are available in Michael E. Stone, *Fourth Ezra*, Hermeneia (Minneapolis: Fortress, 1990); see pages 63–66 for an excursus on Adam's sin.

[54] As mentioned below (under 1 Cor. 15:45), it appears that Paul opposes this approach.

Josephus has a way of writing that is far more accessible to educated Westerners. At times he is literalistic, perhaps writing to connect the Genesis account with the received world picture of the Graeco-Roman world (since one of his purposes was to commend Judaism). He calls Adam "the first man, made from the earth" (*Antiquities*, 1.2.3, line 67). He also says that the gracious God of Israel is the one source of happiness for all mankind (*Antiquities* 4.8.2, line 180), which is connected to his view that all people descend from Adam. This conviction of common humanity apparently underlies his notion that all people should worship the true God, and his explanation for the admission of Gentiles into Jewish worship (*Against Apion*, 2.23, 37 [lines 192, 261]). Josephus is more representative than Philo of the Judaism we find in the other Second Temple sources.

Thus, in the period that bridges the Old Testament and the New, the Jewish authors most representative of the mainstream consistently treat Adam and Eve as actual people, at the head of the human race.

3.d The Gospels

The main reference to early Genesis in the Gospels comes in Matthew 19:3–9 (parallel with Mark 10:2–9). Some Pharisees wanted to test Jesus, probably meaning that they wanted to ensnare him in one of the debates between their own schools of thought. They ask whether it is lawful for a man to divorce his wife "for any cause," and Jesus replies (Matt. 19:4–5):

> 4He answered, "Have you not read that he who created them from the beginning made them male and female, 5and said, 'Therefore a man shall leave his father and his mother and hold fast to his wife, and they shall become one flesh'?

Jesus' answer ties together Genesis 1:27 (cited in verse 4) and Genesis 2:24 (cited in verse 5)—which indicates, by the way, that he read Genesis 1 and 2 as complementary texts. Since the man and woman are now one flesh, joined together by God, they should not be separated. The Pharisees then ask why Moses allowed divorce (Matt. 19:7, citing Deut. 24:1–4), and Jesus explains that it was a concession; "from the beginning it was not so" (Matt. 19:8). This conversation shows that Jesus viewed the creation account of Genesis 1–2 as setting the ideal for a properly functioning marriage for all human beings; this is how it was intended to be "from the beginning."[55] The family legislation of Deuteronomy, on the other hand, does not set the ethical norm but has another function, namely that of preserving civility in Israel: a function that has become necessary by some change of circumstances since "the beginning." The obvious candidate for making that change—indeed, the only one—is the sin of Adam and Eve, with its consequences for all human beings.[56]

Jesus also makes a passing reference to the death of Abel (Gen. 4:8), calling him righteous (Matt. 23:35, see also Luke 11:51). Since this is just in passing we need not make much of it, though we should notice that he refers to the shedding of righteous blood from Abel to Zechariah. It is hard to be certain just who this Zechariah is, though "whom you murdered between the sanctuary and the altar" probably locates him in the shared knowledge of Jesus and his audience, which means he is taking both Abel and Zechariah as historical persons.[57]

There is another passing reference in John 8:44:

You are of your father the devil, and your will is to do your father's desires. He was a murderer from the beginning, and has nothing to do with the truth, because there is no truth in him. When he lies, he speaks out of his own character, for he is a liar and the father of lies.

This is generally held to agree with the reading of the serpent as the mouthpiece of the Evil One that I have argued for above, and with the interpretation found in Wisdom 2:24. The expression "from

---

[55]The "beginning" found in the expressions "from the beginning" (Matt. 19:4) and "from the beginning of creation" (Mark 10:6) is the beginning of human existence; see my discussion in *Science and Faith*, 106–107. For a mid-nineteenth century source in support of this, see J. A. Alexander, *The Gospel according to Mark* (Grand Rapids, MI: Baker, 1980 [1858]), 274.

[56]See discussion in Christopher Wright, *Old Testament Ethics for the People of God* (Downers Grove, IL: InterVarsity Press, 2004), 349–51; Collins, *Genesis 1–4*, 144–45.

[57]For an exhaustive discussion of the possibilities, concluding that Zechariah refers to the man in 2 Chron. 24:20–22, see R. T. Beckwith, *The Old Testament Canon of the New Testament Church* (London: SPCK, 1985), 212–22.

the beginning" (Greek *ap' archês*) certainly points this way, with its reference to the beginning of creation (see John 1:1; 1 John 3:8).

Hence it is fair to say that the Gospel writers portray Jesus as someone who believed both that Adam and Eve were actual people, and that their disobedience changed things for us their descendants.

3.e The Pauline Writings

In this section I will include materials that are traditionally associated with the apostle Paul, even if their actual authorship is disputed (such as the Pastoral Epistles). I will also cover the presentation of Paul found in Acts.[58]

This material mentions parts of Genesis 1–3 in passing, in places such as 1 Corinthians 11:7–12; 2 Corinthians 11:3; and 1 Timothy 2:13–14. Although there is no reason to doubt that these references share the usual assumption of Second Temple Jews that Adam and Eve were historical, it is not easy to insist that the argument *depends* on this assumption for its validity.

The case is different with three other passages: 1 Corinthians 15:20–23, 42–49; Romans 5:12–19; and Acts 17:26, and thus we will spend our time on these. I think these passages will show that Paul's teaching is founded on his understanding of the narrative about Adam and Eve that we have already seen.

In 1 Corinthians 15 Paul is arguing for the historical resurrection of Jesus as essential to his "gospel," the elements of which he narrates in verses 3–8. When Paul uses the Greek word that we translate "gospel," he is generally talking about a story of public events that have earth-shaking significance; specifically, Paul's story culminates with the resurrection of Jesus, by which Jesus takes his Davidic throne (see Rom. 1:1–6) and begins to bring light to the Gentiles.[59] I will leave aside a full exposition of all the theological ramifications of the idea

---

[58]There is a strong case to be made for Paul's actual authorship of the Pastoral Epistles, and for the reliability of the portrayal of Paul in Acts, but I am seeking to keep my discussion from being tightly tethered to the outcome of that debate.

[59]For a fuller discussion of Paul's use of the term "gospel" in Romans, see my study, "Echoes of Aristotle in Romans 2:14–15: Or, Maybe Abimelech Was Not So Bad After All," *Journal of Markets and Morality* 13:1 (2010): 123–73.

of Jesus' bodily resurrection, and refer the reader to the monumental work by N. T. Wright, *The Resurrection of the Son of God*.[60]

In 1 Corinthians 15:20–23, Paul is not simply arguing that Jesus did rise from the dead; he is also explaining why Jesus' resurrection provides certainty for the future resurrection of all Christians:[61]

> [20]But in fact Christ has been raised from the dead, the firstfruits of those who have fallen asleep. [21]For as by a man came death, by a man has come also the resurrection of the dead. [22]For as in Adam all die, so also in Christ shall all be made alive. [23]But each in his own order: Christ the firstfruits, then at his coming those who belong to Christ.

When Paul in verse 21 refers to "a man" (Greek *anthrôpos*), he is referring to a single human being, as verse 22 clarifies: Adam is the human being by whom came death, while Christ is the human being by whom the resurrection of the dead has come. Then in verse 22 Paul uses one of his characteristic formulae, "in Adam" and "in Christ."

To explain these expressions, I shall cut a long story short and simply say that in my judgment, to be "in A" means to be a member of the people for which A serves as the covenantal representative.[62] This membership sets up a kind of solidarity, where what happens to the representative affects all members of the group, and vice-versa. One prominent Pauline scholar has used the term "interchange" to describe the notion of mutual participation in a common life.[63]

This person A is an individual who serves a public role as a representative, and there is no evidence that one can be covenantally "in"

---

[60]N. T. Wright, *The Resurrection of the Son of God* (Minneapolis: Fortress, 2003).

[61]Agreeing with Wright, ibid., 333.

[62]This appears in Gen. 12:3 ("*in* you"); 18:18 ("*in* him"); 22:18 ("*in* your offspring"); 26:4 ("*in* your offspring"), where the Hebrew preposition is *be-*, in each case rendered into Greek with *en*. The New Testament phrase "in Christ" is *en Christô*. Compare the discussion in A. J. M. Wedderburn, "Some observations on Paul's use of the phrases 'in Christ' and 'with Christ'," *Journal for the Study of the New Testament* 25 (1985): 83–97, for similar suggestions; cf. N. T. Wright, *Paul in Fresh Perspective* (Minneapolis: Fortress, 2005), 46.

[63]Morna Hooker, *From Adam to Christ: Essays on Paul* (Cambridge: Cambridge University Press, 1990). This is the concept that C. S. Lewis is grasping for as he tries to explain "in Christ/in Adam," in *The Problem of Pain* (London: Geoffrey Bles, 1940), chapter 5 (see my discussion in section 5.d below).

someone who had no historical existence.[64] Indeed, Paul seems to take for granted that something happened to "all" as a result of Adam's deeds as a representative, just as something will happen to "all" as a result of Christ's representative deeds. And this representation is not done by legal fiction or by an arbitrary divine decree: there is some connection between the representative and the represented people, as is indicated by the analogy with "firstfruits." As Anthony Thiselton recognizes, "Paul accepted the traditional Rabbinic doctrine of the unity of mankind in Adam," though neither those rabbinic passages, nor Paul for that matter, explain unambiguously just *how* they are "in" Adam.[65]

Although C. K. Barrett acknowledges that Paul treats Adam as an historical character, he goes on to assert,[66]

> Sin and death, traced back by Paul to Adam, are a description of humanity as it empirically is. For this reason the historicity of Adam is unimportant.

This assessment underestimates the role of the Biblical story in Paul's argument. Paul rather presents Adam as having *introduced* a problem for mankind, which Jesus has now addressed. He affirms the goodness of the original creation (as in 1 Tim. 4:4); human sin is not inherent in the creation. That is, the "empirical fact" that all humans share a sinful condition has an explanation in a particular event. Thus, as Gordon Fee noted,[67]

> Although Paul's stress is on the common humanity all share in Adam, there can be little question that he considered Adam to be a real person in the same sense as Christ.

---

[64] As Anthony Thiselton puts it (quoting F. F. Bruce), "Adam is, for Paul, both an individual and a corporate entity: 'he was what his Hebrew name signifies—"mankind." The whole of mankind is viewed as originally existing in Adam.'" See Thiselton, *1 Corinthians*, New International Greek Text Commentary (Grand Rapids, MI: Eerdmans, 2000), 1225.
[65] Ibid., 1225 (quoting W. D. Davies).
[66] C. K. Barrett, *1 Corinthians*, Harper's New Testament Commentary (Peabody, MA: Hendrickson, 1968), 351, 353.
[67] Gordon Fee, *1 Corinthians*, New International Commentary on the New Testament (Grand Rapids, MI: Eerdmans, 1987), 751 n. 23.

Indeed, Paul's argument is historical and narratival: one person did something to cause the problem for those he represented, a later person did something to rescue from the problem those he represented Jesus' bodily resurrection is the down payment on the final restoration of the entire physical world from the problems of sin and death—problems that, according to Paul, were introduced by the sin of Adam and Eve. John's Revelation envisions a similar future, with a similar rationale (see 3.f below).

This pattern continues in 1 Corinthians 15, in verses 42–49:

> [42]So is it with the resurrection of the dead. What is sown is perishable; what is raised is imperishable. [43]It is sown in dishonor; it is raised in glory. It is sown in weakness; it is raised in power. [44]It is sown a natural body; it is raised a spiritual body. If there is a natural body, there is also a spiritual body. [45]Thus it is written, "The first man Adam became a living being"; the last Adam became a life-giving spirit. [46]But it is not the spiritual that is first but the natural, and then the spiritual. [47]The first man was from the earth, a man of dust; the second man is from heaven. [48]As was the man of dust, so also are those who are of the dust, and as is the man of heaven, so also are those who are of heaven. [49]Just as we have borne the image of the man of dust, we shall also bear the image of the man of heaven.

As N. T. Wright comments, "our present passage [1 Cor. 15:12–58 as a whole] is one of Paul's more dense and allusive pieces of writing."[68] This means that there are plenty of questions we might like to ask, and we could spend a great deal of time discussing them. At this point, though, I will simply cite some of Wright's conclusions with approval, and refer the reader to his fuller treatment:[69]

> The whole argument establishes, with rock-solid theology and considerable rhetorical power, the point that the resurrection of Jesus the Messiah is the starting-point and means whereby the creator, in completing the work of rescuing and renewing the original creation, will raise all the Messiah's people to new bodily life. . . .

---

[68]Wright, *Resurrection of the Son of God*, 337.
[69]Ibid., 337, 346.

Being human is good; being an embodied human is good; what is bad is being a rebellious human, a decaying human, a human dishonoured through bodily sin and bodily death.

In regard to verses 42–49, Wright notes that verse 45 is citing Genesis 2:7 (the formation of Adam), and concludes:[70]

> When Genesis 2 speaks of the creator making Adam as a living *psyche* [rendered "living creature" in the ESV], this was not a secondary form of humanity, but its primary form. What humans now need is not to get away from, or back behind such an existence, but rather to go on to the promised state of the final Adam, in which this physical [ESV "natural" in verses 44, 46] body will not be abandoned, but will be given new animation by the creator's own Spirit.

For this reason, Wright is on solid ground when he rejects the idea that Paul's argument is "typological":[71]

> This [argument from Gen. 2:7] is not typological (two events related in pattern but not necessarily in narrative sequence), but narratival: Gen. 2.7 begins a story which, in the light of vv. 20–28, and the analogies of vv. 35–41, Paul is now in a position to complete.

This narratival quality means that Paul's argument does presuppose Adam as an actual character in the narrative.[72]

The other passage in which Paul contrasts Adam and Christ is Romans 5:12–19:

> [12]Therefore, just as sin came into the world through one man, and death through sin, and so death spread to all men because all sinned— [13]for sin indeed was in the world before the law was given, but sin is not counted where there is no law. [14]Yet death reigned from Adam to

---

[70]Ibid., 353. Wright also shows that Paul is rejecting a line of interpretation associated with Philo (mentioned in 3.c above).

[71]Ibid., 354 n. 128.

[72]Perhaps, if Paul shared the "Irenaean" reading of the garden story mentioned in section 3.a, he thought that the first man's task was to grow from being merely "natural" to being confirmed as fully "spiritual," through his moral obedience.

Moses, even over those whose sinning was not like the transgression of Adam, who was a type of the one who was to come.

[15]But the free gift is not like the trespass. For if many died through one man's trespass, much more have the grace of God and the free gift by the grace of that one man Jesus Christ abounded for many. [16]And the free gift is not like the result of that one man's sin. For the judgment following one trespass brought condemnation, but the free gift following many trespasses brought justification. [17]If, because of one man's trespass, death reigned through that one man, much more will those who receive the abundance of grace and the free gift of righteousness reign in life through the one man Jesus Christ.

[18]Therefore, as one trespass led to condemnation for all men, so one act of righteousness leads to justification and life for all men. [19]For as by the one man's disobedience the many were made sinners, so by the one man's obedience the many will be made righteous.

This passage raises many important questions: How did the deed of the one man, Adam, bring sin into the world? Are individual people to be held responsible for their own sins—and what influence does Adam's disobedience have on them? What kind of "death" does Paul have in mind? But we will keep our focus on the role Adam plays in Paul's argument, and save those other questions for another occasion.

There is little dispute among the commentators that Paul has based his discussion on the way he read Genesis 3. Paul apparently shares with his contemporary Jews the idea that Adam's sin is what brought sin and "death" (whether physical or spiritual or, as is more likely, both) into the world of human experience.[73] Like the presentation in 1 Corinthians 15, the argument is a narratival one: an event that happened in the past (as in, "one man's trespass, one man's sin, one trespass, one man's disobedience") had consequences ("many died"), even from Adam to Moses (another character in the story), that is, before the law of Moses. Verse 17 is explicit: "because of one man's trespass, death reigned through that one man." These events were followed by what Jesus achieved ("one act of righteousness,

---

[73]Observe how similar the Greek of Rom. 5:12 ("and death [came into the world] through sin") is to the Greek of Wisd. Sol. 2:24 ("by the devil's envy death came into the world").

one man's obedience"), both in his death and in his resurrection (cf. Rom. 4:25).

Many scholars who reject the idea of Adam as a real person whose sin has affected us all say that the notion of "original sin" comes from a Western church father, Augustine (A.D. 354–430). According to this argument, we ought to give more consideration to the Greek church, which does not follow Augustine. Now it is certainly true that the different major factions of the Christian church think differently about how to describe the effects of Adam's sin on the rest of mankind, but we should be careful not to let this fact mislead us. They both agree that the sin of Adam and Eve *does* have an effect, which presupposes our actual descent from this original pair. Besides, some of the allegations of difference are mistaken; we have already seen (section 2.c) how some have misread Irenaeus (an Eastern father). Another Eastern representative is the Greek church father John Chrysostom (c. 344–407), who at one point was bishop of Constantinople. Chrysostom tended to avoid speculative theology, and his interpretations of Greek expressions are often still worth studying today. Even so, Chrysostom explained Romans 5:12 as follows:[74]

---

[74]John Chrysostom, *Homilies on Romans*, Homily x. I have improved the Post-Nicene Fathers translation from the Greek original. It is interesting that Chrysostom has used the term "having fallen" (the Greek verb *piptô*); see also Eusebius, *Preparation for the Gospel*, 7.8 (307d) where "Adam . . . *fell from* [Greek, *apopiptô*] his better lot" (c. A.D. 315). I do not know at what point the term "fall" became common vocabulary for describing Adam's sin (the Bible does not use it, so far as I can tell). Of course there are many differences between Augustine and Chrysostom, and it is not part of my task here to adjudicate. See Panayiotis Papageorgiou, "Chrysostom and Augustine on the sin of Adam and its consequences," *St Vladimir's Theological Quarterly* 39:4 (1995): 361–78, for a presentation that favors the Greek father. Although Christian authors before Augustine did not construe "original sin" in the same way as Augustine did, that does not mean that they lack the idea that somehow the sin of historical Adam and Eve has affected us their children. Besides the Greek speakers Irenaeus and Chrysostom, mentioned already in this work, see also, e.g., Origen (185–254), *Homily on Luke*, at Luke 2:22 ("stains of our birth"), Athanasius (293–373), *On the Incarnation*, 1:3–5 ("the loveliness of their original innocence"), and Theodore of Mopsuestia (350–428), *Catechetical Homilies*, 14 ("we fell and sin corrupted us"); the Syriac speaker Ephraem the Syrian (306–73), *Commentary on 1 Corinthians*, 1:30 (speaking of the forgiveness we need as mediated through baptism); and the Latin-speaking Tertullian (c. 160–220), *On the Soul*, 16, 40–41 ("corruption" that came from the sin of Adam), and Cyprian (d. 258), *Letters*, 58.5 (to Fidus: the sin of Adam affects even newly born infants).

What does "because all sinned" mean? He [Adam] having fallen, even those who did not eat from the tree, all of them, became mortal because of him.

He refers to the rest of mankind as "those who came from him [Adam]," indicating that he read this as a narrative involving actual people. One does not have to be an Augustinian to see this. (Like Paul, Chrysostom shows no undue literalism.)

Modern commentaries tend to see in Paul's argument a similarity to the Second Temple ideas about Adam and the origin of sin, tracing Paul's overall argument ultimately to his reading of Genesis 3; some of these commentators admire Paul's restraint and sobriety in contrast to some of the wilder speculations. They generally agree that Paul took Adam to be an historical person.

We can trace an interesting pattern in the more prominent English commentaries if we observe them in sequence: the commentators have increasingly recognized the narrative basis for Paul's instruction.[75] Cranfield's exhaustive work (1975) displays a clear sympathy with Paul:[76]

> The third and fourth clauses of [Rom. 5:12], however, say something which is not explicit in the Genesis narrative or anywhere else in the OT, though it is the natural inference to be drawn from the Genesis narrative and is surely its intention, namely, that as a result of the entrance of sin followed by death, death in time reached all men because they all sinned.

Cranfield's reading of Genesis 3 agrees with mine, and displays a commendable awareness of the appropriate "inference to be drawn" (without using the terms "showing" and "telling").

---

[75]These are the commentaries that seem to get the most notice in the academic literature. I do not mean to suggest that such commentaries as John Stott's or Thomas Schreiner's are unworthy of notice, as they certainly are worthy.

[76]C. E. B. Cranfield, *Romans*, International Critical Commentary (Edinburgh: T & T Clark, 1975), 279–80. He adds in a footnote, "That the Genesis narrative is intended as an account of the origin of human sinfulness and death can hardly be denied. Note the way in which Gen 4 follows Gen 3, the explicit involvement of Eve's seed in 3.15 and the implicit involvement of future generations in what is said in 3.17–19." Cf. Collins, *Genesis 1–4*, 175–76, for similar opinions.

James Dunn's commentary appeared in 1988, and he agrees that Paul is using Genesis 3 and referring to Adam as an individual, an "epochal figure," by which he means "the one who initiated the first major phase of human history and thereby determined the character of that phase for those belonging to it."[77] At the same time,

> It would not be true to say that Paul's theological point depends on Adam being a "historical" individual or on his disobedience being a historical event as such. Such an implication does not necessarily follow from the fact that a parallel is drawn with Christ's single act: an act in mythic history can be paralleled to an act in living history without the point of comparison being lost. . . . The effect of the comparison between the two epochal figures, Adam and Christ, is not so much to historicize the individual Adam as to bring out the more than individual significance of the historic Christ.

Dunn does not explain why he takes Genesis as "mythic history"; nor does he explain why Adam's role has no necessary place in the narrative. In fact, he seems to have underplayed the narratival nature of Paul's argument, as well as the "more than individual significance" that Adam is thought to have had as a representative.

In 1993 Joseph Fitzmyer's commentary appeared. There he observes,[78]

> Paul treats Adam as a historical human being, humanity's first parent, and contrasts him with the historical Jesus Christ. But in Genesis itself 'Adam is a symbolic figure, denoting humanity. Some commentators on Romans have tried to interpret Adam in this symbolic sense here (thus Barth, *Romans*, 170–71 . . .); but that reading does violence to the contrast that Paul uses in this paragraph between Adam as "one man" and Christ as "one man," which implies that Adam was a historical individual as much as was Jesus Christ. So Paul has historicized the symbolic Adam of Genesis.

---

[77]James D. G. Dunn, *Romans*, Word Biblical Commentary (Dallas: Word, 1988), 289–90.
[78]J. A. Fitzmyer, *Romans*, Anchor Bible (New York: Doubleday, 1993), 407–408.

Fitzmyer seems to *assume* that Adam in Genesis is "symbolic"—at least he does not give reasons for thinking it. When he goes on to say, "'Adam' for Paul is *Adam in the book of Genesis*; he is a literary individual, like Hamlet, but not symbolic, like Everyman,"[79] it is not entirely clear whether he thinks either that Adam existed or that it matters one way or the other to Paul's argument. He finishes his discussion by expressing his uncertainty whether Catholic doctrine is opposed to all forms of polygenism (humans having arisen from more than one ancestor), or if some form of polygenism can be reconciled with that doctrine.

The most recent of these prominent commentaries on Romans is that of N. T. Wright (2002). There Wright comments that Paul's theological context is "the fairly widespread Second Temple Jewish belief not merely about Adam as the progenitor of the human race, and indeed the fountainhead of human sin."[80] He goes on to insist, in terms that deserve serious reflection,[81]

> Paul clearly believed that there had been a single first pair, whose male, Adam, had been given a commandment and had broken it. Paul was, we may be sure, aware of what we would call mythical or metaphorical dimensions to the story, but he would not have regarded these as throwing doubt on the existence, and primal sin, of the first historical pair. Our knowledge of early anthropology is sketchy, to put it mildly. Each time another very early skull is dug up the newspapers exclaim over the discovery of the first human beings; we have consigned Adam and Eve entirely to the world of mythology, but we are still looking for their replacements. What "sin" would have looked like in the early dawn of the human race it is impossible to say; but the turning away from open and obedient relationship with the loving creator, and the turning toward that which, though beautiful and enticing, is not God, is such a many-sided phenomenon that it is not hard to envisage it at any stage of anthropoid development. The general popular belief that the early stories of Genesis were straightforwardly disproved by Charles Darwin is of course nonsense, however many times it is

---

[79] Ibid., 410.
[80] N. T. Wright, "Romans," in Leander Keck et al., eds., *The New Interpreter's Bible* (Nashville: Abingdon, 2002), 10:393–770, at 524ab.
[81] Ibid., 526a.

reinforced in contemporary myth-making. Things are just not that simple, in biblical theology or science.

Wright does not say anything further on this subject in his "Reflections" section (I might have expected him to observe that human unity entails the obligation to equal justice for all people), but these remarks do seem to indicate that Wright prefers to believe what Paul believed on this topic—at least he is laudably skeptical of sensationalistic popular claims about the scientific evidence.[82]

Of these four, only Dunn is hesitant to say that Paul himself held Adam to be an historical person. Indeed, the two that follow him (Fitzmyer and Wright) seem to be turning the tide back to the position represented by Cranfield.[83] And the force of the evidence from Second Temple Judaism is decidedly in their favor. Now, Paul has rooted his behavioral goals for the Roman Christians in the way the Biblical story has led to their present time as the era of bringing God's light to the Gentiles, including those in Spain. And the more clearly we perceive Paul's narratival argument of Romans the more we will see the reality of Adam as the ancestor of all people being tied up with his argument. All people are in need of the gospel's light, and all people are reachable with that light.[84]

One last text will join those in 1 Corinthians and Romans, namely Acts 17:26, which is part of Paul's speech to the Athenian philosophers. After explaining to them that God is not "served by human hands, as though he needed anything, since he himself gives to all mankind life and breath and everything" (v. 25), he goes on to say:

> [26]And he made from one man every nation of mankind to live on all the face of the earth, having determined allotted periods and the boundaries of their dwelling place, [27]that they should seek God, and perhaps feel their way toward him and find him.

---

[82]The way Wright speaks of "the early dawn of the human race" may mean that Wright considers John Stott's suggestions worth considering (section 5.d below).
[83]I should note that Fitzmyer has made an assertion about Adam in Genesis that needs discussion; the treatment in my section 3.a gives reasons for disagreeing with him.
[84]For a narratival analysis of Romans and its purpose, see my "Echoes of Aristotle in Romans 2:14–15," 123–73.

Here is how F. F. Bruce, who applied his training as a classicist to his study of the Bible, explained Paul's assertion:[85]

> The Athenians prided themselves in being *autochthones*, sprung from the soil of their native Attica. . . . So the Greeks in general considered themselves superior to non-Greeks, whom they called barbarians. Against such claims of racial superiority Paul asserts the unity of all men. The unity of the human race as descended from Adam is fundamental in Paul's theology (cf. Rom. v.12ff.). This primal unity, impaired by sin, is restored by redemption (Gal. iii.28; Col. iii.11).

In his later and more expansive commentary on Acts, Bruce added,[86]

> This removed all imagined justification for the belief that Greeks were superior to barbarians, as it removes all justification for comparable beliefs today. Neither in nature nor in grace, neither in the old creation nor in the new, is there any room for ideas of racial superiority.

I will discuss below (section 4.b) how human unity is indeed part of the Biblical foundation for racial justice;[87] for the present I want to focus on the role Paul's assertion played in the whole speech.[88]

Generally in this speech Paul is telling the philosophers (perhaps especially the Stoics) that they have perceived some things that are true about God and mankind; he uses the Old Testament extensively, though without explicit citation, to show them that it supplies the full explanation for the truths they grasp. It may be that Paul needs to assert common humanity with the Athenians in order to clear away any suspicions they might have of him as a foreigner (see Acts 17:18); but there is some evidence that at least some Stoics of the

---

[85] F. F. Bruce, *Acts: Greek Text with Introduction and Commentary* (London: Tyndale Press, 1970), 337. Bruce adds a "Euhemeristic" explanation for the Athenian belief in the ellipsis of this quotation: "a claim which simply means that they belonged to the earliest wave of Greek immigration into the land, so early that, unlike the later arrivals, the Achaeans and Dorians, they had lost all memory of their immigration."

[86] Bruce, *Acts*, New International Commentary on the New Testament (Grand Rapids, MI: Eerdmans, 1988), 337.

[87] I am told that African-American Christians under slavery, when they learned of this passage, took great comfort in it.

[88] I have given a brief exposition of this speech in Collins, *Science and Faith*, 190–95 (with notes and bibliography, 384–86).

first century were appreciating what is common to mankind over the accidents of birth and ethnicity (though they might not have put it the way that Paul did).[89] Further, Paul is using a basic tenet of the Old Testament story, that all mankind were made to know God, to prepare these Gentiles for his declaration in verses 30–31 of God's universal offer:

> [30]The times of ignorance God overlooked, but now he commands *all people everywhere* to repent, [31]because he has fixed a day on which he will judge *the world* in righteousness by *a man* whom he has appointed; and of this he has given assurance *to all* by raising him from the dead.

The making of all kinds of people from one person is an historical statement, which grounds the universal invitation—an invitation that itself is established by an event (the resurrection), in the light of a sure-to-come future event (a day of judgment).

God called Abraham in order to make him the vehicle of blessing to "all people everywhere," and the era for achieving that has now arrived with the resurrection of Jesus. Further, we should recall Bruce's connection of this idea to other passages that insist that in the new people of God, "there is not Greek and Jew, circumcised and uncircumcised, barbarian, Scythian, slave, free; but Christ is all, and in all" (Col. 3:11; cf. Gal. 3:28): through faith in Christ, divisions among Adam's offspring are to be healed.

3.f Elsewhere in the New Testament

Other places in the New Testament give us incidental mentions of characters in Genesis 1–5, which are inconclusive as to whether the historicity of these characters is tightly bound up with the New Testament truth claims.

A likely exception is Hebrews 11:4–7, which lists Abel, Enoch, and Noah as exemplars of faith. Hebrews 11, as everyone recognizes, is a list of outstanding people of faith in the Old Testament. Now,

---

[89]Cf. C. K. Barrett, *Acts*, International Critical Commentary (Edinburgh: T & T Clark, 1998), 842: Paul "referred to the creation of the one man, Adam, the father of all; there was no clear parallel to this in Greek thought and mythology."

that in itself does not necessarily establish that the characters are all historical: in a list of moral examples, it is not necessary that the members of the list be historical persons. After all, a modern Christian might draw lessons from Frodo or Sam, for example, and C. S. Lewis's writings are filled with appeals to characters found in classic novels and legends. At the same time, the rest of the list in Hebrews 11 is composed of historical characters, called "the people of old" (v. 2; literally, "the old-timers"). Further, the list begins with an affirmation about the creation of the universe, which is taken to be an actual event. Finally, the author expects these people to be "made perfect" along with himself and his audience (v. 40), which means that they are more than simple exemplars, they are witnesses whom the readers may hope to join through persevering in their Christian faith.

If, as seems most likely, the author of Hebrews assumes the historicity of these characters from Genesis 4–5, there is no reason to exclude Adam and Eve from the same assumption.

Finally, the book of Revelation has references and allusions to elements of the fall story. I have already mentioned the "tree of life" (Rev. 2:7; 22:2, 14, 19)—the idea here seems to be the promise of reentry to the conditions of Paradise. I have also already shown that Revelation identifies the "serpent" as Satan, or his mouthpiece (Rev. 12:9; 20:2). Consider now Revelation 21:1–4; 22:1–5, which most take to describe the perfected state after God's final victory:

> **21:1** Then I saw *a new heaven and a new earth*, for the first heaven and the first earth had passed away, and the sea was no more. ²And I saw the holy city, new Jerusalem, coming down out of heaven from God, prepared as a bride adorned for her husband. ³And I heard a loud voice from the throne saying, "Behold, the dwelling place [or, *tabernacle*] of God is with man. He will dwell with them, and they will be his people [or, peoples], and God himself will be with them as their God. ⁴He will wipe away every tear from their eyes, and *death shall be no more*, neither shall there be mourning, nor crying, nor pain anymore, for the former things have passed away." . . .
>
> **22:1** Then the angel showed me the river of the water of life, bright as crystal, flowing from the throne of God and of the Lamb ²through

the middle of the street of the city; also, on either side of the river, the *tree of life* with its twelve kinds of fruit, yielding its fruit each month. The leaves of the tree were for the healing of the nations. ³No longer will there be anything accursed, but the throne of God and of the Lamb will be in it, and his servants will worship him. ⁴They will see his face, and his name will be on their foreheads. ⁵And night will be no more. They will need no light of lamp or sun, for the Lord God will be their light, and they will reign forever and ever.

John's Revelation is of course rich with symbolism, and we do well to be cautious about undue literalism. Therefore I make no claims to know exactly what the scene he describes will "actually" be like; but John portrays it as the Edenic state come to its full fruition. Notice how he mentions the tree of life and the rivers; notice too the sanctuary idea (tabernacle, 21:3), of which the garden was the precursor. In 21:4, "death" is a foreign element, to be eliminated (death having been thrown into the lake of fire, 20:14).

This symbolism has its hold on us who believe because we recognize that "death" is a pollution of God's good world, introduced at some point in the unfolding story of the world (in Eden, most believers would say). God's final triumph will include human resurrection and the renewal of the physical creation, as a reversal of that curse brought upon mankind by the defiling work of sin (cf. 22:14–15).

It is time to bring this long—and doubtless tedious to some—discussion of the New Testament passages to a close. We can conclude that, while some texts do not absolutely *require* historical Adam and Eve for their truth value, others look like they do in fact require it. The more we are aware of how the New Testament authors invoke the Biblical story and base their own message upon it, the more clearly we can grasp their message, and the more we can see how Adam and Eve figure into the story.

4

HUMAN UNIQUENESS AND DIGNITY

In this chapter I want to take up a few remaining topics dealing with the nature of human life and God's expectations for human communities. I will contend that the Biblical treatment of these subjects takes for granted some kind of common origin of all human beings in Adam. But I will not stop there, on the purely theological level: there are ways in which these Biblical doctrines actually link up with everyday human experience, of believer and non-believer alike. It is the Biblical picture, based on the Biblical story line, that actually makes sense of this experience—and this very act of making sense commends the Biblical picture to us all.

4.a The Image of God

The very first passage in the Bible, Genesis 1, has God determining to make man "in our image, after our likeness" (italics added):

> [26]Then God said, "Let us make man *in our image, after our likeness.* And let them have dominion over the fish of the sea and over the birds of the heavens and over the livestock and over all the earth and over every creeping thing that creeps on the earth."

[27]So God created man *in his own image,*
in the image of God he created him;
male and female he created them.

There is no unanimity among Biblical scholars on just what the image and likeness of God means, and I will here only summarize the leading positions.

Some suppose that this means that human beings will be like God in some respects, such as intellectual, moral, and aesthetic experience. We will call this the *resemblance* view. This was once the most common interpretation among Christians and Jews, but nowadays two others are much more common. Some theologians today think that the image of God refers to the way that humans are appointed to rule the creation on God's behalf, since verse 26 goes on to say, "and let them have dominion"; we will call this the *representative* view. Others are struck by the way in which the fulfillment (v. 27) describes human beings as "male and female," and conclude that it is male and female together, or more broadly, humans in community, that functions as the image of God. We will call this the *relational* view.

Scholars commonly speak as if these categories are mutually exclusive. My view is that the linguistic and exegetical details favor the idea that "in our image, after our likeness" implies that humans were made with some kind of resemblance to God, which was to enable them to represent God as benevolent rulers, and to find their fulfillment in their relationships with each other and with God. That is, I have combined all three views, and the challenge is to discern which one to start with. As you can see, I start with the *resemblance* idea, but I do not stop there.[1]

On the other hand, suppose that someone is convinced of the *representative* or *relational* view: this person must nevertheless recognize that these views actually presuppose that there are some distinctive human capacities that make the relationships and ruling possible. Therefore, no matter which interpretation of the image of

---

[1]For my discussion, see my *Genesis 1–4: A Linguistic, Literary, and Theological Commentary* (Phillipsburg, NJ: P&R, 2006), 61–67; *Science and Faith: Friends or Foes?* (Wheaton, IL: Crossway, 2003), 124–32 (with additional notes, 373–76).

God we prefer, we must, if we are to be careful, acknowledge that it implies that there is something about human capacities that is different from those in any other animal.

And what might these capacities be? Based on Genesis 1–2, I concluded:[2]

> In [Genesis 1–2] God displays features of his character: he shows intelligence in designing the world as a place for man to live; he uses language when he says things; he appreciates what is "good" (morally and aesthetically); and he works and rests. He is also relational, in the way he establishes a connection with man that is governed by love and commitment (2:15–17). In all of this God is a pattern for man.

How does the image of God relate to the human "soul"—or may we even talk of such a thing? I am persuaded that the Bible does endorse a form of what is called "body-soul dualism"—though certainly not the Cartesian kind, which stresses an easy separability of these two elements. The Biblical version of body-soul dualism stresses much more the intertwining of these two elements than it does their separability. It is not my purpose here to argue that matter—not least because Genesis presents mankind in bodily form as bearing God's image. Recognizing this body-soul unity as the focus in Genesis will help us to avoid a mistake that has a long history in Christian theology, of seeing the image of God as a property of the soul only: rather, it is the human being as a body-soul tangle that expresses God's image.[3]

There is some sense in which this image, or its proper functioning, is thought to be damaged by human sin, and thus it must be "renewed" in God's faithful people (Col. 3:10, cf. Eph. 4:24). Nevertheless, this image is, in some way, present in all human beings (Gen. 9:6; James 3:9). That is, it is a feature that is *unique* to human beings, distinguishing them from other animals; and it is also *universal* among human beings, appearing in all kinds of people.

---

[2]Collins, *Genesis 1–4*, 66.
[3]See further Collins, *Science and Faith*, 130–31.

The question for us is, how did the "image" come to be bestowed, and how is it transmitted? None of the Biblical authors would support us if we imagined this image to be the outcome of natural processes *alone*; the commentator Derek Kidner, who allows for a kind of "evolutionary" scenario leading up to the first human, still insists that the first man must be the result of a special bestowal; his conclusion, "there is no natural bridge from animal to man," surely captures what the Biblical text implies.[4] Some have suggested it is possible that, to make the first man, God used the body of a preexisting hominid, simply adding a soul to it. We should observe that, in view of the *embodied* image of God in Genesis, if this took place it involved some divine refurbishing of that body in order for it to work together with the soul to display God's image.

It is reasonable, then, to observe how these features distinguish man from the other animals. We do not even have to be Jews or Christians to recognize some of the basic tenets of this position. For example, when the Greek philosopher Aristotle (384–322 B.C.) says that "the human being is by nature a political animal"—meaning an animal that lives in political communities—he was noticing a feature that distinguishes man from other animals. He goes on to argue that human communities go well beyond those of bees or gregarious animals, since mankind alone uses speech to discuss what is right and wrong, and what is advantageous and disadvantageous. Further, man alone perceives moral qualities: "it is partnership in these things that makes a household and a city-state" (*Politics* I.i.9–11). How can we gainsay him?

Other animals may have features that are analogous to these special features of human beings, but the total assembly of characteristics that we find in humans is distinct. Human beings, whether they are discussing mathematics or morals, claim to have access to something that transcends their immediate bodily needs. This is not a merely natural development of the capacities in other animals.[5]

---

[4]Derek Kidner, *Genesis*, Tyndale Old Testament Commentary (Downers Grove, IL: Inter-Varsity Press, 1967), 28–29.

[5]Francis Collins has recognized this in his embrace of C. S. Lewis's "moral argument"; see his *The Language of God* (New York: Free Press, 2006), 21–31 (cf. 200, point 6: "humans are

Some authors seem to be unduly optimistic about what it takes to get a human being. For example, the leading British biologist John Maynard Smith (1920–2004) wrote the first edition of his classic book, *The Theory of Evolution*, in 1958; the third edition came out in 1975. In it he claimed that the chimpanzee Washoe, who learned to use a form of human sign language, proves that "it is no longer possible to assert that there is some peculiar feature of human language forever inaccessible to animals—not that this will stop people asserting it." In 1993 Cambridge University Press published the unchanged 1975 text in its Canto series, but Maynard Smith added a preface that included the following:[6]

> I have been persuaded by my colleagues in linguistics that there really is something peculiar about the human capacity to talk, and that there is a deep difference between the proto-language spoken by the chimpanzee Washoe, and by very young children, and the language of adult humans. The difference lies in grammar.

Maynard Smith has made progress, but has still not quite learned his lesson. That difference—grammar—is also what makes the difference between the chimp and those young children: the children have the built-in equipment to learn the grammar of their surroundings, while the chimps do not. These conclusions about language are widely spread among linguists, especially those in the tradition of Noam Chomsky (born 1928).

A Chomskian who has tried to propose a purely evolutionary scenario is Steven Pinker, who at the time of his writing *The Language Instinct* (1995) was a professor of cognitive sciences at MIT.[7] In his chapter 11 he shows that the apes that are said to have learned language did not actually "learn" a human language; language is

also unique in ways that defy evolutionary explanation"; Collins does not explain how this is coherent with his points 4–5). Bruce Waltke, *An Old Testament Theology* (Grand Rapids, MI: Zondervan, 2007), 202–203, who associates himself with Collins (202 n. 81), nevertheless is clear about both the special creation of Adam and his historical fall.
[6]John Maynard Smith, *The Theory of Evolution* (Cambridge: Cambridge University Press, 1993), 343, and 24–25.
[7]Steven Pinker, *The Language Instinct: The New Science of Language and Mind* (London: Penguin, 1995).

a uniquely human faculty. He mentions Noam Chomsky's doubts about the power of natural selection to produce a linguistic faculty in our ancestors. (That does not mean that Chomsky is a creationist!) Intriguingly, Pinker tries to overcome Chomskian doubts; but he does so by generating a story that he thinks *could be* an evolutionary pathway. To the common objection that a language, to be effective, requires a fully functional grammar, he replies:[8]

> The languages of children, pidgin speakers, immigrants, tourists, aphasics, telegrams, and headlines show that there is a vast continuum of viable language systems varying in efficiency and expressive power, exactly what the theory of natural selection requires.

He says this in order to explain how language could have evolved gradually, as Darwinism would have it. The trouble with such examples, though, is that these kinds of communications function only because there is already a functioning language community that allows them to be used: that is, they are a stripped down version of a living language, while living languages are definitely *not* souped-up versions of these defective language efforts. Pinker also pays no mind to the fact that language use in humans is tied to rationality: that is, when we talk (as Aristotle observed), we claim to have access to *truth*, which transcends our immediate bodily condition.

In effect, proposals like those coming from John Maynard Smith and Steven Pinker have the logical value of the following sentence: "I can get myself into the frame of mind in which this story looks feasible; therefore we should treat the feasibility as established."[9] Unfortunately, the stories they have generated are not really feasible, because they drastically underestimate the problem; and this means that these authors are not epistemically entitled to their feelings of feasibility.[10]

---

[8]Ibid., 403.
[9]For example, see Pinker's explanatory half of the paragraph in *Language Instinct*, 401–402: the modal verb "could" appears several times, and each occurrence is just an assertion.
[10]Pinker is honest enough to explain why he finds his kind of scenarios plausible: he thinks that natural selection is the only alternative to divine creation (*Language Instinct*, 396). This is an ideological criterion, not one based on empirical study of language.

Human language capacity is a fascinating phenomenon: every human child is born ready to learn the language or languages to which he or she is exposed. Had my wife and I taken our fair-skinned and blue-eyed children when they were babies, and brought them to live in a Ugandan village, they would have grown up speaking, not just the English we speak at home, but also the local languages, like natives, with no extra effort on the part of the villagers—unlike the struggle their adult parents would have had.

But wait! There is more than language to distinguish us from the other animals. When we hear, say, of Jewish inmates in some hellhole of a concentration camp keeping up some kind of cultural life in spite of their horrifying surroundings and imminent death, we say that they are "more human" than their tormenters. This is not something we see in the other animals.

Finally, Genesis seems to suggest that the image is transmitted by procreation. God made Adam "in the likeness of God," and Adam "fathered a son in his own likeness" (Gen. 5:1–3). Since Seth is presented positively in Genesis 4–5, we should not think that this is somehow a low evaluation of Seth in comparison to Adam. Rather, it explains how human beings—all of them, and not only the first-created ones—come to be made in God's own image (Gen. 9:6).

Consider in this light the fact that when humans form unions (preferably as loving marriages) across "racial" lines, the children born to them will also bear God's image.[11]

These features of human life that make up the image of God, being uniquely human and universally human and transmitted by procreation, strongly favor the idea that all human beings descend from the same source. The conventional alternative, some form of what is called "polygenesis" (from Greek *poly*, "many," and *genesis*, "origin"), holds that God performed the special bestowal of his image in separate places of the world; a contemporary alternative, that perhaps God did this bestowing among several members of an

---

[11]The Biblical ethic welcomes interracial marriages, when the marriage partners are both believers: see J. Daniel Hays, "A Biblical Perspective on Interracial Marriage," *Criswell Theological Review* 6:2 (Spring 2009): 5–23.

existing population of hominids, is not really the same as polygenism proper—but it will require more discussion below.

4.b Universal Human Experiences: Yearning for Justice, Need for God

The Biblical story line, as outlined in chapter 2, is one in which God's originally good creature, mankind, has been corrupted by sin; that is, sin is not part of mankind's created constitution. One of the major effects of that corruption, as highlighted in Genesis, was social: Adam against Eve, Cain against Abel, Lamech the bigamist against everyone. One effect of redemption is to heal these ancient breaches, and one purpose of the Mosaic law was to make possible a just social system in one people, as an invitation for the rest of the peoples to come to know the true God (Deut. 4:5–8). God called Abram with a view toward bringing healing to the rest of the world, and the Old Testament nurtured the hope that the trickle of believing Gentiles (e.g., 1 Kings 8:41–43) would one day become a river, with widespread healing for all the world (e.g., Isa. 2:1–5; Psalm 87). The book of Revelation anticipates "a great multitude that no one could number, from every nation, from all tribes and peoples and languages, standing before the throne and before the Lamb" (Rev. 7:9); the New Testament authors insist on bringing this future reality into the present among Christian people (e.g., Rom. 15:5–7). When Christians call each other "brother" and "sister" (a manner of address inherited from the Jews), this is most naturally understood as more than a convention, and more than a legal fiction: it is an embracing of our common humanity as heirs of Adam rescued by God's grace.

In my discussion of Acts 17:26 (section 3.e), I quoted the offhand remark of F. F. Bruce: "This primal unity, impaired by sin, is restored by redemption." The pagan despisers of Christianity also noticed that. The worldly and Epicurean Lucian of Samosata (c. A.D. 120–200) observed of the second-century Christians:[12]

---

[12]Lucian, *On the Death of Peregrinus*, c. 13; cited from J. Stevenson, *A New Eusebius: Documents Illustrative of the History of the Church to A.D. 337* (London: SPCK, 1968), 135–36. The Greek text is available in the Loeb series, *Lucian* (volume v).

Their first lawgiver [he probably means Jesus] persuaded them that they are all brethren of one another after they have transgressed once for all by denying the Greek gods and by worshipping that crucified sophist himself and living under his laws.

The Rabbis articulated an ideal for mankind (Sanhedrin 4:5):[13]

But a single man was created [first] . . . for the sake of peace among mankind, that none should say to his fellow, 'My father was greater than your father.' Again, [a single man was created] to proclaim the greatness of the Holy One, blessed is he; for man stamps many coins with the one seal and they are all like one another; but the King of kings, the Holy One, blessed is he, has stamped every man with the seal of the first man, yet not one of them is like his fellow.

It was among the early Christians that some small measure of this ideal of peacefully enjoying human diversity came to fruition; and we must make it a major goal of all church life to bring this ideal into more and more complete and convincing expression.

It is a fact that the Christian message has reached, and been embraced by, all kinds of people. Human beings are able to find ways to communicate with one another—not simply by learning each other's languages, but also by finding cultural analogies that illuminate the Christian message (think of the book *Peace Child* [1974], or of the film *The End of the Spear* [2006]). Even when some ignorant Europeans denied that some races were fully human—which removed all barriers to exploiting these "uncivilized" peoples—Christian missionaries stepped in on behalf of the oppressed (though not always, unfortunately).[14]

---

[13]Cited from Herbert Danby, *The Mishnah* (Oxford: Oxford University Press, 1933), 388, with comparison of the Hebrew. In the Talmud, see Sanhedrin 38a.
[14]For an example, see John Paton, *John G. Paton, D.D., Missionary to the New Hebrides: An Autobiography,* ed. James Paton (London: Hodder & Stoughton, 1894). Paton worked primarily among the Melanesian islanders in the New Hebrides, often protecting them from exploitation by French, British, and Americans. On pages 259–75 he tells an episode of his time in Australia (1863), when he combated the abhorrent idea that the Australian Aboriginals were nothing more than "brutes in human shape." Paton gained the trust of the Aboriginals, and proved that they really did have a religion; and he picked out an Aboriginal Christian woman for special praise.

There are many avenues along which we might discuss the shared human experience of redemption, such as the moral sense, the craving for a just society, the concern for an afterlife. I will focus on the general human sense of being lost—of feeling that something is wrong with ourselves, something that demands an explanation. Blaise Pascal put his finger on this when he wrote in his *Pensées*:[15]

Man's greatness is so obvious that it can even be deduced from his wretchedness, for what is nature in animals we call wretchedness in man, thus recognizing that, if his nature is today like that of the animals, he must have fallen from some better state which was once his own.

Who indeed would think himself unhappy not to be king except one who had been dispossessed? . . . Who would think himself unhappy if he had only one mouth and who would not if he had only one eye? It has probably never occurred to anyone to be distressed at not having three eyes, but those who have none are inconsolable.

Man's greatness and wretchedness are so evident that the true religion must necessarily teach us that there is in man some great principle of greatness and some great principle of wretchedness. It must also account for such amazing contradictions.

To make man happy it must show him that a God exists whom we are bound to love; that our true bliss is to be in him, and our sole ill is to be cut off from him. It must acknowledge that we are full of darkness which prevents us from knowing and loving him, and so, with our duty obliging us to love God and our concupiscence leading us astray, we are full of unrighteousness. It must account to us for the way in which we thus go against God and our own good. It must teach us the cure for our helplessness and the means of obtaining this cure. Let us examine all the religions of the world on that point and let us see whether any but the Christian religion meets it.

---

[15]Blaise Pascal, *Pensées*, A. J. Krailsheimer, ed. (London: Penguin, 1995), nos. 117, 149. The French original can be found in Blaise Pascal, *Pensées*, Ch.-M. des Granges, ed. (Paris: Éditions Garnier Frères, 1964), nos. 409, 430 (using the Brunschvicg numbers). For insightful application of this line of reasoning, see Douglas Groothuis, "Deposed Royalty: Pascal's Anthropological Argument," *Journal of the Evangelical Theological Society* 41:2 (1998): 297–312.

Pascal imagines God saying to mankind, "You are no longer in the state in which I made you." Anyone who wishes to be taken seriously must face this and account for it—and who has done this better than Genesis?

Evidence that Pascal is right comes from an unexpected quarter, namely Leon Kass's commentary on Genesis. I call it "unexpected" because Kass insists vigorously on a purely symbolic reading of Adam and Eve, as we already saw in section 2.b above:[16]

> We can learn most from the story by regarding it as a mythical yet realistic portrait of permanent truths about our humanity, rather than as a historical yet idealized portrait of a blissful existence we once enjoyed but lost.

In my earlier discussion I commented on Kass's preference for "permanent truths"; however, he makes a key admission that opens the way to undoing his whole position:

> No matter how sophisticated and civilized we have become, most of us respond to this portrait of our mythical remotest past with *something that feels, in fact, like nostalgia.*

His explanation for that "nostalgia" is less convincing than Pascal's. It is Pascal who has captured the experience of many all over the world who become Christian believers, and who has provided a way of relating this nostalgia to human life in such a way that answers Kass's contention that, "Read as history, the text fails to persuade the skeptical reader." With all due respect to Kass, if we *fail* to read the Genesis story as some kind of history, we fail to persuade the perceptive reader, because we fail to do justice to this nostalgia.

For me, it is G. K. Chesterton who best captures the refreshment that comes from realizing this:[17]

---

[16]Leon Kass, *The Beginning of Wisdom: Reading Genesis* (New York: Free Press, 2003), 58–61 (italics added).

[17]G. K. Chesterton, *As I Was Saying*, ed. Robert Knille (Grand Rapids, MI: Eerdmans, 1985), 160.

The Fall is a view of life. It is not only the only enlightening, but the only encouraging view of life. It holds, as against the only real alternative philosophies, those of the Buddhist or the Pessimist or the Promethean, that we have misused a good world, and not merely been entrapped into a bad one. It refers evil back to the wrong use of the will, and thus declares that it can eventually be righted by the right use of the will. Every other creed except that one is some form of surrender to fate. A man who holds this view of life will find it giving light on a thousand things; on which mere evolutionary ethics have not a word to say. For instance, on the colossal contrast between the completeness of man's machines and the continued corruption of his motives; on the fact that no social progress really seems to leave self behind; . . . . on that proverb that says "the price of liberty is eternal vigilance," which is only what the theologians say of every other virtue, and is itself only a way of stating the truth of original sin; on those extremes of good and evil by which man exceeds all the animals by the measure of heaven and hell; on that sublime sense of loss that is in the very sound of all great poetry, and nowhere more than in the poetry of pagans and sceptics: "We look before and after, and pine for what is not"; which cries against all prigs and progressives out of the very depths and abysses of the broken heart of man, that happiness is not only a hope, but also in some strange manner a memory; and that we are all kings in exile.

If we say, as I think we should, that there is a level of figurative and symbolic description in Genesis 1–4, we must still allow that the story we find there provides the best explanation for our lives now, and for our hunger for things to be better.

5

CAN SCIENCE HELP US
PINPOINT "ADAM AND EVE"?

There are those who claim that the evidence from human DNA "points to a population of several thousand people from whom all humans have descended, not just two."[1] I am not sure whether the words "points to"—rather than, say, "demands"—were chosen to clarify the kind of inference that lies behind this conclusion; for now, I prefer to contend that a good theory must account for *all of the data*, and not just the biochemistry. My discussion in chapter 4 above offers some of the data that it may be easy for biologists to overlook.

Any attempt to relate the Biblical teaching to scientific theories runs into the challenges of what is called "concordism"—that is, the process of seeking to harmonize the conclusions of these two separate fields of study. I will therefore first discuss whether "concordism" of any kind is proper. After this I will consider some further exegetical questions (mostly coming from Genesis 3–5), to see

---

[1]Francis Collins et al., "Question 15: How does the Fall fit into evolutionary history? Were Adam and Eve historical figures?" in *The Biologos Foundation: Questions*, (2009), http://www.biologos.org (accessed July 13, 2009).

whether the Biblical materials point to a specific time period for the origin and development of mankind. In keeping with my plan to consider the whole range of data, I will then examine ways in which the data of human experience may guide us in how we tell the story of mankind's history. Finally, I will list some of the approaches to human origins that have been proposed by various Christians, with a view toward evaluating them for their compliance with the guidelines I have found.

5.a Does the Bible Connect to History and Science? The Problem of "Concordism"

First, let us define "concordism." Strictly speaking, it is the effort to find some kind of agreement between two possibly conflicting accounts. When applied to the Bible, it is especially referring to ways in which Bible believers have tried to coordinate the findings of science with the teachings of Genesis.

For example, it was popular in the nineteenth century to connect the days of Genesis 1 with the newly discovered geological ages. Thus faithful Christians could say that their holy book had anticipated the findings of the modern sciences, even down to details of sequence and timing.[2] This should strengthen the faith of believers and commend the faith to unbelievers.

There are several obvious problems with this approach. To begin with, the scientific theories change. Geologists do not describe the earth's history in 2010 the way they did in 1871. Does the apparent agreement of the Bible with the geology of 1871 mean that we should reject contemporary geology, or that the Bible was *wrong*?

Further, this approach can easily lead believers to suppose that the Bible's own right to refer to historical events depends on our ability to confirm its statements. The Biblical writers do, of course, open some historical claims to public inspection: Paul does this with the resurrection of Jesus, for example (cf. 1 Cor. 15:6). But many events are much harder to confirm, such as the lives of the patriarchs (Genesis 12–50). We can support the generally authentic air of these

---

[2]See, e.g., how Charles Hodge treats the subject in his *Systematic Theology* (Grand Rapids, MI: Eerdmans, 1981 [1871–73]), 1:570–74.

accounts (a worthy endeavor, as I see it), but we cannot say that we have *demonstrated* their truthfulness.

More significantly from an exegetical standpoint, the kind of concordism on display in nineteenth century studies of Genesis assumes that the Bible writer's purpose was to describe the same sorts of things as the contemporary scientist does. This is a highly problematic assumption, when one considers the audience for whom Genesis was written—Old Testament Israel, whose main concerns were dominated by subsistence agriculture. Further, it also assumes that truth and scientific detail are the same thing, which is absurd.

On the other hand, *anti*-concordism, which tends to reject concordism out of hand, is not the only alternative. Anti-concordism, as applied to Genesis, tends to assume that the Biblical account has little or no historical referent.[3]

If the account in Genesis intends to make an historical reference, then—at least in theory—it may be *possible* to find some connection between its subject matter and the results of other fields of study. But "possibility" is not the same as "likelihood," and still less as "necessity."

Sometimes anti-concordism stems from the view that the proper relationship between science and faith is one of complementarity: that is, they are two aspects of a whole description of the world. For example, a faith-based assertion that God gave to my wife and me a child with the specific mix of features from each of us, and a scientific description of chromosomes and cell division, go together to make a more accurate account of what has happened. The science-based and the faith-based statements do not conflict with each other, nor do they compete for primacy: both are correct, but neither is complete. Now, there is much to be said in favor of this general approach: it

---

[3]This seems to underlie Daniel Harlow's rejection of concordism in "Creation According to Genesis: Literary Genre, Cultural Context, Theological Truth," *Christian Scholars Review* 37:2 (2008): 163–98, at 198, where he insists that "the theological truths that Genesis reveals are both timeless and vital" (see discussion in section 2.b above). Likewise when Denis Lamoureux, *Evolutionary Creation: A Christian Approach to Evolution* (Eugene, OR: Wipf & Stock, 2008), rejects concordism in favor of what he calls the "Message-Incident Principle" (pages 110–11 and throughout), it appears to be because he first assumes historical or scientific concordism requires literalism, and second because he thinks a timeless message can be abstracted from the story.

is a helpful tool in discerning what a Bible writer might mean, for example, when he attributes events to God's activity. In such a case, the events may have "natural" causes, and still be God's work. There are two very obvious drawbacks, however, of a strict insistence on science-faith complementarity. First, it can lead to the idea that a scientific account of *all* events will depict purely natural causes, while it is clear that, Biblically, at least some events, such as the resurrection of Jesus, have supernatural components as well.[4] The second drawback, which is especially pertinent here, is that it is probably impossible for anyone actually to practice strict complementarity when it comes to specific historical events. For example, if a Bible writer insists that a person did some action (such as Adam and Eve committing the first sin, and thereby damaging their descendants and the world), and a scientist insists that this is not correct, the disagreement cannot be resolved by an appeal to complementarity. It may be that we should refine our reading of the Bible writer in light of the scientist's opinions; but sooner or later we will have to decide whether the Bible can actually refer to real persons and events or not.[5]

Let us back away from the case of Genesis 1–11, and take an example that should be less emotionally charged. Consider Israel's departure from Egypt. Certainly the Biblical writers depicted this as an actual event; this implies that there was a real Pharaoh, or perhaps a group of Pharaohs, behind the oppression. Some Biblical scholars think

---

[4]In my *God of Miracles: An Exegetical Examination of God's Action in the World* (Wheaton, IL: Crossway, 2000), I explain why I think it is Biblically and philosophically proper to speak of "natural" and "supernatural" factors in events; see also the summary in *Science and Faith: Friends or Foes?* (Wheaton, IL: Crossway, 2003), chapters 3, 11, 14. For discussion of one of the chief objections to my position (namely that it is "just God-of-the-gaps"), see my "Miracles, Intelligent Design, and God-of-the-Gaps," *Perspectives on Science and Christian Faith* 55:1 (2003): 22–29.

[5]John Walton, *The Lost World of Genesis One: Ancient Cosmology and the Origins Debate* (Downers Grove, IL: InterVarsity Press, 2009), makes life difficult for himself when he denies that the distinction between "natural" and "supernatural" is Biblically valid (pages 16–22), while at the same time he affirms that the process by which God produced Adam and Eve as historical persons was qualitatively different from any natural evolutionary process (page 139). The proper word for that qualitative difference is "supernatural," that is, the outcome goes beyond what natural processes on their own would have produced. In any case, for all the differences between Walton and myself on the specifics of reading Genesis, we nevertheless agree when it comes to Adam and Eve.

the time reference in 1 Kings 6:1 (480 years) implies that Israel left Egypt around 1446 B.C. This leads to one scheme for coordinating the Biblical account with what is known from other sources on Egyptian and Canaanite history. Other scholars think that the situation in the book of Exodus comports very well with the Egyptian Nineteenth Dynasty, especially Rameses II (reigned 1279–1213 B.C.), giving an exodus somewhere around 1260 B.C. Neither of these options is completely free of difficulties; but neither is impossible. The evidence with which I am familiar tends to favor the later date, and people whose Egyptological learning I respect highly lean strongly in that direction. It makes good sense to me, but I cannot thereby say that this *proves the truth* of the exodus: rather, it provides a reasonable scenario by which I can connect the Biblical account to contemporary events in its world. At least I can proceed, responsibly confident that the Biblical account has not been shown false. The earlier date is likewise a workable scenario for those who think that date more likely (though to me it seems weaker).

Of course, if the Pentateuch story of the exodus has no historical referent, if the Biblical writers simply wanted to make a kind of timeless theological statement about Israel being under God's care, then the entire effort to connect the story with external events is foolish. But I am sure that the Biblical writers do in fact refer to an historical exodus, and no allowance for literary devices should detract from that.

So then, how should we think about Genesis and science? We should begin by observing the literary conventions, rhetorical purpose, and original audience of the author of Genesis. I have already remarked on the way that Genesis sets itself over against other origins stories from the ancient Near East, especially those from Mesopotamia. Genesis 1–11 provides an alternative front end for its worldview story; its author and audience thought the alternative was in some sense "more true" than the other stories. Those other stories manifest some level of intended historical referentiality, clothed in what we might call imaginative description. It is reasonable to expect that in the same way Genesis intends to use imaginative description to tell us of actual events.

Further, we should appreciate the way in which Genesis tends to speak of the phenomena that the sciences study. Certainly Genesis does not use technical language: a "kind" is not the same as a "species." As a matter of fact, a close inspection shows us that it is probably a mistake to read Genesis 1 as talking about the kinds of plants and animals in a taxonomic sense (or even as implying that the kinds are fixed barriers to evolution). Rather, the passage makes plenty of sense if we consider the perspective of an ancient Israelite: such a person already knew full well that if you want to grow wheat or barley, you plant wheat or barley seeds; if you want more sheep, you breed them from other sheep. The point of Genesis 1 is not to "teach" these facts, but instead to put these already-known facts into a proper worldview context: the world works this way because it is the good creation of a good and magnificent Creator.

It is my hunch that most Israelites were aware, as most people everywhere are, that there is a dissonance between what we feel the world should be and what we experience. They would judge other attempts to account for this dissonance, or to explain it away (including ancient Near Eastern ones), as inadequate, and therefore unsatisfying. We did not need Genesis 3 to inform us of the problem; we can instead be grateful for the way its narrative of a primal disobedience clears away the cobwebs of our own hearts and of our own culture.

But, one may ask, may one legitimately use the Bible to inform scientific theorizing? One straightforward reply is to say, this will depend on the subject matter of the theory. The Bible will not speak one way or the other about relativistic mechanics, solid-state physics, or the circulatory system. Its focus is on events, and on the worldview its telling of those events conveys. This worldview certainly provides a grounding for a version of optimism, though, that scientific study really will uncover true things.[6]

---

[6]It was proper, therefore, for Georges Lemaître, the Belgian priest who did so much to found Big Bang cosmology, to insist that his theories sprang from his equations, and not from Genesis; see Marcia Bartusiak, "Before the Big Bang," *Technology Review* 112:5 (September/October 2009), MIT News Section, M14–15. If the theory should be discarded, that need not falsify Genesis. On the other hand, the theory provides many people with a useful scenario for envisioning the creation event.

At the same time, the Biblical events tend to be public ones, with universal significance; they cannot be restricted to personal religious experience—though their telling can indeed foster intense religious experience, with a whole range of emotions (from fear to exultation to grief to joy). When Paul told the Roman magistrate Festus that he was sure King Agrippa knew the key events of Paul's Christian story, "for this has not been done in a corner" (Acts 26:26), he was insisting on this public character of the events. So no complete account of the world ought to leave these out.[7]

However, one purpose of these chapters in Genesis is to help us hold on to good common sense, to the knowledge we all share as humans (such as what I covered in chapter 4 above)—though many suppress that knowledge—as we think about ourselves and about others.[8] This is how I intend to "use the Bible" in setting up some good criteria for evaluating proposed historical-scientific scenarios for the origin and fall of mankind.

5.b Making Sure We Read the Bible Well

Some people think that features of Genesis 3–5 make a claim about the intended time period for their events, and therefore for Adam and Eve.

I begin by considering features of Genesis 4 that suggest to some that Adam and Eve are not alone. For example, in Genesis 4:14 Cain is afraid that "whoever finds me will kill me." Then we read of Cain's

---

[7]N. T. Wright makes this point forcefully when he writes in *The New Testament and the People of God* (Minneapolis: Fortress, 1992), "It is ironic that many people in the modern world have regarded Christianity as a private worldview, a set of private stories. Some Christians have actually played right into this trap. But in principle the whole point of Christianity is that it offers a story which is the story of the whole world. It is public truth. Otherwise it collapses into some version of Gnosticism" (41–42).

[8]This should make it clear how I differ from Marcus Ross and Paul Nelson, who think that it is the young-earth creationists who really attend to Biblical authority in scientific theorizing. In my view, the proper question is the intention of the Biblical authors, which I see as worldview formation. Since I consider the insistence on young-earth science to be based on a misinterpretation of the Bible, I do not agree that it actually is employing Biblical authority! See Marcus Ross and Paul Nelson, "A Taxonomy of Teleology: Phillip Johnson, the Intelligent Design Community, and Young-Earth Creationism," in William Dembski, ed., *Darwin's Nemesis: Phillip Johnson and the Intelligent Design Movement* (Downers Grove, IL: InterVarsity Press, 2006), 261–75, at 266–67.

"wife" (v. 17), who arrives without any warning. Surely these texts imply that other people are in view?

If it is true that these texts imply the presence of other people, then someone might simply conclude that the author of Genesis 1–4 knew he was writing fiction to illustrate timeless truths, and, not being a compulsive like Tolkien, did not mind leaving a few loose ends.[9] Or maybe he even left in these incongruities to alert us to his fictive intent?

The right reply to these suggestions is, "Not so fast." First, our discussion so far gives us plenty of reason to believe that Genesis 1–5 comes from a careful writer or editor. Second, we also have good reason to believe, according to my discussion in chapter 3, that these stories are woven into the historical framework of Genesis as a whole, and that this is the way that subsequent readers have taken it. And third, we need not declare these texts incongruous with Genesis 1–3.

We should read Genesis 4 under the assumption that the author is using Cain's speech as a way of showing the readers the condition of Cain's inner life.[10] He could be afraid—perhaps God even considered his fear to be legitimate, since he put a "mark" on him (v. 15)—of what his siblings might carry out in due course, along the lines of what came to be known as the "avenger of blood" (see Num. 35:9–34, where it is presented as an institution already familiar to the audience who received the Pentateuch).[11] Some Jewish interpreters have taken the expression "whoever finds me" to refer, not to people, but to animals—an interpretation the Hebrew might allow (albeit with a little stretch).[12] It is also possible that the author wants

---

[9]On Tolkien's perfectionism, see Humphrey Carpenter, *J. R. R. Tolkien: A Biography* (London: George Allen & Unwin, 1976), 142–43, 198–99, 232.

[10]See my *Genesis 1–4: A Linguistic, Literary, and Theological Commentary* (Phillipsburg, NJ: P&R, 2006), 11, on the kinds of literary techniques the Biblical writers used.

[11]See, e.g., Umberto Cassuto, *Genesis, Part I: From Adam to Noah (Genesis i-iv 8)* (Jerusalem: Magnes, 1961 [1944]), 225.

[12]See Yehudah Kiel, *Sefer Bereshit*, Da'at Miqra' (Jerusalem: Mossad Harav Kook, 1997), קיג (on Gen. 4:14), recording some Rabbinic precedents. See also Josephus, *Antiquities*, 1.2.1, line 59. The grammatical difficulty is that the Hebrew word "finds" is masculine, while the usual terms for a "dangerous wild animal" are feminine (e.g., *khayyâ ra'â*, Gen. 37:20, 33). This means that if dangerous beasts are included, the idea is "whoever finds me, man or beast" (Kiel's interpretation).

us to think that Cain's fears are exaggerated, the result of his evil deed upon his conscience. In this case God put a mark on Cain in order to reassure him.

As for Cain's wife, it is true that we know nothing of her until Genesis 4:17. The traditional Jewish interpretation is that she came from among Cain's sisters (compare Gen. 5:4, mentioning the sisters).[13]

In both of these cases, it is important to recall that nothing in the Hebrew tells us how long Adam and Eve took before having their first child, nor does it tell us how old Cain and Abel are supposed to be in these events. There could be a small population resulting from Adam and Eve themselves. Some, however, have concluded from these details of Genesis 4 that there might be another source of people contemporary with Adam and Eve; I will take this up in section 5.d below.

Another exegetical consideration is whether the descriptions of Genesis 4, and the genealogy of Genesis 5, enable us to locate Adam and Eve in our historical timeframe. For example, some have suggested that Cain the farmer and Abel the keeper of sheep, together with the crafts described in 4:17–22, fit in the Neolithic period (no earlier than about 10,000 B.C.);[14] others have argued for an even more recent situation, assuming the genealogies have little or no gaps in them. But neither of these positions follows from the text of Genesis. To begin with, the description of Cain and Abel is fairly vague as it is, and the literary features of Genesis 1–11 lead us to allow for a level of anachronism (as already observed).[15]

When I use the term "anachronism," I mean that a text may well have described aspects of the older times in terms of what the writer and his audience are familiar with. This does not necessarily detract from the historicity of the text, since the text still refers to actual

---

[13]Kiel, *Sefer Bereshit*, קים (on Gen. 4:17); so too Cassuto, *Genesis, Part I*, 229, who adds, "this explanation is given by all the commentators from Talmudic times to our own day."

[14]E.g., Davis Young, "The Antiquity and the Unity of the Human Race Revisited," *Christian Scholars Review* 24:4 (1995): 380–396. For more discussion, see my *Genesis 1–4*, 201–203.

[15]There may be some evidence that the earliest stages of what became farming long pre-date the Neolithic period: see D. R. Piperno et al., "Processing of Wild Cereal Grains in the Upper Paleolithic Revealed by Starch Grain Analysis," *Nature* 430 (August 2004), 670–73, which reports findings that people were processing wild cereal grains—a predecessor to cultivation—more than 20,000 years ago.

events. The Greek poet Homer, for example, could talk about real events (the Trojan War) in his poem *The Iliad*, albeit with a lot of imaginative elements mixed in. If Homer, who apparently lived in the eighth century B.C., wanted to describe the armor and weapons of the warriors in his tale, he probably would base those descriptions on the equipment of his own day, without a serious concern for what they "actually" were as many as four or five centuries earlier. In Genesis 1–11, we have Noah taking aboard the ark extra specimens of the "clean animals," presumably because these were fit for sacrifice (Gen. 7:2, 8; 8:20). Now there is no hint in the creation account that the clean-unclean distinction is inherent in the nature of the animals, and in the Bible this distinction served to set Israel apart from the Gentiles (see Lev. 20:24–26); this is why the early Christians did away with these laws (see Acts 10:9–29; Mark 7:19).[16] The very first mention of a "clean" animal occurs right here; we do not even know what they are unless we turn to Leviticus 11. Perhaps we are to think that Noah had some idea of what kinds of animals are right for sacrifice, but we need not suppose that it was identical to the system found in the books of Moses. How could it be, when Noah was not an Israelite?[17] Perhaps the specific "burnt offering" is also anachronistic—that is, Noah made a sacrifice, but the term "burnt offering" had a very precise sense in Israel that may go beyond what Noah thought.[18] Genesis interprets Noah's behavior in line with Israelite practice. Nothing makes this literary practice unhistorical, since we are recognizing a literary device.

The literary features of Genesis 4 also allow us to read the records of various crafts in 4:20–22 as describing the pioneers of the skills that eventually led to the crafts the audience would be familiar with.

---

[16]For a very helpful discussion of these laws from a Jewish perspective, see Meir Soloveichik, "Locusts, Giraffes, and the Meaning of *Kashrut*," *Azure* 23 (Winter 5766/2006): 62–96.

[17]See Ezek. 14:14, 20, which mentions Noah, Daniel, and Job as ancient exemplars. "Daniel" in this context is probably the figure known as Dan'il in the Ugaritic poem (although I expect that, in order to commend the man, Ezekiel knew more about him than what we find in that particular story).

[18]Perhaps the two kinds of sacrifice in Gen. 4:3–4, which are recognizable in the Israelite system, can be treated the same way.

Umberto Cassuto argued that the Hebrew terms "father" and "forger" can be read with these nuances.[19] Likewise, the genealogies in this kind of literature do not claim to name every person in the line of descent, and thus are not aimed at providing detailed chronological information. Further, I know of no way to ascertain what size gaps these genealogies allow; it does not appear that they are intended to tell us what kind of time period they are describing.[20]

There is, therefore, good reason to steer away from the idea that Genesis 4–5 makes any kind of claim about the dates of the events and people involved.

There is also the question of "death": Does Genesis 3 imply that there was no "death" before Adam and Eve sinned? I have already stated, in section 3.a, that the "death threat" of Genesis 2:17 should be taken to refer to what we can call "spiritual" death. This follows pretty easily if we take it as a given that God is a reliable character in the Bible: he means what he says, and if he seems to deceive, or to change his mind, the reasons are clear from the context. Well, then: in Genesis 3, after the couple have disobeyed God, they feel shame, they try to hide from God, and they avoid taking personal responsibility. They are alienated from God, and from each other: something inside them has died, the bliss they had known is gone. Since this alienation is a legitimate sense of the words "die" and "death" in Hebrew, we are reading the passage well—or taking the words "at face value"—when we find this as God's intended meaning in Genesis 2:17.[21]

But Genesis 3:19 says that, in addition, the human being will "return to the ground." Does that imply that there was no physical death before this event? This question arises from two main motives: first, the likelihood that the earth is far older than 6,000 years, based

---

[19]Cassuto, *Genesis, Part I*, 235–37. I provide some philological support for this in Collins, *Homonymous Verbs in Biblical Hebrew: An Investigation of the Role of Comparative Philology* (University of Liverpool Ph.D. Thesis, 1988), 232–33.

[20]For fuller argument, see Collins, *Genesis 1–4*, 203–207.

[21]Lamoureux, *Evolutionary Creation*, insists on "literalism" in his reading of the Bible passages in order to argue that they are not "historical." He seems unaware of the lexical and literary issues mentioned here (see his pages 305–306).

on geology and the fossil record, implies that animals had been dying long before human beings came on the scene. Second, some Christians suppose that the first true human beings had ancestors (see below), which would then imply that there had been death in the human family line before this event. Perhaps, they say, the first true humans were originally made mortal, and death is a "natural" part of human existence.

To answer that question, we first recognize that, whatever the verse talks about, it is referring to humans. Therefore Genesis is not at all suggesting that no other animals had ever died before this point: the teeth and claws of a lion are not a decoration, nor have they been perverted from their "pre-fall" use. Further, *if* God made the first humans from preexisting animals, we still should suppose that the lives and self-awareness of these first humans were different from those of their animal predecessors. In my treatment of Genesis 3, I have indicated that I am very wary of trying any detailed description of what the moral and mental life of these first human beings was like: after all, their condition, as I read the account, was intended to be temporary, and they were to grow into maturity and confirmation. Nevertheless, bodily death for such creatures does not fit well with the condition in which they were first made, and we their heirs do not welcome death. We can accept the death of our bodies, we can acquire the spiritual skills to die well; but we still see death as an enemy. Hence we have grounds for thinking that bodily death was never God's intended outcome for his human creatures.

Therefore the fossils that record the bodily deaths of animals provide no difficulty for taking Genesis 3 at *its own* face value. Neither are we forced, if we think that Adam and Eve had animal predecessors, to believe that bodily death was the "natural" end for them.

5.c Criteria for Good Scenarios

Sections 5.a and 5.b give us good reasons to be very cautious about a literalistic form of concordism for the early chapters of Genesis. It is easy to go wrong by ignoring some of the literary conventions. Another good reason for being cautious in thinking about historical-scientific scenarios comes from Henri Blocher, who appealed for modesty:[22]

> It is also difficult to forecast what aspect of being the image of God would actually show up in a scientific description of mankind; so it is not quite certain what it is we are looking for when we try to discover the first man largely in terms of incomplete skeletons.

He is speaking, of course, about reconstruction from the fossils; but the same would apply to the biochemical evidence. Thus I have further reasons why I will focus on what I have called "scenarios," ways that can help us to picture events that really took place.

We are still wise, on the other hand, to see if there are some boundaries to what makes for a good scenario. My discussion so far does in fact provide some criteria for sound thinking about human origins and sin.

But first, what are some of the relevant findings from the sciences that we should try to account for?

One consideration is the evidence from the study of human fossils and cultural remains. If Adam and Eve are indeed at the headwaters of the human race, they must come before such events as the arrival of modern humans in Australia, which means before about 40,000 B.C. In popular presentations of human history, it is easy to get the impression that there is an unbroken procession from the apes, through the early hominins, to the genus *Homo* (of which we are members), right up to modern human beings. However, according to John Bloom's survey, there are two important gaps in the available data. The first occurs with the appearance of anatomically modern humans around 130,000 B.C. The second gap occurs when culture appears, around 40,000 B.C. At this point we find art, and "the complexity and variety of artifacts greatly increases." As Bloom observes,[23]

---

[22]Henri Blocher, *In the Beginning* (Downers Grove, IL: InterVarsity Press, 1984), 231. See more recently his "The Theology of the Fall and the Origins of Evil," in R. J. Berry and T. A. Noble, eds., *Darwin, Creation and the Fall: Theological Challenges* (Leicester, U.K.: Apollos, 2009), 149–72, at 169–72.

[23]John Bloom, "On Human Origins: A Survey" *Christian Scholars Review* 27:2 (1997): 181–203, at 199–200.

At present either of these transitions seems sharp enough that we can propose that the special creation of man occurred in one of these gaps and that it was not bridged by purely natural means.

On the genetic side, there are two related conclusions that we must account for. One is the idea that the genetic similarities between humans and chimpanzees require that these species have some kind of "common ancestor." A second conclusion is that the features of the human genome—particularly genetic diversity—imply that the human population needs to have been a thousand or more individuals, even at its beginning.[24]

I am not sure how to assess this DNA evidence; I do not know whether the evidence is only *compatible* with these conclusions, or if it *strongly favors* them. I cannot predict whether future geneticists will still think the same way about DNA as contemporary ones do. I know that biologists' understanding of DNA has changed over the years (e.g., so-called "junk DNA," the majority of the genome that was once thought to be nonfunctional, now appears to have a function),[25] but I have no idea what views biologists might hold in the future.

At the same time, it is worth observing that Francis Collins's presentation of the argument for common ancestry between humans and chimpanzees seems to depend a great deal on the "junk DNA" that humans and chimps have in common.[26] If the argument gains its force from the assumption that junk DNA is best viewed as a sort of evolutionary attic filled with relics no longer functional, then it loses its force as we learn more about what functions junk DNA actually performs. These functions include such tasks as regulating, maintaining, and reprogramming genetic processes, and possibly disabling some genes and activating genes that had been

[24]See Francis Collins et al., "Question 21: Who Was Mitochondrial Eve? Who Was Y-Chromosome Adam? How Do They Relate to Genesis?" in *The Biologos Foundation: Questions* (2009), http://www.biologos.org (accessed July 13, 2009). The research behind this comes from Francisco Ayala et al., e.g., "Molecular Genetics of Speciation and Human Origins," *Proceedings of the National Academy of the Sciences* 91 (July 1994): 6787–94.
[25]See, e.g., Erika Check Hayden, "Life Is Complicated," *Nature* 464 (2010): 664–67 (published online, March 31, 2010).
[26]Francis Collins, *The Language of God: A Scientist Presents Evidence for Belief* (New York: Free Press, 2006), 135–36.

inactive; since these are vital to both humans and chimpanzees, the fact that we have them in common is not *of itself* evidence of common ancestry.

Further, I am aware that John Bloom has suggested that population size studies relied on processes that were poorly understood (at least in 1997), and there may be other ways to explain the features of the human genome that led to the conclusion about a minimal human population.[27] Studies published as recently as 2006 show that there are apparently mechanisms by which the relevant kinds of genetic diversity can increase faster than the population size models had predicted, which means that caution is in order.[28] Thus it is reasonable to think of calculations based on genetic diversity as giving us a rough idea of the population size, with the evidence pointing toward a small population.

I have encountered at least one biologist who has insisted, however, that it is a scientifically established "fact" that it is just not possible for only two people to be the ancestors of the entire human race. But this is an overstatement: after all, it is not a *fact*, it is an *inference*, which means that it is the result of a process of reasoning. It may be a good inference, given today's state of biological thinking, but that does not make it automatically true. Not long ago many biologists treated as "fact" the notion that most of the genome has no function; had they been more careful, they would have said, it has no *known* function. No one knows, of course, whether future biologists will still use these same population size models.

Finally, I do not know whether these positions make use of assumptions that we really ought to be questioning. In view of my limitations, this is not the place, and I am not the person, to say whether these inferences are good or bad—though I wish that there were more critical discussion in the popular literature, laying out

---

[27]Bloom, "On Human Origins," 195–96.
[28]Takashi Shiina et al., "Rapid Evolution of MHC Class I Genes in Primates Generates New Disease Alleles in Man via Hitchhiking Diversity," *Genetics: Published Articles Ahead of Print*, May 15, 2006: published online as 10.1534/genetics.106.057034; Renaud Kaeuffer et al., "Unexpected Heterozygosity in an Island Mouflon Population Founded by a Single Pair of Individuals," *Proceedings of the Royal Society B*, September 24, 2006: published online as doi:10.1098/rspb.2006.3743.

strengths and weaknesses. At this point I am mostly asking that we be careful. This is why I have sought ways to allow advocates of these conclusions to stay within the bounds of sound thinking. In other words, even if someone is persuaded that humans had "ancestors," and that the human population has always been more than two, he does not *necessarily* have to ditch all traditional views of Adam and Eve, and I have tried to provide for these possibilities more than to contend for my particular preferences on these matters.

Now then: how do we stay within the bounds of sound thinking? What criteria do all our reflections so far lead us to?

(1) To begin with, we should see that the origin of the human race goes beyond a merely natural process. This follows from how hard it is to get a human being, or, more theologically, how distinctive the image of God is.

(2) We should see Adam and Eve at the headwaters of the human race. This follows from the unified experience of mankind, as discussed in chapter 4: where else could human beings come to bear God's image?

(3) The "fall," in whatever form it took, was both historical (it happened) and moral (it involved disobeying God), and occurred at the beginning of the human race. The universal sense of loss described in chapter 4 makes no sense without this. Where else could this universality have come from?

Someone could reply that the moral sense is a delusion, and thus human life only *looks* nasty: we call it "wrong" only because we do not like it. Or someone else might think that God somehow created the world with sin as a part of it, either because he could not help it, or because sin has some sort of existence independent of God, and forced its way in. As I have already argued, all of these answers produce more problems than they solve. Thus even though conventional Christian theism may leave us with some kinds of discomfort (how could God have allowed evil, if he knew about it beforehand, and is all-powerful?), it is a discomfort that we can find resources to live with.

Applying criteria (2) and (3) means that any valid model will cover, not only Middle Easterners and Europeans, but also those peoples who were the first to populate what is now Australia and the Americas.

Theories about multiple origins for human beings, the lines developing in parallel in different regions ("polygenesis"), do crop up from time to time.[29] These theories posit a natural transition from pre-human to human, which is unreasonable. A Christian should not find these attractive, either, even if a theory suggests separate *creations*. These theories will be unsatisfactory, because they imply that there are some humans who do not need the Christian message because they are not "fallen"—or else that every time God made human beings they "fell," or that there is some other means of transmitting sin. It looks like the models that are more in favor among paleoanthropologists today focus more on unified origin (as in the "out of Africa" hypothesis).

(4) If someone should decide that there were, in fact, more human beings than just Adam and Eve at the beginning of mankind, then, in order to maintain good sense, he should envision these humans as a single tribe. Adam would then be the chieftain of this tribe (preferably produced before the others), and Eve would be his wife. This tribe "fell" under the leadership of Adam and Eve. This follows from the notion of solidarity in a representative. Some may call this a form of "polygenesis," but this is quite distinct from the more conventional, and unacceptable, kind.[30]

5.d A Sampling of Scenarios Examined
Now we are in a position to list a few scenarios, and see what we might have to do to bring them into compliance with the criteria that I just offered. I do not claim thereby to have established the likelihood of any of these scenarios; that is not my purpose. They

---

[29]Described in Fazale Rana with Hugh Ross, *Who Was Adam? A Creation Model Approach to the Origin of Man* (Colorado Springs: NavPress, 2005), 36–37, 124–26.

[30]It appears that Bruce Waltke, *An Old Testament Theology* (Grand Rapids, MI: Zondervan, 2007), 202–203, would agree with my first three criteria, and perhaps the fourth. I consider his description of the fall, that 'adam [man or mankind?] freely chose to "follow their primitive animal nature," to be inadequate, but it is still moral. I cannot say whether in referring to 'adam and saying "their" he means to leave open how many humans there were to begin with. Waltke associates himself with Francis Collins's perspective (202 n. 81), but he is clearer than Collins on the special origin and importance of Adam and Eve.

are instead ways of envisioning the events, and I present them here in order to foster conversation and creativity.[31]

The standard young earth creationist understanding would have Adam and Eve as fresh, *de novo* creations, with no animal forebears. Some old earth creationist models share this view, while others allow for God to have refurbished a preexisting hominid into Adam. For the purposes of this work I do not intend to make this an issue. On the other hand, my first criterion in section 5.c shows why I think the *metaphysics* by which the first human beings came about—namely, it was not by a purely natural process—matters a great deal. This common ground matters more than the differences over where God got the raw material, because either way we are saying that humans are the result of "special creation."

An obvious scenario has Adam and Eve as the first members of the genus *Homo*. Some young earth creationists have favored this, as have some old earth creationists. A major difficulty with this proposal is that the earliest *Homo* is dated at two million years ago, and this leaves a very long time without any specific cultural remains in the paleontological record; this makes the alternatives more attractive.[32]

A sophisticated model, up-to-date with the genetic evidence, comes from Fazale Rana of the Christian apologetics organization Reasons to Believe (RTB).[33] Rana traces human ancestry to an original woman (Eve) and to one man who comes later (Noah). The overall Reasons to Believe model would place the origin of humanity somewhere between 10,000 and 100,000 years ago. More precisely, Rana suggests,[34]

---

[31]In keeping with my plan of outlining "mere-historical-Adam-and-Eve-ism," I am not arguing for my own preference out of all these. Indeed, my four criteria in section 5.c are what counts; but I have shown what I prefer and why in *Science and Faith*, 267–69; *Genesis 1–4*, 253–55.

[32]See further John Bloom, "On Human Origins," 199 n. 72.

[33]Fazale Rana with Hugh Ross, *Who Was Adam?* They discuss the genetic issues in chapter 4, pages 55–75. This general approach finds support in John Bloom, "On Human Origins." Bloom tells me (personal communication, 7-9-2009) that he has updated his essay in light of new genetic evidence, and generally supports Rana's approach—though he does not claim that the scientific evidence *proves* the model, or a single first pair. Bloom's background in both physics and ancient Near Eastern studies makes his opinions worthy of attention.

[34]Rana, *Who Was Adam?* 248.

The RTB model views Adam and Eve as historical individuals—the first human beings—originating by God's miraculous intervention approximately 70,000 to 50,000 years ago. Adam and Eve's descendants formed a small initial population that eventually gave rise to all human population groups around the world.

In addition to Adam and Eve, this model explicitly includes the great flood, reading Genesis 6–9 as implying that all mankind, except Noah and his immediate family, perished in it. The overall model does not depend on this last point, however.

Rana's model does not require the use of an earlier hominid to produce Adam's body. An "evolutionary creationist," Gavin Basil McGrath, offers a scheme that explicitly involves pre-Adamic hominids:[35]

God took two hominids to become the first human beings, Adam and Eve (1 Tim. 2:13). In Eve's case, God provided the new genetic information needed to make her human by using some genetic material taken from "one of" Adam's "ribs," so she too would be of Adam's race. . . . Thus Eve's existence as a person was made racially dependant upon Adam; and these two *alone* are the rest of the human race's progenitors.

He dates Adam to around 45,000 B.C. (± 20,000 years), which is still in the same ballpark as Rana's model.

John Stott is somewhat similar to McGrath, though he reads Genesis 2–4 as implying that Adam corresponds to a Neolithic farmer (c. 10,000 B.C.).[36] Since, he says, the evidence from ancient skeletons is "anatomical rather than behavioural," it is hard to tell when the pre-Adamic hominids were "still *homo sapiens* and not yet *homo divinus*, if we may so style Adam." This has received some scientific critique;[37] but, from the perspective of this study, its Neolithic set-

---

[35]Gavin Basil McGrath, "Soteriology: Adam and the Fall," *Perspectives on Science and Christian Faith* 49:4 (1997): 252–63. Philosopher David Siemens commended aspects of McGrath's approach in a letter in *Perspectives on Science and Christian Faith* 50:1 (1998): 78, including his orthodox soteriology (involving human unity and an historical fall).
[36]John Stott, *Romans* (Downers Grove, IL: InterVarsity Press, 1995), 162–66.
[37]Allan J. Day, "Adam, Anthropology and the Genesis Record: Taking Genesis Seriously," *Science and Christian Belief* 10 (1998), 115–43, at 136.

ting treats the material in Genesis with a higher degree of literalism than the literary genre calls for. It also does not account for all humans, unless we wish to argue that Australia and the Americas were populated much more recently than paleontologists currently interpret the data to imply. These factors make the proposal less attractive (though Stott has a clear eye for what matters, namely human uniqueness and unity in both dignity and need).

Stott draws attention to an idea of Derek Kidner, which Kidner himself calls "an exploratory suggestion," which "is only tentative, as it must be, and it is a personal view."[38] Kidner was struck by the pointers in Genesis 4 that seem to indicate that there were other human beings at the time of Cain and Abel (see section 5.b above). He wonders if Cain's fears of others and the source of his wife (Gen. 4:14, 17) favor, or at least allow for this, though he also acknowledges that traditional answers (other descendants of Adam and Eve) are "valid enough." Kidner was also well aware, from the theological angle, of the kinds of criteria that I posited in section 5.c (although he does not spell them out as I have done).

In this arrangement, we have the special creation of Adam and Eve, perhaps refurbishing an existing hominid. Then,[39]

It is at least conceivable that after the special creation of Eve, which established the first human pair as God's vice regents (Gn. 1:27, 28) and clinched the fact that there is no natural bridge from animal to man, God may now have conferred his image on Adam's collaterals, to bring them into the same realm of being. Adam's 'federal' headship of humanity extended, if that was the case, outwards to his contemporaries as well as onwards to his offspring, and his disobedience disinherited both alike.

Kidner argues that "the unity of mankind 'in Adam' and our common status as sinners through his offence are expressed in Scripture in terms not of heredity but simply of solidarity."

---

[38]Kidner, Genesis, Tyndale OT Commentary (Downers Grove, IL: InterVarsity Press, 1967), 26–31 (quotation from 30).
[39]Ibid., 29.

This suggestion is moving us away from the simplicity of the Biblical picture, though it does have the virtue of seeking to preserve the "doctrine that mankind is a unity, created in God's image, and fallen in Adam by the one act of disobedience."[40] Further, solidarity in the Bible is not based on legal fiction but on some actual connection; perhaps this can still apply to the "collaterals," provided they are closely enough related. In order to ensure that Kidner's proposal meets the criteria of section 5.c, and is worthy of consideration, one would need to imagine Adam as chieftain, or "king," whose task it is not simply to *rule* a people but more importantly to *represent* them (the basic idea of a king in the Bible).

Kidner does acknowledge that his proposal becomes unlikely if Eve's name, *Khawwâ*, implies that she is the physical mother of all humans. He takes the name to mean "Life" (as in Greek *Zoe* at Gen. 3:20); but her name more likely means "Life-giver" (see section 3.a above). Nevertheless, a king and queen under the arrangement that Kidner envisions are legitimately the father and mother of their people, so Kidner's own reservation is not fatal.

Still another suggestion comes from Denis Alexander, an eminent British biologist who is also a Christian, serving as Director of the Faraday Institute for Science and Religion in Cambridge. His well-written book, *Creation or Evolution: Do We Have to Choose?* (2008), is becoming very influential in science-religion discussions in Britain.[41] Alexander presents the case for the biological continuity between humans and their animal ancestors, rejecting any idea of a *special* creative action that bestowed the image of God on the first human beings. He finds in Genesis 4 "the clear implication that 'the man' and 'the woman' were not the only people around at that time"; indeed, he reads the agriculture and gardening of Genesis 2–4 as implying a Neolithic setting (some time since 10,000 B.C.): "God in his grace chose a couple of Neolithic farmers in the Near East, or

---

[40]Ibid., 30.

[41]Denis Alexander, *Creation or Evolution: Do We Have to Choose?* (Oxford: Monarch/Grand Rapids, MI: Kregel, 2008). There is much to appreciate about this book, and a number of things to differ with; the book deserves a proper review (which I hope one day to provide). Although the entire book is relevant here, the key material comes in his chapters 9–13.

maybe a community of farmers, to whom he chose to reveal himself in a special way." That is to say, these were the first people to have a personal relationship with God, real spiritual life; presumably they were to spread the knowledge of God through the rest of mankind (between one and ten million people, spread over the globe, according to the estimates). Although Alexander calls Adam "the federal head of the whole of humanity alive at that time," it is unclear just what he thinks that means: there is no discussion of what he thinks the "in" expressions of the Bible might mean, and one wonders if the "representation" is an arbitrary one. As a Christian, Alexander feels obligated to come to grips with all of the Bible; since Paul, for example, took Adam to be just as historical as Jesus, therefore Alexander intends to take Adam as an actual person.[42]

The consequence of Alexander's view is that death is a "natural" end of the life of every human being; Adam's selection for spiritual life did not change that. Further, the "fall" of Adam led to sin coming into the rest of mankind, "spreading the spiritual contamination of sin around the world." He is clear about how this works: "spiritual death came to all men by them actually sinning. Each person is responsible for his or her own sin." At the same time, "there is no doubt that in the New Testament physical death is an enemy to be destroyed, because it has no place in the fulfilled kingdom of God." He interprets I Corinthians 15:50 ("flesh and blood cannot inherit the kingdom of God, nor does the perishable inherit the imperishable") to imply that, by the very nature of things, we must die in order to receive the resurrection body.[43]

Alexander certainly wants to take the Bible as seriously as he takes the science. The difficulty with his position is twofold, however: first, he has assumed too easily that human capacities could arise in the natural course of evolution. As I have already argued, one need not be a Christian to see how hard it is to get a human being; in my conversations with evolutionary biologists who are not Christians, I have found those who readily acknowledge this point. The second difficulty is that, not being a Bible specialist, he is at the mercy of

---

[42]Ibid., 265.
[43]Ibid., 250.

whatever sources he chose to use, and his Biblical resources have, in my judgment, misled him. Indeed, he is aware of the Genesis commentaries of Derek Kidner and Gordon Wenham,[44] both of whom are closer to the traditional Christian understanding of Adam and Eve and their relation to the rest of mankind. Unfortunately, he does not even count Kidner's suggestion as one of the "models" he considers for evaluation, and I would be very interested in why he leaves it out. I have already given reasons (in section 5.b) why I do not think that a Neolithic setting is required by Genesis 4. Further, Alexander does no justice to the ideas of covenantal inclusion conveyed by the terms "in Adam" and "in Christ," as already discussed here. I cannot see how his version of "representation" is much more than the setting of a good or bad example. The distinguished work of N. T. Wright, *The Resurrection of the Son of God*, contains an excellent treatment of 1 Corinthians 15; even if one disagrees with Wright's conclusions, he should at least interact with this work. I find Wright's view of 1 Corinthians 15:50 to be compelling: namely, "flesh and blood cannot inherit the kingdom of God" refers to flesh and blood *as it now is* after Adam's sin—that is, the perishability came through the sin, not by virtue of creation.[45] In Paul, the term "the perishable" is also rendered "corruption," referring to the corrupting effect of sin (cf. Gal. 6:8; Eph. 4:22; 2 Cor. 7:2).[46]

I find that when Alexander treats human death as something "natural," he never considers whether the "fall" has changed circumstances:[47] after all, every Biblical character who dies does so after Genesis 3. In addition, even though he properly recognizes that death is an enemy in the New Testament, his overall discussion does not take seriously the human reaction to death as something unwelcome, as something we are right to grieve. When he argues that human pain is a normal part of the good creation order he limits that to the physical sensation. I agree that the ability to feel such

---

[44]Ibid., 360–61 n. 108.
[45]N. T. Wright, *The Resurrection of the Son of God* (Minneapolis: Fortress, 2003), 359.
[46]For my discussion of the effects of the fall on "nature," see my *Genesis 1–4*, 162–66 (on Gen. 3:16–19), 182–84 (on Rom. 8:18–25); see further my *Science and Faith*, chapters 9–10.
[47]Alexander, *Creation or Evolution*, 246–49.

pain is good, but this is not the "pain" we have in mind when we talk about "the *problem* of pain." We are instead thinking of despair, of grinding oppression, of anxiety and anguish, of the waste of a life that yearns for eternity. This seems to be the kind of pain that Genesis describes as God's verdict for the humans as a consequence of their disobedience (Gen. 3:16, 17).[48]

There is more to say on specific topics in Alexander's whole discussion; but for our purposes we will notice that his proposal falls short of the criteria given in section 5.c, and that neither the science nor the Bible demands such a scenario. Therefore we should find some other approach more satisfying.

The last scenario I will present gets its place of honor from the one who offered it, namely C. S. Lewis. Francis Collins, who—as both an accomplished biologist and also a Christian—is a kind of American counterpart to Denis Alexander, finds the scenario appealing. In his *Problem of Pain* Lewis devotes chapter 5 to "The Fall of Man."[49] The chapter's thesis is "that man, as a species, spoiled himself, and that good, to us in our present state, must therefore mean primarily remedial or corrective good." But in the course of developing this thesis, Lewis offers a suggestion that he calls "a 'myth' in the Socratic sense." By this he refers to what one can find in Plato's dialogues, a story that *may have been* historical fact, "a not unlikely tale"—indeed, it is along the lines of what I am calling a scenario. I will excerpt from his highly pictorial description for the sake of brevity:[50]

> For long centuries, God perfected the animal form which was to become the vehicle of humanity and the image of Himself. He gave it hands whose thumb could be applied to each of the fingers, and

---

[48]Alexander gives a touching anecdote on how members of a Japanese family became Christians through suffering (*Creation or Evolution*, 289–90), illustrating his view that this present life is "a vale of soul-making." But this misses the point: the suffering undermines our self-sufficiency because it reveals that something is wrong, and we are helpless to fix it; we need God's help, but we are estranged from him. That is what makes pain "God's megaphone" (to use C. S. Lewis's phrase).

[49]This has appeared in several editions. My copy is the 1943 printing of the 1940 text, published in London by Geoffrey Bles.

[50]The portion of text in this block quote is the same as that excerpted in Francis Collins, *The Language of God*, 208–209, and in Collins et al., "Question 15." Unfortunately, neither place addresses Lewis's own reservations about his scenario, as discussed here.

jaws and teeth and throat capable of articulation, and a brain sufficiently complex to execute all of the material motions whereby rational thought is incarnated. . . . Then, in the fullness of time, God caused to descend upon this organism, both on its psychology and physiology, a new kind of consciousness which could say "I" and "me", which could look upon itself as an object, which knew God, which could make judgments of truth, beauty and goodness, and which was so far above time that it could perceive time flowing past. . . . We do not know how many of these creatures God made, nor how long they continued in the Paradisal state. But sooner or later they fell. Someone or something whispered that they could become as gods. . . . They wanted some corner in the universe of which they could say to God, "This is our business, not yours." But there is no such corner. They wanted to be nouns, but they were, and eternally must be, mere adjectives. We have no idea in what particular act, or series of acts, the self-contradictory, impossible wish found expression. For all I can see, it might have concerned the literal eating of a fruit, but the question is of no consequence.

Lewis admits that the Greek word "in" ("*in* Christ, *in* Adam") is a challenge to his own understanding, as is the sense of inclusion or solidarity we encounter in the Old Testament. He can be excused for not quite getting these clear, as there was probably no one in Oxford in the 1930s to lend clarity on these points; the ideas presented in the book you are now reading, with its narrative orientation and its notion of covenantal inclusion, steer us away from any approach that does not involve these concepts. Also, Lewis calls the story in Genesis a "myth," by which he apparently means of limited historical value. I am not sure why he did not treat it as "a 'myth' in the Socratic sense"; I suspect it was because he viewed its intended effect to be primarily on the imagination.

Lewis certainly preserves important features of the Biblical presentation; indeed, I would say that he meets the first three criteria of section 5.c, and it will take only a small tweak to bring it into line with the fourth criterion. Lewis is clear on the kind of divine supervision necessary (that is, man did not result from a purely natural process) and on the moral issues involved. Also to Lewis's credit, whenever it comes to imaginative presentation of the ideas in his other books, he keeps to a particular Adam and Eve, as he has great respect for the form of the story in Genesis.[51] But Lewis's imaginative exercise here has really moved us away from the Biblical story line.

Further, Lewis preserves the historical character of the fall: that is, it is an event—or cluster of events—that actually took place, and changed human life forever. This certainly sets his view apart from all views that see sin as the result of something "timeless and eternal" and thus non-historical (as in Karl Barth), or as something inherent in God's creation (as in many modern theologians).

The main difficulty with Lewis's view lies in his clause, "We do not know *how many* of these creatures God made."[52] He is not asserting that there *must* have been more than Adam and Eve; he is declaring the question immaterial to the discussion. If, however, we take our cue from Lewis's own mention of solidarity and "in Adam," and reflect on what we saw in Derek Kidner's tentative suggestion, then we have a way of pushing Lewis's scenario into a more acceptable direction. That is, we should make it more like Kidner's scenario, with Adam as the chieftain and Eve as his queen.

Two of these scenarios, from Derek Kidner and C. S. Lewis, may be attractive to those who favor the "population size approaches" based on human DNA. As I have indicated, my goal here is not to assess the science but to display how to keep the reasoning within the bounds of sound thinking. Nothing requires us to abandon monogenesis altogether for some form of polygenesis; rather, a modified monogenesis, which keeps Adam and Eve, can do the job.

---

[51]E.g., in his novel *Perelandra* (from the Space Trilogy), and in Aslan's words to Prince Caspian at the end of that story: "You come of the Lord Adam and the Lady Eve. And that is both honour enough to erect the head of the poorest beggar, and shame enough to bow the shoulders of the greatest emperor in earth. Be content." See C. S. Lewis, *Prince Caspian* (New York: Macmillan, 1951), chapter 15.

[52]There are further demurrals from Lewis's full presentation in Henri Blocher, *Original Sin: Illuminating the Riddle*, New Studies in Biblical Theology (Grand Rapids, MI: Eerdmans, 1997), 56–57 (Lewis could be taken to imply that sin was a natural consequence of human free will), 89 (did humans by their fall actually lose their proper nature?). These are insightful, but do not affect our topic. (On pages 97–98 Blocher approves Lewis's recognition of solidarity.)

I admit that these scenarios leave us with many uncertainties, but these uncertainties in no way undermine our right to hold fast to the Biblical story line with full confidence. In fact, this holding fast actually helps us to think well about the scientific questions!

6

CONCLUSIONS

6.a What I Think I Have Shown

I do not claim to have solved every problem or to have dealt with every possible objection. But I trust I have shown why the traditional understanding of Adam and Eve as our first parents who brought sin into human experience is worthy of our confidence and adherence. It does justice to specific Biblical texts, and suits the Biblical story line, with its notions of representation and covenantal inclusion; it also provides a meaningful explanation for everyday experience. It is the view articulated or presupposed in Genesis, in Paul, and, above all, in the Gospel presentation of Jesus. The alternatives are less satisfactory, and possibly even disastrous, on all these counts.

6.b Why I Think It Matters

Let me summarize why I think it is important for Christians to affirm the results of this study.

First, I have emphasized throughout that I am sure that a major goal of the Christian story is to enable those who believe it to make sense of the world. If we abandon the conventional way of telling the Christian story, with its components of a good creation marred by the fall, redemption as God's ongoing work to restore the creatures to their proper functioning, and the consummation in which the restoration will be complete and confirmed, then we really give up all chance of understanding the world. Specifically, if we deny that all people have a common source that was originally good but through which sin came into the world, then the existence of sin becomes God's fault, or even something that God could not avoid. In either case there is little reason to be confident that any relief is headed our way.

Second, the notions of sin as an alien invader that affects all people, and of atonement as God's way of dealing with the guilt and pollution that comes from this defiling influence, depend on the story of the original family and their original disobedience. The Biblical terms for atonement, which have the associated ideas of propitiation, expiation, and cleansing, become meaningless without this part of the story. If this is so, then the death of Jesus loses a crucial aspect of its meaning as well.

Third, if we cannot insist on a common origin for all mankind, then we have given up the grounds, from both the Bible and common sense, for affirming the common dignity of all people, and their common need of the solution that the Biblical faith claims to offer. Therefore abandoning our common origin looks like a dangerous mistake.

Fourth, how we relate to the story of Adam and Eve does, sooner or later, face us with what stance we will take toward Biblical authority. There are many subtleties and nuances to this whole matter, to be sure, and I have discussed some of them in another place: for example, I make a distinction between "world picture" and "worldview," and how they function in what I have called "good faith communication."[1] The Bible is more concerned with the world-*view* than with the world *picture*. Even so, we must decide whether we accept the authority of Jesus; and that authority includes his right to have people like Moses, Paul, and John as his authorized

---

[1] E.g., in C. John Collins, *Genesis 1–4: A Linguistic, Literary, and Theological Commentary* (Phillipsburg, NJ: P&R, 2006), 260–65.

messengers, who show us how to interpret the redemptive story. I, acting as an individual, hardly have the right to declare any part of Christian teaching so foundational that if you remove it you have destroyed Christian faith. Paul, acting as God's messenger, can make that kind of pronouncement about the resurrection of Jesus (1 Cor. 15:14-17). But it seems to me that Adam and Eve at the headwaters of the human family, and their fall, are not only what Jesus believed but also an irremovable part of that whole story.

6.c A Concluding (and Unacademic) Anecdote: How to Grieve

When I was in the midst of researching and writing this study, an unpleasant thing happened that helped to put it all into perspective. Early one summer Saturday morning a phone call from the police awakened my wife and me. Some dear friends of ours, Jim and Jackie, were having a medical emergency, and could we go to their house to let the first responders in? It turned out that their son Jimmy, a 37-year old man with severe physical and mental handicaps, had died suddenly, while the mother was out. My wife and children and I were deeply involved in offering love and care and understanding for them in their grief.

Jimmy dwelt in an assisted living home, and had two roommates, Mike and Nick, men who also have mental handicaps (though nowhere near as severe). Our friends were often hosts to all three of the handicapped men; on this particular weekend only their son Jimmy was staying with them. On the day Jimmy died, the two roommates came over to our friends' house to be part of the family circle. Mike was very broken up; several times during the weekend I held him in my arms while he sobbed on my shoulder about how much he missed Jimmy, and how he could not believe he was gone.

I realized that a person would grieve very differently depending on what he thought about the introduction of sin into our world. I told Mike that he was right to feel the way he did, because it does indeed hurt. And the hurt shows us that something in the world is not right, and we need God's help.

I also conducted the funeral. My homily, which was based on John 11:25-26, included the following words:

On Saturday, I heard Jackie say, "No parent should ever have to outlive their own child." I heard the same words from my father's mother when my father died; and my wife and I said the same thing when we lost our first child. The pain is horrible; the loss is beyond our ability to describe.

When we feel this grief, we are feeling that it's just not right for this to happen. We don't want our loved ones to suffer; we don't want to be separated from them by death. We want to be sure that they are happy, and we want to be able to enjoy their company always.

The Bible tells us that these feelings we have are *right*. Death and suffering are intruders in God's good world; they don't belong here. And the story of Adam and Eve, the first human beings, tells us how these evil things came in: When these, the parents of us all, disobeyed God, they opened the door to all manner of sin and evil, not only for themselves, but also for us.

You don't need me to prove it; it's all around us. It's why we are here today.

But the Bible story doesn't end there: instead it tells us about how God wants to help us, to heal us of what is wrong with us. And you can see that here in the passage I am talking about: Jesus wept with them in their sorrow, he was deeply moved; and he did something about it: he went on to raise Lazarus from the dead.

There is indeed comfort in the Biblical story that has a real Adam and Eve at its front end: the comfort of finding assurance that we will indeed receive relief and healing and *restoration and final bliss*, when God has finally banished the intruder forever. This comfort helps us to live fully human lives, as God's beloved people, even now.

APPENDIX 1

ANCIENT NEAR EASTERN TEXTS AND GENESIS 1–11

Readers of the Old Testament have long understood that its authors knew about the cultures of the other nations of the ancient Near East. Generally speaking, these authors set themselves against the basic values of these other cultures, as in the book of Deuteronomy:

> **6:14** You shall not go after other gods, the gods of the peoples who are around you.

> **17:14** When you come to the land that the LORD your God is giving you, and you possess it and dwell in it and then say, "I will set a king over me, like all the nations that are around me . . ."

At times, however, the attitude expressed is more "tolerant," as in Judges 11:24, where the Israelite Jephthah acknowledges to the Ammonite king that "Chemosh your god" has given the Ammonites a land to possess, just as the LORD had given Israel a land to possess.

Similarly, students of the New Testament have long considered the ways in which its authors might have commented on their contemporary Jewish and Graeco-Roman cultures. Until about 1800, there was a great deal more contemporary textual information available to the New Testament students than to their Old Testament counterparts. Knowledge of the ancient cultures of the Old Testament period came primarily through Greek-speaking authors, such as the native Greek Herodotus of Halicarnassus (c. 484–430 B.C.), who told his audience what he had learned from the Persians, Syrians, and Egyptians. One always has to be cautious about his accuracy—although, for example, certainly his description of the ruthlessness of the Persian emperors serves to illuminate the practice found in Dan. 6:24 (it also relieves believers of any need to justify the Persian king's actions). Other materials in Greek came from natives of the other cultures who wrote for their Hellenistic audience (i.e., after Alexander the Great had incorporated these lands into a Greek-speaking empire). Good examples of this kind of author are the Egyptian Manetho (c. 240 B.C.) and the Babylonian Berossus (ca. 290 B.C.). Such authors seem to be more reliable in explaining their cultures, though their works have only been available in excerpts found in other authors (such as Josephus).

Up until about 1800, texts in the ancient languages themselves were largely unknown, and the languages were long forgotten. Since then, however, there has been an explosion of new knowledge about the ancient Near East and its cultures, imperial (e.g., Egyptians, Mesopotamians, Hittites) and more local (e.g., Phoenicians, Moabites, Ugaritians).[1] The texts from these countries allow us to compare their beliefs and values with those of the Biblical authors, for similarities and dissimilarities.[2]

The peoples of the ancient Near East include the Sumerians of southern Mesopotamia, who spoke a language of no known relation-

---

[1] For a nice popular-level account of how this new knowledge became available, see Alan Millard, *Treasures from Bible Times* (Tring, Hertfordshire, U.K.: Lion, 1985). Millard is a highly accomplished scholar of ancient Near Eastern languages and literature.

[2] I am not implying that there have been no new discoveries for New Testament backgrounds since 1800, nor even that these are unimportant!

ship to any other language family; they are the oldest civilization, going back as far as the fourth millennium B.C., or perhaps earlier; their oldest known writings come from about 3100 B.C. Speakers of the Semitic language Akkadian, who became the Assyrians and Babylonians, inherited their culture; they became dominant in Mesopotamia after the middle of the third millennium B.C. The Egyptian civilization goes back to around 3000 B.C. or even earlier. The Hittites occupied what is now Turkey, and spoke an Indo-European language; their empire was founded around 1800 B.C. These were the main civilized powers in the second millennium B.C., and they vied for control of the areas between them. Lesser peoples from whom we have writings included the various speakers of Northwest Semitic dialects, such as the Hebrews, the Canaanites and their heirs the Phoenicians, the Ugaritians, the Ammonites, and the Moabites. These show up in the later second millennium and on into the first millennium B.C.[3]

Before we get into specifics for the Genesis story, it is worthwhile to think a little about the whole process of comparing the literatures of Israel and other ancient Near Eastern peoples. There is no question that such comparisons will help us understand the Bible better: after all, the Biblical writings came to a people with real pastoral needs, and generally those needs had to do with staying faithful to the Lord and to his way of living in the world. These other writings help us to appreciate the world in which God's ancient people struggled to survive. At the same time, just because there seems to be a parallel does not mean that there is one: we must justify our claims to have found parallels. Further, we must never forget that the Biblical writings are coherent texts in Hebrew, and not simply instantiations of things we find elsewhere. The supposed Near Eastern parallels need to be evaluated for how they fit into the Hebrew context—the Hebrew words, sentences, paragraphs, and texts—and not the other way around.[4]

---

[3]For a nice catalogue of the materials available, see John Walton, *Ancient Near Eastern Thought and the Old Testament: Introducing the Conceptual World of the Hebrew Bible* (Grand Rapids, MI: Baker, 2006), 29–83 (his chapter 2).
[4]John Walton, *The Lost World of Genesis One: Ancient Cosmology and the Origins Debate* (Downers Grove, IL: InterVarsity Press, 2009), falls afoul of these guidelines in his approach, when he carries out very little linguistic or literary analysis of Genesis 1 itself,

The number of texts is vast, and the major languages are very different from one another. There are several candidates for the background of Genesis 1–11; Egypt is an obvious one. Fortunately, a number of scholars have shown that the most likely primary interpretive backcloth comes from Mesopotamia.[5] (This is hardly surprising, given that Abram came from Ur of the Chaldeans, Gen. 11:27–31.) The Egyptologist Kenneth Kitchen, for example, has argued that there are really four "primeval protohistories" that show important parallels. These are three texts from Mesopotamia, and Genesis 1–11. The Mesopotamian texts are:[6]

(1) the *Sumerian King List* (c. eighteenth century B.C.), which gives the dynasties of the rulers of the cities of Sumer, before and after "the flood";[7]

---

and emphasizes themes he finds in other ancient Near Eastern literatures. A predictable result of his method comes in this admission (page 104): "The view presented in this book has emphasized the similarities between the ways the Israelites thought and the ideas reflected in the ancient world, rather than the differences." That is, Walton's approach does not allow an Israelite author (who may or may not represent the ways the rest of the Israelites thought) to challenge the ideas found in other peoples. Only by attending to the Hebrew text, and to reflections on it in the rest of the Bible, do we actually see what specific message the Biblical writer had.

[5] See, e.g., David T. Tsumura, "Genesis and Ancient Near Eastern Stories of Creation and Flood: An Introduction," in Richard S. Hess and David T. Tsumura, eds., *I Studied Inscriptions from before the Flood: Ancient Near Eastern, Literary, and Linguistic Approaches to Genesis 1–11* (Winona Lake, IN: Eisenbrauns, 1994), 27–57 (especially pages 44–57); Richard Averbeck, "The Sumerian Historiographic Tradition and Its Implications for Genesis 1–11," in A. R. Millard, James K. Hoffmeier and David W. Baker, eds., *Faith, Tradition, and History: Old Testament Historiography in Its Near Eastern Context* (Winona Lake, IN: Eisenbrauns, 1994), 79–102; Kenneth A. Kitchen, *On the Reliability of the Old Testament* (Grand Rapids, MI: Eerdmans, 2003), 423–25; Anne Drafkorn Kilmer, "The Mesopotamian Counterparts of the Biblical *Nephilim*," in Edgar W. Conrad, ed., *Perspectives on Language and Text* (Winona Lake, IN: Eisenbrauns, 1987), 39–43. Richard S. Hess, "The Genealogies of Genesis 1–11 and Comparative Literature," *Biblica* 70 (1989): 241–54 (reprinted in Hess and Tsumura, *I Studied Inscriptions*, 58–72), adds some helpful cautions about the differences between the Biblical genealogies and the king lists.

[6] All of these are available in English translation in a number of places: a source that includes them all is James B. Pritchard, ed., *Ancient Near Eastern Texts* (Princeton, NJ: Princeton University Press, 1969). Other sources will be noted for each item.

[7] The prime publication is Thorkild Jacobsen, *The Sumerian King List* (Chicago: University of Chicago Press, 1939); Sumerian material is now online at The Electronic Text Corpus of Sumerian Literature <etcsl.orinst.ox.ac.uk>.

(2) the *Atrahasis Epic* (c. eighteenth century B.C.), which describes the creation of mankind, and then the great flood and how Atrahasis was preserved, along with his family, by the help of the god Enki;[8]

(3) the *Eridu Genesis*, also called the *Sumerian Flood Tale* (c. 1600 B.C.), which may have included a creation story, but whose currently known fragments focus on the flood and the deliverance of king Ziusudra.[9]

Kitchen provides a table showing the connections between these sources (see table I).[10]

Sumerian King List	Atrahasis Epic	Eridu Genesis	Genesis 1–11
1. Creation assumed; kingship came down from heaven	1. Creation assumed, gods create humans to do their work	1. Creation; cities are instituted	1. Creation (Gen. 1–2)
2. Series of eight kings in five cities	2. Noisy humans alienate deities	2. [Alienation]	2. Alienation (Gen. 3), genealogies (Gen. 4–5)
3. The flood	3. The flood; ark	3. The flood; ark	3. The flood; ark (Gen. 6–9)
4. Kingship again; dynasties follow, leading to —	4. New start	4. New start	4. New start; then genealogies, down to —
5. "Modern times"	(5. Modern times, implied)	(5. Modern times, implied)	5. "Modern times"

Table I

---

[8]The prime source is W. G. Lambert and A. R. Millard, *Atra-hasis: The Babylonian Story of the Flood* (Winona Lake, IN: Eisenbrauns, 1999 [1969]); see also Stephanie Dalley, *Myths from Mesopotamia: Creation, the Flood, Gilgamesh and Others* (Oxford: Oxford University Press, 1989), 1–38.

[9]See Alexander Heidel, *The Gilgamesh Epic and Old Testament Parallels* (Chicago: University of Chicago, 1949), 102–105; M. Civil, in Lambert and Millard, *Atra-hasis*, 138–45; Thorkild Jacobsen, "The Eridu Genesis," *Journal of Biblical Literature* 100:4 (1981): 513–29; and the online edition at <etcsl.orinst.ox.ac.uk>.

[10]This table is based on Kitchen, *On the Reliability of the Old Testament*, 424 (Table 34).

Once we see the pattern as Kitchen has laid it out, we can see that there must be some relationship between Genesis 1–11 and these Mesopotamian stories. In fact, though there may be additional connections to stories from Egypt and Canaan (as attested in the Ugaritic texts), the Mesopotamian stories are the chief literary milieu, in view of this overarching pattern.

But just what is the nature of that "relationship"? Did the Hebrew stories *borrow* from the Mesopotamian? Or did the Mesopotamians *borrow* from the Hebrews? Or did they share a common source? Should we even talk about *borrowing*?

To answer this question it will help us to reflect on what the Mesopotamians thought they were doing when they wrote and read works like these.

The Sumerian King List was produced, apparently, by "a Babylonian scholar" who "compiled a list of kings who had ruled the land from the institution of kingship by the gods until his own day."[11] The list begins with, "When kingship was lowered from heaven, kingship was (first) in Eridu." There are five dynasties, in the five leading cities of Sumer; then the flood "swept over," and then kingship is lowered again from heaven.

There seems little reason to doubt that the author thought he was writing about real people and real events. A peculiarity of this list, however, is that the kings before the flood are said to have ruled for an enormous amount of time, ranging from 18,600 years (the last king before the flood) to 43,200 years. After the flood, the reigns shorten, but are still quite long: e.g., 1,200 years, 690 years, and so on; they show a trend until Gilgamesh, who reigned for 126 years, and his son, who reigned for 30 years (the first reasonable number).[12] No one really knows what to make of the extraordinarily high numbers: perhaps there is a rhetorical device being employed, to which we are not (yet) initiated, for example involving base 60 or 360.

---

[11] A. R. Millard, "King Lists," in Piotr Bienkowski and A. R. Millard, eds., *Dictionary of the Ancient Near East* (Philadelphia: University of Pennsylvania Press, 2000), 169.
[12] It is generally thought that the pre-flood section is a separate composition from the post-flood list.

There are further questions as to whether the dynasties mentioned in the list were strictly sequential: some seem to have been in parallel. No one knows whether the compiler of the list was aware of this.

But our (and perhaps the Babylonians') inability to take these numbers and the sequences "literally" does not entitle us to call the list "unhistorical." It is better to say that it has an historical core, and that this core is presented with various rhetorical purposes in mind that go beyond the simple conveyance of information—even if we do not know all the devices to achieve that rhetorical purpose.

Consider as well the theme of the flood, which is common to these sources. The form of the flood story in the Atrahasis Epic seems to lie behind the flood story found in the Gilgamesh Epic; and it is this form that shows the most similarity with that in Genesis.[13] Gilgamesh appears in the Sumerian King List; in his story he searches for and finds the survivor of the flood (called Utnapishtim in the Gilgamesh story; he is apparently the same person as Atrahasis and Ziusudra). This flood may well be the great flood mentioned in the Sumerian King List.

Floods in this part of the world, with the rivers Tigris and Euphrates nearby, are common enough; but this flood seems to be especially catastrophic. Is there any evidence of such a flood from the ground beneath the present landscape? Sir Leonard Woolley, one of the first British archaeologists to excavate the Sumerian cities, famously thought he had found evidence of the great flood at the site of Ur.[14] This evidence goes back to about 3500 B.C., and most people think that this is too early to be the flood of the King List, since Gilgamesh is thought to have lived around 2700 to 2600 B.C.[15] This would make the flood of the King List somewhere around 2900 B.C., and there do appear to be remains of a major flooding event around that time.[16]

---

[13]The classic study is Heidel, *Gilgamesh Epic and Old Testament Parallels*, to which I will refer.
[14]Described in Millard, *Treasures from Bible Times*, 38–41.
[15]See M. E. L. Mallowan (the husband of Agatha Christie), "Noah's Flood Reconsidered," *Iraq* 26 (1964): 62–82 (with plates 16–20), at 67–68.
[16]Ibid., 80–81; see also Samuel Noah Kramer, "Reflections on the Mesopotamian Flood," *Expedition* 9 (Summer 1967): 12–18.

This is, perhaps, the flood that provides the historical referent of the Sumerian King List, and thus of the other Mesopotamian flood stories. There may be reasons why we might hesitate to identify these events too quickly, however: for example, the flood of 2900 B.C. was not universal, nor was it large enough to interrupt the continuity of Mesopotamian civilization.[17] We might answer this hesitation by saying that the storytellers no doubt exaggerated. But another difficulty is more serious: in Gilgamesh (and in the Bible), the "boat" ends up on a mountain, while the current of an ordinary flood would have taken the boat into the Persian Gulf. Again, poetic license may be the explanation, but there are additional features of the stories that lead R. L. Raikes to say,[18]

> That people, to whom regular annual flooding was one of the inescapable facts of life, should have singled out one event (or possibly more) for description to their children, seems, even allowing for the natural tendency for oral tradition to exaggerate, to point to a flood of a different type as the origin of the legends. . . .
>
> Any idea of a vastly expanded version of the annual Euphrates flood can be dismissed as a prime reason for the legend, for its results would be entirely different in every conceivable way from those described in the legend.

Raikes goes on to suggest avenues for further study, particularly taking seriously the Biblical statement, "the fountains of the great deep burst forth" (Gen. 7:11), which makes him wonder about a sudden subsidence.

Before I offer my proposal for handling these questions, I cannot avoid a comment on methodology. I am used to reading Biblical scholars who are skeptical about whether this or that Biblical passage can really be historical; therefore it strikes me like a brisk wind to read in these students of the ancient Near East a respect for the historical basis of their sources. To them it is perfectly reasonable to affirm that "the earliest Flood stories themselves were not merely vague echoes of natural disaster, but were legends related

---

[17]As Mallowan, "Noah's Flood," 81, points out.
[18]R. L. Raikes, "The Physical Evidence for Noah's Flood," *Iraq* 28 (1966): 52–63, at 61.

to one definite event, a catastrophic Flood which occurred, if not in historic, then in prehistoric times."[19] For this reason it seems that a scholar like Kenneth Kitchen—an Egyptologist who is also well accomplished in studying the whole of the ancient Near East and is convinced that the Bible gives soundly historical accounts—is within his rights when he chides Biblical scholars about not being sufficiently in touch with conclusions from the rest of the ancient Near East. When he insists, "Assyriologists have no problem on this score" (i.e., on the matter of an historical flood), he is fairly representing this discipline.[20]

Perhaps, in view of all this, the Mesopotamian flood tradition does preserve the memory of an especially catastrophic flood. Maybe that flood is the one with which the evidence is now associated, and it was a flood more severe than scholars think. Possibly, though, the descriptions of that flood are merged with the memory of one even bigger, further back into antiquity. It could be that the flood of 2900 B.C. was treated as an exemplar, or the latest instance, of a series of floods; or that the whole array of floods was merged into one. In any event, we have no need to label the Mesopotamian tradition unhistorical.

How does the flood in Genesis connect with the Mesopotamian tradition? Some scholars simply accept that Genesis borrowed the Mesopotamian story: even if Moses wrote Genesis, the Mesopotamian tradition still predates him. The difficulty with that position, however, is that while there are plenty of parallels between the two traditions, there are so many stark differences as well, reflecting the strongly differing ideologies behind the two stories. The Assyriologist Alexander Heidel extensively compared the two traditions and concluded,[21]

> That the Babylonian and Hebrew versions are genetically related is too obvious to require proof; the only problem that needs to be discussed is the degree of relationship.

---

[19]Mallowan, "Noah's Flood," 66.
[20]Kitchen, *On the Reliability of the Old Testament*, 426.
[21]Heidel, *Gilgamesh Epic and Old Testament Parallels*, 260.

The three possible relationships, of course, are (1) the Hebrew story borrows from the Babylonian; (2) the Babylonian borrows from the Hebrew; and (3) both stories share a common source. Heidel finds the case between these options ultimately indecisive, and that is where we should leave it for now, except to point out that, whatever the relationship, one cannot say that the Biblical version is a straightforward *copy* of the Mesopotamian.

What was the nature and purpose of the Mesopotamian stories? Generally, we classify them as "myths and legends," but these terms can be confusing, because in ordinary English these terms imply that the stories have minimal historical intention or value. It should be clear from the discussion above that the tales have *some* historical content, even if we cannot be sure just how much. It would seem that "pre- and proto-history of the worldview story" is the best designation; this corresponds to what the philosopher Richard Purtill sees as the function of "myth":[22]

Myths in the original, unstretched sense were stories of gods or heroes that usually had a religious or moral purpose. . . . When human beings begin to tell myths, they sometimes do so because they think, for whatever reason, that the stories are true. But the mythmaker need not think that every detail, or even every important element, of the story is true. . . .

The original mythmakers did not aim only to tell an interesting story (though it is important to remember that they did intend at least that). They aimed to do something that they would probably have expressed as a desire to *honor* the gods and heroes and to *inspire* their listeners.

Thinking of the Mesopotamian stories this way finds support from Richard Averbeck's observations:[23]

The ancients, it seems, did "speculative thought" largely through "mythography." They understood cause and effect and were fully

[22]Richard Purtill, *J. R. R. Tolkien: Myth, Morality, and Religion* (San Francisco: Ignatius, 2003 [1984]), 1–2.
[23]Averbeck, "Sumerian Historiographic Tradition," at 87 n. 20.

capable of logical induction and deduction, but their application of these human capacities toward understanding and handling their world on a speculative level took mythological and ritual form.

Worldview stories "inspire their listeners" by putting their lives into historical perspective: we are here, they say, as heirs, beneficiaries, or victims of these events that have preceded us. Probably in the case of Mesopotamia, the idea of the protohistories is to encourage people willingly to maintain the order of their stratified society.[24] This seems to follow from, for example, the reason for which the gods are said to have made mankind: according to Atrahasis, it was to do the work that the junior gods, the Igigi, were so tired of doing that they went on strike against the senior gods.

Therefore Kitchen is on solid ground when he denies the term "myth" (understood as nonhistorical) for describing the intent behind the Mesopotamian flood tradition, and prefers the term "protohistory":[25]

So, an epochally important flood in far antiquity has come down in a tradition shared by both early Mesopotamian culture and Gen. 6–9, but which found clearly separate and distinct expression in the written forms left us by the two cultures. . . . Genesis . . . offers a more concise, simpler account, and *not* an elaboration of a Mesopotamian composition. As to definition, myth or "protohistory," it should be noted that the Sumerians and Babylonians had no doubts on that score. They included it squarely in the middle of their earliest historical tradition, with kings before it and kings after it, the flood acting as a dividing point in that tradition, from long before 1900.

Lambert and Millard show a number of ways in which the Atrahasis Epic served to shape the worldview of its hearers.[26] They say

---

[24]Cf. how Brevard Childs described the function of myth, in his *Myth and Reality in the Old Testament* (London: SCM, 1960), 27–28: "Myth is a form by which the existing structure of reality is understood and maintained. It concerns itself with showing how the action of a deity, conceived of as occurring in the primeval age, determines a phase of contemporary world order."

[25]Kitchen, *On the Reliability of the Old Testament*, 425–26.

[26]Lambert and Millard, *Atra-hasis*; quotations are from the Introduction (pages 8, 13, 21, 13).

that its "content gives the impression of having been intended for public recitation." Further,

> the first hearers of this epic were vitally concerned with many of the issues presented. The sociological system described was that which they actually knew, and they conceived that their existence was really dependent on what Enki and Enlil did. . . . Thus every aspect of civilized life, public or private, important or trivial, was looked on as ideally conforming to a divine pattern.

An example of this pattern is childbirth: "By insisting on the view that what happened at the first creation of man is repeated with every human birth, the author brings home the relevance of his myth." (This shows, by the way, that intention to relate an historical event, and to evoke the ongoing pattern set by that event, are not at odds with each other.)

Some scholars have concluded that the author of Genesis wrote an explicit *polemic* against these Mesopotamian views—and really, against all the views of the pagan peoples around Israel. To support this, we can notice that the sun and moon are called "the greater light" and "the lesser light" in Genesis 1:16: by not using the ordinary Hebrew words for these lights in the sky, *Shemesh* and *Yareakh*,[27] which are also the names of deities, the story puts them in their place as things that the one God made. The trouble with this example is that, apart from God and mankind, *nothing* gets its ordinary Hebrew name in Genesis 1. After all, terms like "plants yielding seed," "fruit trees," "swarms of living creatures," "birds [or flying things]," and "livestock and creeping things and beasts of the earth" are very general: the narrator is not offering us a "scientific" taxonomy, but a broad-stroke description of all the different sorts of things a nomadic shepherd might encounter in God's world.

---

[27]These are the standard names; much less common ones include the more poetic *Khammâ* (the sun as "heat source") and *Lebanâ* (the moon as "white lady"; cf. Gollum's name for the moon in *The Two Towers*, "White Face").

Therefore, if Genesis is providing a "polemic," it is a very gentle one. As Umberto Cassuto observed,[28]

> The purpose of the Torah in this section [1:1–2:3] is to teach us that the whole world and all that it contains were created by the word of One God, according to His will, which operates without restraint. It is thus opposed to the concepts current among the peoples of the ancient East who were Israel's neighbours; and in some respects it is also in conflict with certain ideas that had already found their way into the ranks of our [Israelite] people. The language, however, is tranquil, undisturbed by polemic or dispute; the controversial note is heard indirectly, as it were, through the deliberate, quiet utterances of Scripture, which sets the opposing views at nought by silence or by subtle hint.

It is probably more accurate, then, to describe Genesis 1–11 as providing the front end to an alternative worldview story—a story whose purpose is to shape Israel's stance toward God, the world, and the rest of mankind. As Kitchen noted,[29]

> Gen. 1–11 is the Hebrew answer on how to present "prehistory/protohistory" before the time of their first fully "historical" people, the patriarchs Abraham to Jacob. Again, the approach they adopted was common to their neighbors, using the same basic tools and concepts of that time: the succession of human generations, and how to span them. Mesopotamia chose to expand "heroically" the too-few reigns available. The Hebrew genealogies became telescoped through time, keeping a representative number.

The Biblical alternative story certainly does reject or correct many elements of the other stories available (and perhaps attractive) to Israel: Genesis tells of one true God, who alone made and rules the heavens and the earth, and all that is in them; there is nothing left for any other god—if it exists—to do. There is coherence to the world, as the wisdom literature of other cultures presupposes; Genesis provides the true explanation for this, namely the one good God who

---

[28]Umberto Cassuto, *From Adam to Noah: Genesis I–VI.8* (Jerusalem: Magnes, 1961 [1944]), 7.
[29]Kitchen, *On the Reliability of the Old Testament*, 447.

made it all as the right kind of place for human beings to live, and love, and serve. And far from mankind being made to relieve God of work he did not like doing, they are dignified with his image, and with the task of ruling the creation in a wise and benevolent way. Human "work" at the beginning was to enjoy Eden, and to spread its blessings throughout the world. The painful toil people now experience is not a proper part of the creation; it results from human disobedience, which requires divine redemption.

By affirming human unity in Adam and Eve, Genesis lays the foundation for Israel's calling to bring light to the world. It should also foster a respect for common human dignity in those who believe it, though not everyone who has *professed* such belief has shown this respect. God does not endorse a stratified society for his people, treating people differently depending on their social or economic status (cf. Lev. 19:9–18); even slaves are human beings.[30]

In this light we can appreciate why Genesis 4 describes the development of arts and crafts, such as city building, musical instruments, and metalworking. The Mesopotamian stories describe kingship and the crafts as gifts from the gods; they are therefore an unqualified good.[31] When Genesis attributes these skills to Cain's offspring in Genesis 4:17–24—a passage that is noteworthy for the complete absence of any mention of God—it puts these things into a proper perspective. An Israelite could recognize that these skills can accomplish much that is good; but he is also likely to look around at other cultures, whether Egyptian or Canaanite or Mesopotamian, and feel drawn to them because their achievements had far outpaced those in backward Israel (cf. 1 Sam. 13:19–22; Deut. 1:28). Thus the skills are *relatively* good, both because they express human ingenuity and because they can be used to bring benefits: but they are not good in themselves, and God's faithful people must strive after moral purity first.

---

[30]On this point see Christopher Wright, *Old Testament Ethics for the People of God* (Downers Grove, IL: InterVarsity Press, 2004), 292–93, 333–37.

[31]Cf. Lambert and Millard, *Atra-hasis*, 18: "From Sumerian literature to Berossus it is everywhere assumed that the human race was at first and naturally barbarous. Civilization was a gift of the gods, and that is the way to understand kingship coming down from heaven [as in the Sumerian King List]. The gods gave it as an institution for regulating society."

The life spans of the pre-flood patriarchs in Genesis 5 are long indeed: Adam lived for 930 years, Seth 912 years, Enosh 905 years, and so on down to Lamech at 777 years, and Noah at 950 (Gen. 9:29). Similarly, the life spans in Genesis 11:10–26 (after the flood) are quite long, though trending downward (the narrator here leaves it to the reader to add up the numbers). Abram, the last one in that list, and the focus of attention, dies at 175 (Gen. 25:7). These spans are far longer than anything the audience would expect: Psalm 90:10 (attributed to Moses) gives the normal life-span at 70–80 years, Joseph died at 110 (Gen. 50:26), Moses at 120 (Deut. 34:7), and Joshua at 110 (Josh. 24:29). At the same time, the spans are not nearly as wild as those in the Sumerian King List. In any event there may be evidence of some kind of rhetorical figures being employed here, even if we do not know what they are. Perhaps, as Cassuto suggested, the Biblical account is scaling down the numbers found in the Mesopotamian stories, though there is no way to be sure of that. We are left with Wenham's very sensible observation:[32]

> These [rhetorically oriented explanations] seem better approaches to these great ages than the attempts to find symbolic or historical [i.e., reading literalistically] truths in the precise ages of the patriarchs. Could it be that the precision of the figures conveys the notion that these patriarchs were real people, while their magnitude conveys their remoteness from the author of Genesis?

When it comes to the flood story, I do not see how we can be sure that Genesis and the Sumerian King List are referring to the same event.[33] Actually, there may well be another event, or even group of events, behind the Atrahasis story, as I have already noted. Perhaps Genesis refers to that greater flood (or collection of floods), or to an even greater flood (or collection of floods): in effect Genesis would be saying (in the style of Crocodile Dundee),[34] "That's [the Mesopotamian] not a flood—*that's* [the Biblical] a flood." I am not sure

[32]Gordon J. Wenham, *Genesis 1–15*, Word Biblical Commentary (Dallas: Word, 1987), 134.
[33]With all due respect to Josephus, *Antiquities*, 1.3.6, line 93.
[34]In the 1986 film *Crocodile Dundee*, a mugger with a switchblade threatens the hero, Mick "Crocodile" Dundee. Mick dismisses the threat by saying of the switchblade, "That's not

whether Genesis is really insisting that its flood was worldwide, or that it at least affected all existing *human* life, any more than the Mesopotamian flood tradition did. After all, the term "all the earth/ the whole earth" (Gen. 7:3; 8:9) appears again in Genesis, when *"all the earth* came to Egypt to Joseph to buy grain, because the famine was severe over *all the earth"* (Gen. 41:57). But the reference here is surely limited to the eastern end of the Mediterranean; so the reference in the flood story *may be* limited as well (but I do not know).[35]

However we may prefer to resolve these difficulties, the point of this story, as over against the Mesopotamian tales,[36] is the reason for the flood: those stories portray the gods as frustrated with human noisiness, with one sly deity who sneaks a message to a man to save his family, while Genesis actually lists recognizable moral causes (Gen. 6:5, 11: "the LORD saw that the *wickedness* of man was great in the earth, and that every intention of the thoughts of his heart was only *evil* continually. . . . The earth was filled with *violence*."). Further, in the Mesopotamian tradition, after the flood the gods felt remorse for what they had done, and were relieved to discover that some humans had actually survived. When Atrahasis made a burnt offering, "the gods sniffed the smell, they gathered like flies over the offering." Apparently without humans to make sacrifices, the gods were not properly fed! In contrast, when Noah makes his burnt offerings, the Lord smelled the pleasing aroma and promised never again to destroy mankind in this fashion. There is no hint of divine dependence on human worship (cf. Ps. 50:7–15, which makes a point that is pretty obvious to anyone who thinks clearly about the creation account!).

Another area in which comparison and contrast are illuminating is the creation of the first human being(s). In Genesis 2:7, God

---

a knife"; he then pulls out his enormous Bowie knife and declares, *"That's* a knife." The mugger runs away.

[35]Scholars are therefore divided on whether the flood stories found throughout the world are related to some ancient archetypal flood, or reflect the common experience of life next to a major body of water.

[36]And, since there is evidence of an edition of the flood story found at Ras Shamra (Ugarit), we might infer that this narrative was known to the peoples that Israel was called to dispossess.

uses "dust" (loose soil) from the ground, "forms" the man like a potter does (the verb "form," Hebrew *yatsar*, suggests this), and then breathes into his nostrils the breath of life. In Atrahasis (I.172ff.), the gods slay a god in order to mix his flesh and blood with clay; this process yields the first seven human couples. Berossus describes the event as, "the other gods mixed the blood which flowed forth [from the slain god] with earth and formed men; that on this account they are rational and partake of divine understanding."[37] Even though Berossus says that the gods used these materials for making the animals as well, he likely thought that rationality and divine understanding belonged distinctively to mankind. We can find this kind of description elsewhere in the ancient world: for example, the Stoic Epictetus (c. A.D. 50–130) wrote of "body, which we have in common with the beasts, and reason and intelligence, which we have in common with the gods" (*Discourses*, I.iii.3). Aristotle (384–322 B.C.) described man as having three parts: the part that has to do with living and growing, which we have in common with the plants; the part that has senses and some form of consciousness, which we have in common with all animals; and the part that acts on reason or principle, which is distinctively human (*Nicomachean Ethics*, I.vii.12–13; I.xiii.9–20). No doubt this motif is trying to explain the fairly straightforward observation that human beings are like other living things (plants and animals) in some respects, and quite different from them in other respects.

Alan Millard summarizes what these "parallels" do and do not imply:[38]

Both the Bible and some Babylonian Creation accounts depict man as created from 'the dust of the earth' or 'clay'. To this is added some divine component, 'breath' in Genesis, flesh and blood of a god, and divine spittle in Babylonia. This concept of clay and divine substance mixed is not exclusive to these two literatures. It is found in Egypt in certain traditions, and, further afield, in China. Common ideas need not share a common source. The earthy concept may be placed in the

---

[37]Berossus as cited from Alexander Heidel, *Babylonian Genesis* (Chicago: University of Chicago Press, 1951), 78.
[38]A. R. Millard, "A New Babylonian 'Genesis' Story," *Tyndale Bulletin* 18 (1967): 15.

category of a deduction from natural processes which could be made independently. The belief in a divine indwelling 'spark' seems to be common to so many faiths and cultures that this also need not be traced to a common origin.

We should be careful not to misunderstand what Millard has called the "divine component" in Genesis: the breath of life comes from God, and animates the "clay" that God has just formed. But it is not actually divine substance; humans have *likeness* to God, but the stuff they are made of is quite distinct from God. This is a difference between Genesis and the Mesopotamian stories, where a "divine substance" (blood or flesh) is an actual component of human nature.

The existence of this motif can help us focus on what Genesis 2:7 is asserting about the first man, namely his special origin that sets him apart from the other animals (in the light of 1:26–27, that includes the image of God). It also leaves us careful about applying too firm a literalism in relating the words of Genesis 2:7 to a physical and biological account of human origins, although it does insist that the process was not a purely natural one.

The differences between the competing visions for human life, and conceptions of human well-being as friends of God, could not be clearer. If we wish to call both sets of stories "propaganda," we may: but we should recall that "the ancients (Near Eastern and Hebrew alike) knew that propaganda based on real events was far more effective than that based on sheer invention."[39] Hence the Hebrew version represents an effort to tell the story of these events as it "should" be told. As Alan Millard argued, "If there was borrowing [by the Hebrews from the Mesopotamians] then it can have extended only as far as the 'historical' framework, and not included intention or interpretation."[40]

Before we finish this section, we should consider some other Mesopotamian stories that have been offered as parallels with Genesis 1–11. For instance, it was once common to see the Babylonian poem called *Enuma Elish* (from its two opening words in Akkadian, "when

---

[39]Kitchen, *On the Reliability of the Old Testament*, 300.
[40]Millard, "New Babylonian 'Genesis' Story," 3–18.

on high") as part of the background for Genesis.[41] This story includes a description of the conflict between the younger god Marduk and the older goddess Tiamat; after Marduk slew Tiamat he used her body to make the world. (The Babylonian version has the god Marduk as its hero, in accord with the preeminence of that deity at Babylon. The Assyrian version, however, has the god Assur as the hero.)

Part of the appeal for this comparison comes from the simple excitement of finding material from the ancient world that covers a similar topic (the making of the world). Further, the Akkadian name Tiamat seemed to be parallel to the Hebrew word for "the deep," $t^{e}h\hat{o}m$ (Gen. 1:2), which led some scholars to think of Genesis 1 as describing a conflict of sorts between God and the forces of nature, or even a sea monster; this gains some traction from the possibility that "without form and void" is a paraphrase for "chaos." The opening words of the Akkadian story, "when on high," also influenced some to argue that the opening words of Genesis should likewise be "when God began to create . . ." (see the alternate translation of the RSV).[42]

Although Biblical scholars continue to make these comparisons, it appears that Assyriologists are now less likely to endorse the comparison than formerly.[43] Partly this is due to the work of W. G. Lambert, who argued:[44]

The first major conclusion is that the *Epic of Creation* [another name for *Enuma Elish*] is not a norm of Babylonian or Sumerian cosmology. It is a sectarian and aberrant combination of mythological threads

[41]The classic study is Alexander Heidel, *The Babylonian Genesis* (Chicago: University of Chicago Press, 1951 [1942]).

[42]For an example, see Cyrus H. Gordon, "Ancient Middle Eastern Religions: The Cultural Context," in Philip W. Goetz et al., eds., *The New Encyclopedia Britannica* (Chicago: University of Chicago Press, 1989), 24:60–64, at 61b.

[43] Kitchen, *On the Reliability of the Old Testament*, 425, says, "most Assyriologists have long since rejected the idea of any direct link between Gen. 1–11 and *Enuma Elish*." Kitchen's sociological claim about "most Assyriologists" may be right, but I cannot know. Millard, "New Babylonian 'Genesis' Story," 4, summarizes some of the reasons for this new attitude. (Millard's title, "A New Babylonian 'Genesis' Story," refers to Heidel's earlier book, giving Millard's view that Atrahasis is a more likely context for Genesis.)

[44]W. G. Lambert, "A New Look at the Babylonian Background of Genesis," *Journal of Theological Studies* n.s. 16:2 (1965): 287–300, at 291.

woven into an unparalleled compositum. In my opinion it is not earlier than 1100 B.C.

Further, Lambert and Millard note that "the *Epic of Creation* is known to have been recited to the statue of the god Marduk in the course of the New Year festival at Babylon from c. 700 B.C. and perhaps earlier."[45] The end of *Enuma Elish* seems to suggest that its primary use is for private reading and reflection, "with which the content wholly agrees" (Lambert and Millard).

For the earlier stages of Biblical history, it may well be that *Enuma Elish* has limited importance; at the same time, Berossus certainly uses material from *Enuma Elish* in his presentation. Unless Berossus was a crank, offering as standard what is really sectarian or idiosyncratic, this means that at some point the story did wield some influence.[46]

Further, the grammar of Genesis 1:1—at least in the Hebrew we have—really does not allow the alternate interpretation: the familiar rendering, "In the beginning, God created the heavens and the earth," is surely right. The only serious linguistic question is whether the verse serves as a summary of the whole account (Gen. 1:2–2:3 describes how it is that God "created" the heavens and the earth), or as an introduction, giving the very first event as part of the setting for the main action sequence. In my view the grammar, together with other factors, strongly favors the opinion of Alexander Heidel:[47]

> The first verse of Genesis briefly records the creation of the universe in its essential form, and the second verse singles out a part of this universe, viz., the earth, and describes its condition in some detail.

These two verses then set out the conditions under which the first main event took place (Gen. 1:3).[48]

---

[45]Lambert and Millard, *Atra-hasis*, 7.
[46]In Dalley's introduction to *Enuma Elish* (*Myths from Mesopotamia*, 231–32), moreover, she finds evidence that at some point the epic was given a reading before an assembly of top officials.
[47]Heidel, *Babylonian Genesis*, 93.
[48]For full grammatical discussion, using the principles of discourse grammar, see my *Genesis 1–4: A Linguistic, Literary, and Theological Commentary* (Phillipsburg, NJ: P&R, 2006), 50–55.

Many have come to acknowledge that the supposed parallel between Babylonian Tiamat and Hebrew $t^e h \hat{o} m$ ("the deep") is very unlikely. The linguistic details show that there is no way that Hebrew $t^e h \hat{o} m$ can be a borrowing from Akkadian Tiamat; likewise, "without form and void" (Gen. 1:2) is a phrase, not for "unruly and disorderly chaos," but for "an unproductive and uninhabited place."[49] Further, nothing in Genesis 1 can be reasonably said to imply any kind of struggle on God's part: Psalm 33:9 ("for he spoke, and it came to be; he commanded, and it stood firm") is an excellent summary of the creation story.

Another Babylonian story is the legend of Adapa, a man to whom many compare the Biblical Adam. In this tale, Adapa was one day fishing in the Persian Gulf when the south wind suddenly overturned his boat. Adapa cursed the wind, breaking one of its wings so that it could not blow for seven days. Hence Anu, the sky god, summoned Adapa to give account for himself; but before Adapa went, the god Ea instructed him on how to conduct himself, and warned him that in heaven they will offer him the food and water of death, which he must not eat or drink. Adapa followed Ea's instructions and found favor with Anu, who decided to offer him the food and water of life—which would have conferred immortality. But Adapa refused, and went back to live among mankind, apparently bringing illness to those among whom he lived.

It is possible that Adapa actually lived; he is listed as the first of the seven Mesopotamian sages who lived before the great flood. Scholars usually identify him with a figure known as Uan, which, as Oannes, is Berossus's name for the first sage. No one knows when the story was first composed: the tablets we have come from Tell el-Amarna in Egypt (fifteenth to fourteenth century B.C.) and from Assur, the traditional capital of Assyria (late second millennium B.C.); all of them are in the Akkadian language.

Some have argued that the name Adapa could be linguistically related to Adam, since there are other examples of the p/m connec-

---

[49] On these points, see Collins, *Genesis 1–4*, 44–45, nn. 15–16, drawing on linguistic work by Heidel, and more recently by David Tsumura.

tion.[50] One difficulty is that forms of the proper name Adam (with an *m*) are attested as far back in West Semitic materials as we can look;[51] this makes it harder to explain how anyone could have "borrowed" a figure named Adapa (with a *p*) into a West Semitic language (such as Hebrew). Indeed, the name Adapa might actually be Sumerian (and thus non-Semitic), rather than Akkadian (a Semitic language, related to Hebrew).[52] These factors do not make it impossible that the Hebrew story is echoing the Babylonian; but they do show why no one should claim that it *does* (the most we can say is that it *might*).

Another hindrance to an easy identification is that Adapa is a sage (Akkadian *apkallu*), an advisor to a king (Alulim, the first King of Sumer, according to the Sumerian King List). The Biblical Adam, if he has any role at all, is "royal" primarily in the sense that he is to rule the world as God's delegate. It is possible, though not certain, that Adapa nevertheless had some kind of representative role for other people: some interpreters render line 6 as "Ea created him [Adapa] as a *leader* (or *model*) among mankind,"[53] while others call him a "protecting spirit" among mankind.[54] If Adapa was a representative of sorts, he might have had the opportunity to gain immortality for himself and also for those he represented (his fellow Sumerians, no doubt; there is no reason to suppose it was for all humanity).

The stories are different thematically as well. Adapa had a chance to gain immortality for himself and others (of whom he was *not* the first),[55] but he missed it out of obedience to instructions given him by a god. There is no indication that his "transgression" (breaking the wing of the south wind) was the first offense committed by a

---

[50]E.g., William H. Shea, "Adam in Ancient Mesopotamian Traditions," *Andrews University Seminary Studies* 15:1 (1977): 27–41.

[51]See Richard Hess, "Adam," in T. Desmond Alexander and David W. Baker, eds., *Dictionary of the Old Testament: Pentateuch* (Downers Grove, IL: InterVarsity Press, 2003), 18a–21b, at 21a.

[52]See William W. Hallo, "Adapa Reconsidered: Life and Death in Contextual Perspective," *Scriptura* 87 (2004): 267–77, at 272.

[53]Heidel, *Babylonian Genesis*, 148; Pritchard, ed., *Ancient Near Eastern Texts*, 101.

[54]Dalley, *Myths from Mesopotamia*, 184 (with uncertainty).

[55]A point acknowledged by Shea, "Adam in Ancient Mesopotamian Traditions": "the Sumerians believed that Alulim and Adapa belonged to the first *significant* generation of mankind" (36).

human being. On the other hand, Adam departed from his pristine state of moral innocence (and perhaps broke the process of maturation) by disobeying God's command.

The only real thematic parallel is the question of personal faith: Adapa exercised it, while Adam failed. As Giorgio Buccelati observed,[56]

> This [story] is, I would submit, one of the few cases where Babylonian mythology presents us with a phenomenon of what one may properly call "faith." Adapa has a personal relationship with Ea which prompts him to bear witness to his god even in front of other gods and even at the risk of dangerous consequences.

It is nevertheless conceivable—though how one could prove it I do not know—that the Genesis account echoes the Adapa story. If so, it is not saying that Adam and Adapa are the same person. It would instead be saying that the missing immortality, for which all people yearn, is due to a greater calamity, a more basic fault, than that connected with Adapa. In other words, the Adapa story, like much Mesopotamian material, identifies a human problem but gives an utterly inadequate explanation.[57]

We occasionally find other suggestions, say, that elements in the Gilgamesh Epic have supplied elements for Genesis. Aside from the flood account (mentioned already), most of the suggestions are far-fetched. One that is worthy of attention, though, occurs after Gilgamesh, who is searching for the key to immortality, has met Utnapishtim (apparently the same person as Atrahasis and Ziusudra, and parallel to Noah), whom the gods have made immortal. Utnap-

---

[56]Giorgio Buccelati, "Adapa, Genesis, and the Notion of Faith," *Ugarit-Forschungen* 5 (1973): 61–66, at 63. Although Buccelati compares Adam and Adapa, he makes no claim of any direct dependence.

[57]Niels-Erik Andreasen, "Adam and Adapa: Two Anthropological Characters," *Andrews University Seminary Studies* 19.3 (1981), 179–94, is more cautious than Shea's article, though he still supports it. He is more aware of the differences between the two figures than Shea seems to be. He sees them as two representations of the same actor, which I do not; but he makes the interesting suggestion that "Adam and Adapa represent two different characterizations of human nature" (194). But I prefer to say that, to the extent there is any connection between the two stories, the two men give different analyses of the human situation.

ishtim tells Gilgamesh of an underwater plant that will grant him constant rejuvenation. Gilgamesh dives for it and retrieves it. On his way home, he stops for the night at a pool and bathes himself in it; while he is not looking, a serpent steals the rejuvenating plant. According to some, this provides the original that Genesis has modified in its story of "the fall."

In reply, the first thing to say is that it would be folly indeed to call these two tales the same story. Each tale has its place in the larger context of which it is part. Further, to the extent that Genesis 3 is about a missed opportunity to acquire immortality (which is not the way I would describe it), it nevertheless sets that opportunity in a moral context. The human beings failed due to their direct disobedience to God's command. If this episode from Gilgamesh has any bearing on how we read Genesis 3 at all, it is by showing us the way that serpents could function in that literary world, as archetypes of forces that thwart human well-being. A careful study of Genesis 3 as a Hebrew story has shown us that the serpent functions there as the mouthpiece of some Dark Power, whom later generations would call Satan (see section 3a). The archetypal role of the serpent in the Gilgamesh story may remind us to sit lightly on the literality with which we take the serpent, but we already knew that.

APPENDIX 2

REVIEW OF JAMES BARR, *THE GARDEN OF EDEN AND THE HOPE OF IMMORTALITY* (MINNEAPOLIS: FORTRESS, 1992)

The late James Barr (1924–2006) was one of the most important voices of the previous generation, with landmark books that introduced Biblical scholars to sound method in lexicography (the study of word meanings) and in comparative philology (using languages related to Hebrew to shed light on Hebrew words). Ironically, Barr held conventional "critical" views of the Bible's origin, but his books inspired many traditionalist students (including me) to serious study of linguistic method.[1] In this short and readable book, Barr addresses questions about Biblical views of immortality. In particular, he que-

---

[1] Barr's books are *The Semantics of Biblical Language* (Oxford: Oxford University Press, 1961) and *Comparative Philology and the Text of the Old Testament* (Oxford: Oxford University Press, 1968). My own doctoral thesis was *Homonymous Verbs in Biblical Hebrew: An Investigation*

ries the opposition between the immortality of the soul and the resurrection of the body—an opposition that is standard fare in the "Biblical theology" movement of which Barr is such an implacable foe.

Barr's plan of attack is to propose a way of reading Genesis 3. He begins by asserting (page ix, and repeated *passim*):

> Old Testament scholars have long known that the reading of the story as the 'Fall of Man' in the traditional sense, though hallowed by St Paul's use of it, cannot stand up to examination through a close reading of the Genesis text.

On page 4 Barr sets out clearly his "basic thesis" about the Genesis narrative:

> My argument is that, taken in itself and for itself, this narrative is not, as it has commonly been understood in our tradition, basically a story of the origins of sin and evil, still less a depiction of absolute evil or total depravity: it is a story of how human immortality was almost gained, but in fact was lost.

Barr's argument spans five chapters. In the first, he lists his reasons for rejecting the "Pauline" reading of Genesis 3. In the second, he argues that in the Old Testament death, far from being an evil invader, is seen as "natural," and that the Old Testament supports a body-soul dualism. In my judgment, this chapter is based on an equivocation on the word "natural." The word *may* refer to the inevitable, and therefore expected, outcome of a human life as we now experience it; in such a case one should be prepared to die well. On the other hand, it may refer to the intended pattern in the creation, a pattern that might have been interrupted by the sin of Genesis 3. To assert that death is "natural" in the first sense does not decide whether it is "natural" in the second, and certainly cannot be used

---

of the Role of Comparative Philology (University of Liverpool, 1988), whose title shows its debt to Barr. Another traditionalist indebted to Barr is Moisés Silva, *Biblical Words and Their Meaning: An Introduction to Lexical Semantics* (Grand Rapids, MI: Zondervan, 1983 [revised 1994]). A key difference is that Barr's work was mainly critical, exposing faulty method; these works inspired by him have sought to articulate constructive methodology.

Appendix 2

as evidence that the second sense is meaningless; and Barr the lexicographer should know that.[2]

The third chapter covers a variety of topics in Genesis 3, such as the tree of life: he takes Genesis as implying that Adam and Eve had not tasted of the tree before their expulsion; that is, they lost their chance of unending life and therefore died in the natural course of things. In the fourth chapter Barr argues that the story of Noah provides a better narrative of a "fall." He also contends that the genealogies in this part of Genesis indicate that the Hebrews had a keen interest in chronology—hence they could have cared about the "chronological" side of eternal life (a point denied by leading "Biblical theology" proponents). The title of the final chapter indicates its theme: "Immortality and resurrection: Conflict or Complementarity?" We have been faced with an either-or choice between the two, based supposedly on the features of "Hebrew thought"; but surely it can be both-and?

This book alternates between the enlightening and the frustrating. The enlightening part is the discussion of body-soul dualism in "Hebrew thought," pages 36–47. After extensive (and generally effective) discussion he concludes (page 44):

> The ancient Hebrew conceptions of humanity were such that conceptions differentiating body and soul could be built upon them, already within later Old Testament strata—as, in later Judaism and early Christianity, they certainly were.

There is today a trend toward "monistic" views of human nature—that is, to insist that human beings are composed of only one substance (usually the body) as opposed to "dualism," which sees people as having two components (usually body and soul). This tendency is gaining popularity among science-and-religion writers, and they mistakenly think it is the "Hebrew" view of man. To the extent that this tendency relies on the arguments that Barr here shreds, it is

---

[2]Barr coined a term to name a fallacious lexical procedure, "illegitimate totality transfer," in his well-justified critique of sloppy lexical semantics; this is a kind of equivocation error. See his *Semantics of Biblical Language*, 218.

unworthy of serious confidence. Barr is at his best when he exposes sloppy argumentation.

The frustrating part of the book derives from several factors. In the first place, Barr presents himself as a spokesman for responsible mainstream Old Testament scholarship. He is of course a leading voice; but how do we define "responsible"? A few sentences on page 91 reveal the answer: "competent" scholarship has agreed that the story of Adam and Eve was not the story of the "Fall of Man" in the traditional sense. This he also calls "mainstream modern scholarship." Unfortunately, this approach *leaves out* (and does not even stoop to refute) the work of theologically conservative scholars such as Franz Delitzsch or Gordon Wenham. Barr's discussion of Noah, and of death and the afterlife, makes no mention at all of Alexander Heidel's valuable work comparing views of death and afterlife in Gilgamesh with those of the Old Testament. This means that when Barr describes traditional views, he often paints a caricature. An example comes on pages 80–81, where he refers to "total depravity," and what that would have led us to expect in the fallen Adam as a "foul wretch and miserable sinner." I have not encountered a traditional source that would have led us to expect such a description; I have to conclude that Barr is either reacting to some kind of abuse, or else that he is setting up a straw man.

Even more telling is the way the argument is conducted. There is no reflection on method, nor is there much effort to make use of the sophisticated tools that have been developed in literary and discourse-linguistic studies, which are aimed at helping us toward ancient literary competence. Barr had led me to expect some attention to this when he spoke of a "close reading" in the first quotation above. This calls into question his entitlement to the confidence with which he writes.

It is surprising to find Barr, who did so much to promote the careful use of linguistic principles among Biblical students, dropping some pretty loud clangers in this book. For example, on page 6 he makes a really stunning argument about the story of Genesis 3:

First, it is not without importance that the term 'sin' is not used any-
where in the story . . . nor do we find any of the terms usually understood as 'evil', 'rebellion', 'transgression' or 'guilt'.

This is stunning on the linguistic level, because and Barr the
semanticist knew this full well—for a thing to be present in a text
it is not necessary to have the usual words for it. Besides, Genesis
3:11, where God asks Adam, "Have you done what I told you not to
do?" is as good a paraphrase for "Have you disobeyed me?" as we
could ask for. On the literary level, the author is *showing* their sin
and its effects, and not *telling*: this is a recognized aspect of narrative
style, which Barr has missed.

Later (page 65) he proposes an etymological connection between
the name "Eve" (Hebrew *khawwâ*) and an Aramaic word for "snake"
(*khewyâ*): thus "the mythological ancestor of Eve was some sort of
'serpent goddess' who was, perhaps, the goddess of life." Barr does
concede, "The point has never been proved and is perhaps incapable
of proof, and yet it has much that is attractive about it." Barr, who
wrote an important book on the misuse of comparative philology
(*Comparative Philology and the Text of the Old Testament*), falls into
the traps that he had so incisively described. The etymological connection that he alleges is a tenuous one, with little bearing on the
Hebrew story we have as Genesis 3; and the connection with the roots
kh-y-h / kh-w-h "to be alive" is far more likely. In fact, in 1997 Scott
Layton's article established that connection solidly, showing that
the likely meaning of the name Eve is "Life-giver."[3] Of course Barr
could not have known of Layton's work before its publication; but
this conclusion is just what the Hebrew story itself implies, a point
that apparently did not occur to Barr.

At the literary level, Barr shows dubious sensitivity. For example,
in his discussion of the divine threat (pages 8–14), "in the day that
you eat of it you shall surely die" (Gen. 2:17), and the serpent's denial
of that threat, he never stops to consider the obvious: namely, God is
a reliable character in Old Testament narration. The semantic range

---

[3]Scott C. Layton, "Remarks on the Canaanite Origin of Eve," *Catholic Biblical Quarterly*
59:1 (1997): 22–32.

of "die" includes what we call physical death, but it also includes "spiritual death," which is surely what happens in Genesis 3. Further, when Barr insists that "the story nowhere says that Adam, before his disobedience, was immortal, was never going to die" (page 5), and claims that in Genesis 3 we have "the absence from the text of the atmosphere of guilt and tragedy" (page 11), he is again failing to account for showing in place of telling, and therefore he is not reading the Bible text well.

The best response to this, however, is not a retreat into dogmatism. Instead Barr's book is a call to theological traditionalists to employ the best tools available to achieve a sound reading, both of Genesis and of Paul. I have made some effort toward this in "What Happened to Adam and Eve? A Literary-Theological Approach to Genesis 3," *Presbyterion* 27:1 (Spring 2001): 12–44, and more fully in my *Genesis 1–4: A Linguistic, Literary, and Theological Commentary* (Phillipsburg, NJ: P&R, 2006)—studies stimulated (or provoked!), in part, by reading Barr's book. To that extent, Barr has helped us immeasurably. But my conclusions about Paul as a reader of Genesis are radically different from Barr's: I find Paul very capable, seeing things in the sacred text that a careful linguistically oriented literary method supports. To the extent that a reading disagrees with Paul, then that reading shows less ancient literary competence than Paul's.

APPENDIX 3

THE DATE OF GENESIS

In the text of chapter 3, I have not made my argument depend very much on views about when Genesis came into being. Through the centuries, most Jews and Christians took it as the work of Moses (which would date it around either 1440 or 1250 B.C.), with hardly a thought about the process by which Moses composed it. In the later eighteenth century, however, scholars began wondering about that process of composition, and whether there were identifiable sources behind the current form of Genesis (and of the Pentateuch as a whole). Initially, they still took Moses as the author, or at least compiler, of Genesis; but as the theories developed, it became more common to date the sources, and thus the book, after the time of Moses.

In the later nineteenth century, and through most of the twentieth, the dominant form of these theories held that there were four main sources for the Pentateuch. These sources had distinctive features, and were named J (the Yahwist, because the main name for God is Yahweh, "the LORD," spelled in German *Jahwe*); E (the Elohist, because his main name for God is *ᵉlôhîm*, or "God"); D (the Deuteronomist, reflecting the concerns especially visible in the book of

Deuteronomy); and P (the Priestly writer). There are many varia-
tions on this theory, though in general the view is that the sources
follow that order. This approach is called "source criticism." There
are also other theories that do not rely on sources, arguing that the
Pentateuch as we have it was composed all at once (during or after
the exile), using sources that are now unrecoverable.

According to most source-critical models, the book of Genesis
is mostly composed of material from J and E, with a good deal of
P mixed in. According to a fairly standard analysis, Genesis 1–11
breaks down roughly as follows: 1:1–2:4a is from P, while the rest of
Genesis 2–4 comes from J; then most of Genesis 5 (the genealogy)
is P, the flood story of Genesis 6–9 is a pastiche of P and J, and the
genealogies of Genesis 10–11 are from P, with the Tower of Babel
story (11:1–9) being from J.[1]

I have no intention of evaluating the source theories here, and
my conclusions in chapters 2 and 3 do not rely on any view of the
sources or of how they were brought together. The important thing
is to recognize that, whatever the pre-history of these materials, they
now flow as a coherent literary product. In fact, they show signs of
being edited to display that coherence (as I already argued for Genesis 1–5 in section 3a, and the connection with the rest of Genesis
in section 3b). That means that it makes no sense to talk about what
function these sources performed *before* they were part of Genesis;
what matters is how they hang together in the book of Genesis that
we have.

The advance of literary appreciation for Biblical narrative has further reduced the attractions of source criticism. Regardless of where
the materials came from, it is becoming more clear that whoever put
Genesis together has shown a pretty sophisticated literary ability.
Many of the features that were once taken as evidence of disparate
sources—and may indeed reflect that pre-history—are being seen to
carry out a function in the present shape of Genesis. For example, it
is common to infer from the change in divine name, from "God" in
Genesis 1:1–2:3, to "the LORD God" in 2:4, that these two narratives

---

[1]Based on S. R. Driver, *The Book of Genesis*, Westminster Commentary (London: Methuen,
1904).

came from separate sources. Whatever we might think of that, it is now obvious that the switch in name has a rhetorical function: it identifies the majestic, transcendent Creator of 1:1–2:3 with "the LORD" (Yahweh), the covenant God of Israel. This supplies the warrant for the way Genesis presents Israel as a people with a calling to be a blessing, an avenue of the one true God's light, to all the nations of the world.

At the same time, we can say more about *when* Genesis came to be in the form we have it. It used to be said that P was the latest, coming from the exilic period (or even later). Studies based on the history of the Hebrew language, however, point us in the direction of P being *pre*-exilic.[2] Further, the patriarchal narratives, to the extent we can tell, seem to reflect the customs of the patriarchs' own times (first half of the second millennium B.C.) more than they do the later times of Israel as a settled people. This means that these stories preserve authentic memories. All of the Mesopotamian materials that provide the literary background for Genesis 1–11 were finished by about 1600 B.C., and at least some of them were available to a well-educated Egyptian (such as Moses was supposed to be). The material in Exodus fits well with the time of Rameses II, as in the names of the store cities Pithom and Raamses (Ex. 1:11); these names were forgotten soon afterward. The pattern of the plagues also shows pretty good knowledge of the annual cycle of Egypt. The covenant formulations in Exodus–Numbers and in Deuteronomy reflect covenant forms found elsewhere in the late second millennium B.C., and are different from the forms found in the first millennium.[3]

---

[2] Avi Hurvitz, *A Linguistic Study of the Relationship between the Priestly Source and the Book of Ezekiel: A New Approach to an Old Problem* (Paris: Gabalda, 1982). See further Gordon Wenham, *Genesis 1–15*, Word Biblical Commentary (Dallas: Word, 1987), xxxi–xxxii.

[3] In this paragraph I am drawing on arguments found in Kenneth A. Kitchen, *On the Reliability of the Old Testament* (Grand Rapids, MI: Eerdmans, 2003), e.g., his chapters 6–7. I am aware that his conclusions are controversial: see Hendel's critique in Ronald S. Hendel, William W. Hallo, and Kenneth A. Kitchen, "The Kitchen Debate," *Biblical Archaeology Review* 31:4 (2005): 48–53. Hendel adopts a condescending tone, and Kitchen meets his every criticism with arguments well-supported by data; the result of this combination is that Hendel's whole case sounds like petty carping. The one criticism that has some traction is his complaint that Kitchen "tends to characterize his own views and interpretations as objective facts" (49a). However, Kitchen's mastery of the data (and I have checked the data where I could) certainly entitles us to see his views as what I prefer to

The literary evidence allows us to say that if we have a man with the kind of education that the Biblical Moses had, then he could easily have put together the basic material of the Pentateuch. (Obviously he did not write Deuteronomy 34, which describes his death!) We are often told, however, that the kind of Hebrew we encounter in the Pentateuch cannot be from Moses' time; its form is what we would expect from much later.[4] But there is a ready reply to that: there was an apparently well-established scribal practice in the ancient world, of copying manuscripts and updating any grammatical forms and spellings that were going out of fashion, perhaps even adding an explanatory gloss here and there to identify a place with its contemporary name.[5]

The outcome of all this is that the traditional picture of a Pentateuch that is substantially from Moses, with small updates and tweaks, is consistent with the evidence, and this is my view. A few difficulties remain, and some prefer to suppose that the substantially Mosaic materials took their final shape during the time of David and Solomon,[6] though this later date does not affect conclusions for Genesis 1–11.

---

call well-established conclusions. I do not think a sensible person would count either Kitchen's feisty writing style (which is usually entertaining) or the terminological quibble as in any way undermining the basic case Kitchen makes.

[4] E.g., Peter Enns, *Inspiration and Incarnation: Evangelicals and the Problem of the Old Testament* (Grand Rapids, MI: Baker, 2005), 51–52; Daniel Harlow, "Creation according to Genesis: Literary Genre, Cultural Context, Theological Truth," *Christian Scholars Review* 37:2 (2008): 163–98, at 168–69. Neither of these authors even mentions the possibility of scribal updating; I cannot tell whether they know of it and reject it, or simply have never considered it.

[5] Although Kitchen, *On the Reliability of the Old Testament*, 305–306, is one source that makes this point, I have always encountered it as standard fare among scholars associated with the Tyndale Fellowship in Great Britain.

[6] E.g., Gordon Wenham, *Story as Torah: Reading Old Testament Narratives Ethically* (Grand Rapids, MI: Baker, 2000), 41, notes that "the Mosaic era certainly accounts for many of the key features in Genesis"; in the face of observations from "critical orthodoxy," he argues (42) "none of these observations are problems for a date in the united monarchy period" (David and Solomon).

BIBLIOGRAPHY

Adler, Jerry. "Thinking Like a Monkey: What Do Our Primate Cousins Know and When Do They Know It? Researcher Laurie Santos Is Trying to Read Their Minds." *Smithsonian* 38.10 (January 2008): 58(5).

Alexander, Denis. *Creation or Evolution: Do We Have to Choose?* Oxford: Monarch/ Grand Rapids, MI: Kregel, 2008.

Alexander, T. Desmond. "From Adam to Judah: The Significance of the Family Tree in Genesis." *Evangelical Quarterly* 61.1 (1989): 5–19.

———. "Genealogies, Seed and the Compositional Unity of Genesis." *Tyndale Bulletin* 44.2 (1993): 255–70.

———. "Further Observations on the Term 'Seed' in Genesis." *Tyndale Bulletin* 48.2 (1997): 363–67.

Anderson, Gary A. "Necessarium adae peccatum: An Essay on Original Sin." *Pro Ecclesia* 8.3 (1999): 319–37.

Andreasen, Niels-Erik. "Adam and Adapa: Two Anthropological Characters." *Andrews University Seminary Studies* 19.3 (1981): 179–94.

Averbeck, Richard E. "The Sumerian Historiographical Tradition and Its Implications for Genesis 1–11." In *Faith, Tradition, and History: Old Testament Historiography in Its Near Eastern Context*, edited by A. R. Millard, James K. Hoffmeier and David W. Baker, 79–102. Winona Lake, IN: Eisenbrauns, 1994.

Ayala, Francisco, et al. "Molecular genetics of speciation and human origins." *Proceedings of the National Academy of the Sciences* 91 (July 1994): 6787–94.

Baker, David W. "Scribes as Transmitters of Tradition." In *Faith, Tradition, and History: Old Testament Historiography in Its Near Eastern Context*, edited by

A. R. Millard, James K. Hoffmeier, and David W. Baker, 65–77. Winona Lake, IN: Eisenbrauns, 1994.

Barr, James. *The Garden of Eden and the Hope of Immortality.* Minneapolis: Fortress, 1992.

———. "One Man, or All Humanity? A Question in the Anthropology of Genesis I." In *Recycling Biblical Figures: Papers Read at a NOSTER Colloquium in Amsterdam, 12–13 May 1997,* edited by Athalya Brenner and Jan Willem van Henten, 3–21. Studies in Theology and Religion. Leiden: Deo, 1999.

Barrett, Charles K. *1 Corinthians.* Harper's New Testament Commentary. Peabody, MA: Hendrickson, 1968.

———. *Acts 15–28.* International Critical Commentary. Edinburgh: T & T Clark, 1998.

Barth, Karl. *Romans.* Translated by E. C. Hoskyns. London: Oxford University Press, 1933 [1921].

Bartholomew, Craig, and Michael W. Goheen. *The Drama of Scripture: Finding Our Place in the Biblical Story.* Grand Rapids, MI: Baker, 2004.

Bartusiak, Marcia. "Before the Big Bang." *Technology Review* 112.5 (September/October 2009): MIT News Section, M14–15.

Beale, Gregory. *The Temple and the Church's Mission: A Biblical Theology of the Dwelling Place of God.* New Studies in Biblical Theology, edited by Donald A. Carson, Downers Grove, IL: InterVarsity Press, 2004.

Bechtel, Lyn M. "Genesis 2.4b–3.24: A Myth about Human Maturation." *Journal for the Study of the Old Testament* 67 (1995): 3–26.

Beckwith, R. T. *The Old Testament Canon of the New Testament Church.* London: SPCK, 1985.

Bienkowski, Piotr, and A. R. Millard, eds. *Dictionary of the Ancient Near East.* Philadelphia: University of Pennsylvania Press, 2000.

Blocher, Henri. *In the Beginning.* Downers Grove, IL: InterVarsity Press, 1984.

———. *Original Sin: Illuminating the Riddle.* New Studies in Biblical Theology, edited by Donald A. Carson. Grand Rapids, MI: Eerdmans, 1997.

———. "The Theology of the Fall and the Origins of Evil." In *Darwin, Creation and the Fall,* edited by R. J. Berry and T. A. Noble, 149–72. Leicester, U.K.: Apollos, 2009.

Bloom, John A. "On Human Origins: A Survey." *Christian Scholars Review* 27.2 (1997): 181–203.

Brandon, S. G. F. "The Origin of Death in Some Ancient Near Eastern Religions." *Religious Studies* I (1966): 217–28.

Bruce, F. F. *Acts: Greek Text with Introduction and Commentary.* London: Tyndale Press, 1970.

———. *Acts*. New International Commentary on the New Testament. Grand Rapids, MI: Eerdmans, 1988.

Buccelati, Giorgio. "Adapa, Genesis, and the Notion of Faith." *Ugarit-Forschungen* 5 (1973): 61–66.

Bunt, Lucas, Phillip Jones, and Jack Bedient. *The Historical Roots of Elementary Mathematics*. New York: Dover, 1988 [1976].

Caird, G. B. *The Language and Imagery of the Bible*. Philadelphia: Westminster, 1980.

Callender, Dexter E. *Adam in Myth and History: Ancient Israelite Perspectives on the Primal Human*. Harvard Semitic Studies. Winona Lake, IN: Eisenbrauns, 2000.

Carpenter, Humphrey. *J. R. R. Tolkien: A Biography*. London: George Allen & Unwin, 1976.

Cassuto, Umberto. *From Adam to Noah: Genesis I–VI.8*. Jerusalem: Magnes, 1961 [1944].

Chavalas, Mark. "Genealogical History as 'Charter': A Study of Old Babylonian Period Historiography and the Old Testament." In *Faith, Tradition, and History: Old Testament Historiography in Its Near Eastern Context*, edited by A. R. Millard, James K. Hoffmeier and David W. Baker, 103–28. Winona Lake, IN: Eisenbrauns, 1994.

Chesterton, G. K. *The Everlasting Man*. New York: Doubleday, 1955 [1925].

———. *As I Was Saying*. Grand Rapids, MI: Eerdmans, 1985.

Chomsky, Noam. "Universals of Human Nature." *Psychotherapy and Psychosomatics* 74 (2005): 263–68.

Collins, C. John. *Homonymous Verbs in Biblical Hebrew: An Investigation of the Role of Comparative Philology*. Ph.D. thesis, University of Liverpool, 1988.

———. "The Wayyiqtol as 'Pluperfect': When and Why." *Tyndale Bulletin* 46.1 (1995): 117–40.

———. "A Syntactical Note on Genesis 3:15: Is the Woman's Seed Singular or Plural?" *Tyndale Bulletin* 48.1 (1997): 141–48.

———. "Discourse Analysis and the Interpretation of Gen 2:4–7." *Westminster Theological Journal* 61 (1999): 269–76.

———. *The God of Miracles: An Exegetical Examination of God's Action in the World*. Wheaton, IL: Crossway, 2000.

———. *Science and Faith: Friends or Foes?* Wheaton, IL: Crossway, 2003.

———. "Galatians 3:16: What Kind of Exegete Was Paul?" *Tyndale Bulletin* 54.1 (2003): 75–86.

———. "The Eucharist as Christian Sacrifice: How Patristic Authors Can Help Us Read the Bible." *Westminster Theological Journal* 66 (2004): 1–23.

———. *Genesis 1–4: A Linguistic, Literary, and Theological Commentary*. Phillipsburg, NJ: P&R, 2006.

———. "The Theology of the Old Testament." In *The ESV Study Bible*, edited by Lane T. Dennis, et al., 29–31. Wheaton, IL: Crossway, 2008.

———. "Proverbs and the Levitical System." *Presbyterion* 35.1 (2009): 9–34.

———. "Echoes of Aristotle in Romans 2:14–15: Or, Maybe Abimelech Was Not So Bad After All." *Journal of Markets and Morality* 13.1 (2010): 123–73

Collins, Francis. *The Language of God: A Scientist Presents Evidence for Belief*. New York: Free Press, 2006.

Collins, Francis, et al. *The Biologos Foundation: Questions*. 2009.

Cranfield, C. E. B. *Romans 1–8*. International Critical Commentary. Edinburgh: T & T Clark, 1975.

Dalley, Stephanie. *Myths from Mesopotamia: Creation, the Flood, Gilgamesh and Others*. Oxford: Oxford University Press, 1989.

Day, Allan John. "Adam, Anthropology and the Genesis Record: Taking Genesis Seriously." *Science and Christian Belief* 10 (1998): 115–43.

de Moor, Johannes C. "The First Human Being a Male? A Response to Professor Barr." In *Recycling Biblical Figures: Papers Read at a NOSTER Colloquium in Amsterdam, 12–13 May 1997*, edited by Athalya Brenner and Jan Willem van Henten, 22–27. Leiden: Deo, 1999.

Dennis, Lane T., et al., ed. *The ESV Study Bible*. Wheaton, IL: Crossway, 2008.

deSilva, David A. *Introducing the Apocrypha: Message, Context, and Significance*. Grand Rapids, MI: Baker, 2002.

Dillmann, A. *Genesis Critically and Exegetically Expounded*. Edinburgh: T & T Clark, 1897 [1892].

Driver, S. R. *The Book of Genesis*. Westminster Commentary. London: Methuen, 1904.

Dubarle, André-Marie. "Les chromosomes, Adam et Ève: Un nouveau concordisme." In *Revue des Sciences Philosophiques et Théologiques* 61.3 (1977): 429–36.

Dunn, James D. G. *Romans 1–8*. Word Biblical Commentary. Dallas: Word, 1988.

Emmrich, Martin. "The Temptation Narrative of Genesis 3:1–6: A Prelude to the Pentateuch and the History of Israel." *Evangelical Quarterly* 73.1 (2001): 3–20.

Enns, Peter. *Inspiration and Incarnation: Evangelicals and the Problem of the Old Testament*. Grand Rapids, MI: Baker, 2005.

Fee, Gordon D. *1 Corinthians*. New International Commentary on the New Testament. Grand Rapids, MI: Eerdmans, 1987.

Finlay, Graeme. "*Homo divinus*: The Ape that Bears God's Image." *Science and Christian Belief* 15.1 (2003): 17–40.

———. *Human Genomics and the Image of God*. Vol. 14 of Faraday Papers. Cambridge: The Faraday Institute for Science and Religion, 2009.

Fischer, Dick. "In Search of the Historical Adam, part 1." *Perspectives on Science and Christian Faith* 45 (1993): 241–51.

———. "In Search of the Historical Adam, part 2." *Perspectives on Science and Christian Faith* 46 (1994): 47–57.

Fitch, W. Tecumseh, Marc D. Hauser, and Noam Chomsky. "The Evolution of the Language Faculty: Clarifications and Implications." *Cognition* 97 (2005): 179–210.

Fitzmyer, J. A. *Romans*. Anchor Bible. New York: Doubleday, 1993.

Fodor, Jerry. "The Trouble with Psychological Darwinism." *London Review of Books* 20.2 (1998).

Gordon, Cyrus H. "Ancient Middle Eastern Religions: The Cultural Context." In *The New Encyclopedia Britannica*, edited by Philip W. Goetz et al. Vol. 24, 60–64. Chicago: University of Chicago Press, 1989.

Groothuis, Douglas. "Deposed Royalty: Pascal's Anthropological Argument." *Journal of the Evangelical Theological Society* 41.2 (1998): 297–312.

Gunkel, Hermann. *Genesis*. Macon: Mercer University Press, 1997 [German original, 1910].

Hallo, William W. "Part 1: Mesopotamia and the Asiatic Near East." In *The Ancient Near East: A History*, edited by William W. Hallo and William K. Simpson, 3–181. Fort Worth, TX: Harcourt Brace College Publishers, 1998.

———. "Adapa Reconsidered: Life and Death in Contextual Perspective." *Scriptura* 87 (2004): 267–77.

Hamilton, Victor P. *The Book of Genesis, Chapters 1–17*. New International Commentary on the Old Testament. Grand Rapids, MI: Eerdmans, 1990.

Harlow, Daniel C. "Creation according to Genesis: Literary Genre, Cultural Context, Theological Truth." *Christian Scholars Review* 37.2 (2008): 163–98.

Hauser, Marc D., Noam Chomsky, and W. Tecumseh Fitch. "The Faculty of Language: What Is It, Who Has It, and How Did It Evolve?" *Science* 298 (November 22, 2002): 1569–79.

Hayden, Erika Check. "Life Is Complicated." *Nature* 464 (2010): 664–67 (published online, 31 March 2010).

Hays, J. Daniel. "A Biblical Perspective on Interracial Marriage." *Criswell Theological Review* 6.2 (Spring 2009): 5–23.

Heidel, Alexander. *The Gilgamesh Epic and Old Testament Parallels*. Chicago: University of Chicago, 1949.

——. *The Babylonian Genesis.* Chicago: University of Chicago Press, 1951.

Hendel, Ronald S., William W. Hallo, and Kenneth A. Kitchen. "The Kitchen Debate." *Biblical Archaeology Review* 31.4 (2005): 48–53.

Hess, Richard S. "Splitting the Adam: The Usage of *'adam* in Genesis i–iv." In *Studies in the Pentateuch,* edited by John A. Emerton, 1–15. Leiden: Brill, 1990.

——. "Adam." In *Dictionary of the Old Testament: Pentateuch,* edited by T. Desmond Alexander and David W. Baker, 18a–21b. Downers Grove, IL: InterVarsity Press, 2003.

Hess, Richard S., and David T. Tsumura, eds. *I Studied Inscriptions from before the Flood: Ancient Near Eastern, Literary, and Linguistic Approaches to Genesis 1–11.* Winona Lake, IN: Eisenbrauns, 1994.

Hurvitz, Avi. *A Linguistic Study of the Relationship between the Priestly Source and the Book of Ezekiel: A New Approach to an Old Problem.* Paris: Gabalda, 1982.

Jacobs, Alan. "Leon Kass and the Genesis of Wisdom." *First Things* 134 (June/July 2003): 30–35.

Jacobsen, Anders-Christian. "The Importance of Genesis 1–3 in the Theology of Irenaeus." *Zeitschrift für antikes Christentum* 8.2 (2005): 299–316.

Jacobsen, Thorkild. *The Sumerian King List.* Assyriological Studies, Oriental Institute of the University of Chicago. Chicago: University of Chicago Press, 1939.

——. "The Eridu Genesis." *Journal of Biblical Literature* 100.4 (1981): 513–29.

Kaeuffer, Renaud, et al. "Unexpected Heterozygosity in an Island Mouflon Population Founded by a Single Pair of Individuals." *Proceedings of the Royal Society B,* 24 September 2006: published online as doi:10.1098/rspb.2006.3743.

Kass, Leon R. *The Beginning of Wisdom: Reading Genesis.* New York: Free Press, 2003.

Kelly, Douglas F. *Creation and Change: Genesis 1.1–2.4 in the Light of Changing Scientific Paradigms.* Fearn, Ross-shire: Christian Focus, 1997.

Kennedy, James M. "Peasants in Revolt: Political Allegory in Genesis 2–3." *Journal for the Study of the Old Testament* 47 (1990): 3–14.

Kidner, Derek. *Genesis.* Tyndale OT Commentary. Downers Grove, IL: InterVarsity Press, 1967.

Kiel, Yehudah. *Sefer Bereshit, 1–17 (Genesis 1–17).* Da'at Miqra'. Jerusalem: Mossad Harav Kook, 1997.

Kilmer, Anne Drafkorn. "The Mesopotamian Counterparts of the Biblical *Nephilim.*" In *Perspectives on Language and Text,* edited by Edgar W. Conrad, 39–43. Winona Lake, IN: Eisenbrauns, 1987.

Kitchen, Kenneth A. *Ancient Orient and Old Testament.* London: Tyndale Press, 1966.

———. "A Possible Mention of David in the Late Tenth Century BCE, and Deity *Dod as Dead as the Dodo?" *Journal for the Study of the Old Testament* 76 (1997): 29–44.

———. *On the Reliability of the Old Testament.* Grand Rapids, MI: Eerdmans, 2003.

Kramer, Samuel Noah. "Sumerian Historiography." *Israel Exploration Journal* 3.4 (1953): 217–32.

———. "Sumerian Theology and Ethics." *Harvard Theological Review* 49.1 (1956): 45–62.

———. *Sumerian Mythology: A Study of Spiritual and Literary Achievement in the Third Millennium B.C.* New York: Harper & Row, 1961.

———. "Reflections on the Mesopotamian Flood." *Expedition* 9 (Summer 1967): 12–18.

Kreitzer, L. J. "Adam and Christ." In *Dictionary of Paul and His Letters*, edited by Gerald F. Hawthorne and R. P. Martin, 9a–15b. Downers Grove, IL: InterVarsity Press, 1993.

Kufeldt, George. "Were There People before Adam and Eve? No." In *The Genesis Debate: Persistent Questions about Creation and the Flood*, edited by Ronald F. Youngblood, 148–65. Grand Rapids, MI: Baker, 1990.

Ladd, George E. *The Pattern of New Testament Truth.* Grand Rapids, MI: Eerdmans, 1968.

Lambert, W. G. "A New Look at the Babylonian Background of Genesis." *Journal of Theological Studies* n.s. 16.2 (1965): 287–300.

Lambert, W. G., and A. R. Millard. *Atra-hasis: The Babylonian Story of the Flood.* Winona Lake, IN: Eisenbrauns, 1999 [1969].

Lamoureux, Denis. *Evolutionary Creation: A Christian Approach to Evolution.* Eugene, OR: Wipf & Stock, 2008.

Layton, Scott C. "Remarks on the Canaanite Origin of Eve." *Catholic Biblical Quarterly* 59.1 (1997): 22–32.

Lewis, C. S. *The Problem of Pain.* London: Geoffrey Bles, 1940.

———. *Mere Christianity.* New York: Scribner, 1952.

———. *Prayer: Letters to Malcolm.* London: Collins, 1966.

———. *Christian Reflections.* Grand Rapids, MI: Eerdmans, 1967.

———. *Present Concerns.* London: Collins, 1986.

Livingstone, David N. "Preadamites: The History of an Idea from Heresy to Orthodoxy." *Scottish Journal of Theology* 40 (1987): 41–66.

Long, V. Philips. *The Reign and Rejection of King Saul: A Case for Literary and Theological Coherence.* SBL Dissertation Series. Atlanta: Scholars, 1989.

———. *The Art of Biblical History.* Grand Rapids, MI: Zondervan, 1994.

Lucas, Ernest. "Some Scientific Issues Related to the Understanding of Genesis 1–3." *Themelios* 12.2 (1987): 46–51.

———. *Interpreting Genesis in the 21st Century*. Vol. 11 of Faraday Papers. Cambridge: Faraday Institute for Science and Religion, 2007.

Mallowan, M. E. L. "Noah's Flood Reconsidered." *Iraq* 26 (1964): 62–82, with plates 16–20.

Mayell, Hillary. "Documentary Redraws Humans' Family Tree." *National Geographic News*, January 21, 2003.

Maynard Smith, John. *The Theory of Evolution*. Canto. Cambridge: Cambridge University Press, 1993.

McCurdy, J. F., Kaufman Kohler, and Richard Gottheil. "Adam." In *Jewish Encyclopedia*, edited by Isidore Singer. Vol. 1, 173b–79a. New York: Funk & Wagnalls, 1901.

McGrath, Gavin Basil. "Soteriology: Adam and the Fall." *Perspectives on Science and Christian Faith* 49.4 (1997): 252–63.

McIntyre, John A. "The Historical Adam." *Perspectives on Science and Christian Faith* 54.3 (2002): 150–57.

———. "The Real Adam." *Perspectives on Science and Christian Faith* 56.3 (2004): 162–70.

———. "The Real Adam and Original Sin." *Perspectives on Science and Christian Faith* 58.2 (2006): 90–98.

Millard, A. R. "A New Babylonian 'Genesis' Story." *Tyndale Bulletin* 18 (1967): 3–18.

———. "Methods of Studying the Patriarchal Narratives as Ancient Texts." In *Essays on the Patriarchal Narratives*, edited by A. R. Millard and Donald J. Wiseman, 43–58. Leicester, U.K.: Inter-Varsity Press, 1980.

———. *Treasures from Bible Times*. Tring, Hertfordshire: Lion, 1985.

———. "Story, History, and Theology." In *Faith, Tradition, and History: Old Testament Historiography in Its Near Eastern Context*, edited by A. R. Millard, James K. Hoffmeier and David W. Baker, 37–64. Winona Lake, IN: Eisenbrauns, 1994.

Moye, Richard H. "In the Beginning: Myth and History in Genesis and Exodus." *Journal of Biblical Literature* 109.4 (1990): 577–98.

Naugle, David K. *Worldview: The History of a Concept*. Grand Rapids, MI: Eerdmans, 2002.

Noort, Ed. "The Stories of the Great Flood: Notes on Gen 6:5–9:17 in Its Context of the Ancient Near East." In *Interpretations of the Flood*, edited by Florentino G. Martínez and Gerard P. Luttikhuizen, 1–38. Themes in Biblical Narrative: Jewish and Christian Traditions. Leiden: Brill, 1998.

———. "The Creation of Man and Woman in Biblical and Ancient Near Eastern Traditions." In *The Creation of Man and Woman: Interpretations of the Biblical Narratives in Jewish and Christian Traditions*, edited by Gerard P. Luttikhuizen, 1–18. Themes in Biblical Narrative. Leiden: Brill, 2000.

Oakes, Edward T. "Original Sin: A Disputation." *First Things* 87 (November, 1998): 16–24.

Orr, James. *The Christian View of God and the World*. Edinburgh: Andrew Elliott, 1897.

Oswalt, John N. *The Bible Among the Myths*. Grand Rapids, MI: Zondervan, 2009.

Papageorgiou, Panayiotis. "Chrysostom and Augustine on the Sin of Adam and Its Consequences." *St Vladimir's Theological Quarterly* 39.4 (1995): 361–78.

Pascal, Blaise. *Pensées*. Translated by A. J. Krailsheimer. London: Penguin, 1995.

Paton, John G. *John G. Paton, D.D., Missionary to the New Hebrides: An Autobiography*. Edited by James Paton. London: Hodder and Stoughton, 1894.

Pederson, Don. "Biblical Narrative as an Agent for Worldview Change." *International Journal of Frontier Missions* 14.4 (1997): 163–66.

Piperno, D. R. et al. "Processing of Wild Cereal Grains in the Upper Paleolithic Revealed by Starch Grain Analysis." *Nature* 430 (August 2004): 670–73.

Plantinga, Cornelius. *Not the Way It's Supposed to Be: A Breviary of Sin*. Grand Rapids, MI: Eerdmans, 1995.

Plaut, W. G. *Genesis*. Vol. 1 of *The Torah: A Modern Commentary*. New York: Union of American Hebrew Congregations, 1981.

Pollard, Katherine S. "What Makes Us Human? Comparisons of the Genomes of Humans and Chimpanzees Are Revealing Those Rare Stretches of DNA That Are Ours Alone." *Scientific American*, April 20, 2009.

Pope, Marvin H., et al. "Adam." In *Encyclopedia Judaica*, edited by Fred Skolnik. Vol. 1, 371a–76b. Jerusalem: Keter, 2007.

Porter, Stanley. "The Pauline Concept of Original Sin, in Light of Rabbinic Background." *Tyndale Bulletin* 41.1 (1990): 3–30.

Pritchard, James B., ed. *Ancient Near Eastern Texts*. Princeton, NJ: Princeton University Press, 1969.

Purtill, Richard. *J. R. R. Tolkien: Myth, Morality, and Religion*. San Francisco: Ignatius, 2003 [1984].

———. *C. S. Lewis' Case for the Christian Faith*. San Francisco: Ignatius, 2004 [1981].

Raikes, R. L. "The Physical Evidence for Noah's Flood." *Iraq* 28 (1966): 52–63.

Rana, Fazale, with Hugh Ross. *Who Was Adam? A Creation Model Approach to the Origin of Man.* Colorado Springs: NavPress, 2005.

Rogerson, J. W. "Slippery Words, V: Myth." *Expository Times* 90 (1978): 10–14.

Ross, Marcus, and Paul Nelson. "A Taxonomy of Teleology: Phillip Johnson, the Intelligent Design Community, and Young-Earth Creationism." In *Darwin's Nemesis: Phillip Johnson and the Intelligent Design Movement*, edited by William Dembski, 261–75. Downers Grove, IL: InterVarsity Press, 2006.

Ryle, H. E. *Genesis.* Cambridge Bible for Schools and Colleges. Cambridge: Cambridge University Press, 1921.

Sarna, Nahum M. *Genesis.* JPS Torah Commentary. Philadelphia: Jewish Publication Society, 1989.

Schreiner, Thomas. *Romans.* Baker Exegetical Commentary on the New Testament. Grand Rapids, MI: Baker, 1998.

Seaford, H. Wade. "Were There People before Adam and Eve? Yes." In *The Genesis Debate: Persistent Questions about Creation and the Flood*, edited by Ronald F. Youngblood, 148–65. Grand Rapids, MI: Baker, 1990.

Shea, William H. "Adam in Ancient Mesopotamian Traditions." *Andrews University Seminary Studies* 15.1 (1977): 27–41.

Shiina, Takashi, et al. "Rapid Evolution of MHC Class I Genes in Primates Generates New Disease Alleles in Man via Hitchhiking Diversity." *Genetics: Published Articles Ahead of Print*, May 15, 2006: published online as 10.1534/genetics.106.057034

Simpson, George Gaylord. *The Meaning of Evolution.* New Haven, CT: Yale University Press, 1967.

Sklar, Jay. *Sin, Impurity, Sacrifice, Atonement: The Priestly Conceptions.* Sheffield: Sheffield Phoenix Press, 2005.

Sollberger, Edmond. *The Babylonian Legend of the Flood.* London: British Museum, 1966.

Stek, John H. "What Says the Scripture?" In *Portraits of Creation*, edited by Howard J. Van Till, et al., 203–65. Grand Rapids, MI: Eerdmans, 1990.

Sternberg, Meir. *The Poetics of Biblical Narrative: Ideological Literature and the Drama of Reading.* Bloomington: Indiana University Press, 1985.

Stevenson, J. *A New Eusebius: Documents Illustrative of the History of the Church to A.D. 337.* London: SPCK, 1968.

Stone, Michael E. *Fourth Ezra.* Hermeneia. Minneapolis: Fortress, 1990.

Stott, John. *Romans.* Downers Grove, IL: InterVarsity Press, 1995.

Thiselton, Anthony C. *1 Corinthians.* New International Greek Text Commentary. Grand Rapids, MI: Eerdmans, 2000.

Tigay, Jeffrey H. *The Evolution of the Gilgamesh Epic*. Philadelphia: University of Pennsylvania Press, 1982.

Towner, W. Sibley. "Interpretations and Reinterpretations of the Fall." In *Modern Biblical Scholarship: Its Impact on Theology and Proclamation*, edited by Francis A. Eigo, 53–85. Villanova, PA: Villanova University Press, 1984.

Trigg, Roger. "Sin and Freedom." *Religious Studies* 20.2 (1984): 191–202.

Tsumura, David T. "Genesis and Ancient Near Eastern Stories of Creation and Flood: An Introduction." In *I Studied Inscriptions from before the Flood: Ancient Near Eastern, Literary, and Linguistic Approaches to Genesis 1–11*, edited by Richard S. Hess and David T. Tsumura, 27–57. Winona Lake, IN: Eisenbrauns, 1994.

United Bible Societies. *Fauna and Flora of the Bible*. London: United Bible Societies, 1980.

Vermes, Geza. *The Dead Sea Scrolls in English*, 4th ed. London: Penguin, 1995.

von Rad, Gerhard. *Genesis*. London: SCM, 1961 [1956].

Wallace, Howard N. "Adam." In *Anchor Bible Dictionary*, edited by David N. Freedman. Vol. 1, 62b–64a. New York: Doubleday, 1992.

Waltke, Bruce. *An Old Testament Theology*. Grand Rapids, MI: Zondervan, 2007.

Waltke, Bruce, and Cathy J. Fredericks. *Genesis*. Grand Rapids, MI: Zondervan, 2001.

Walton, John H. *Ancient Near Eastern Thought and the Old Testament: Introducing the Conceptual World of the Hebrew Bible*. Grand Rapids, MI: Baker, 2006.

———. *The Lost World of Genesis One: Ancient Cosmology and the Origins Debate*. Downers Grove, IL: InterVarsity Press, 2009.

Ward, Keith. *Divine Action: Examining God's Role in an Open and Emergent Universe*. Philadelphia: Templeton Foundation Press, 2007 [1990].

Wedderburn, A. J. M. "Some Observations on Paul's Use of the Phrases 'In Christ' and 'With Christ.'" *Journal for the Study of the New Testament* 25 (1985): 83–97.

Wenham, Gordon J. *Genesis 1–15*. Word Biblical Commentary. Dallas: Word, 1987.

———. *Story as Torah: Reading Old Testament Narratives Ethically*. Grand Rapids, MI: Baker, 2000.

Wilcox, David L. "Establishing Adam: Recent Evidences for a Late-Date Adam (AMH @ 100,000 BP)." *Perspectives on Science and Christian Faith* 56.1 (2004): 49–54.

———. "The Original Adam and the Reality of Sin." *Perspectives on Science and Christian Faith* 58.2 (2006): 104–05.

Wilkinson, David. *The Message of Creation: Encountering the Lord of the Universe.* The Bible Speaks Today. Downers Grove, IL: InterVarsity Press, 2002.

Williams, Michael D. *Far as the Curse Is Found: The Covenant Story of Redemption.* Phillipsburg, NJ: P&R, 2005.

Wolters, Albert M., and Michael W. Goheen. *Creation Regained: Biblical Basics for a Reformational Worldview,* 2nd ed. Grand Rapids, MI: Eerdmans, 2005.

Wright, Christopher J. H. *Walking in the Ways of the Lord: The Ethical Authority of the Old Testament.* Downers Grove, IL: InterVarsity Press, 1995.

———. *Old Testament Ethics for the People of God.* Downers Grove, IL: InterVarsity Press, 2004.

———. *The Mission of God: Unlocking the Bible's Grand Narrative.* Downers Grove, IL: InterVarsity Press, 2006.

Wright, N. T. *The New Testament and the People of God.* Minneapolis: Fortress, 1992.

———. "Romans." In *The New Interpreter's Bible,* edited by Leander Keck et al. Vol. 10, 393–770. Nashville: Abingdon, 2002.

———. *The Resurrection of the Son of God.* Minneapolis: Fortress, 2003.

———. *Paul in Fresh Perspective.* Minneapolis: Fortress, 2005.

Yoder, Perry. "Will the Real Adam, Please Stand Up!" *Perspectives on Science and Christian Faith* 58.2 (2006): 99–101.

Young, Davis A. "The Antiquity and Unity of the Human Race Revisited." *Christian Scholars Review* 24.4 (1995): 380–96.

GENERAL INDEX

Abel, 77, 90
Abraham, 43, 57, 59, 68, 90
abusus usum non tollit, 15
Adam
    and Adapa, 157–59
    as chieftain, 121, 125
    as "epochal figure," 86
    federal headship of, 124–25, 126
    Josephus on, 75–76
    name, 55–56
    Paul on, 79–87
Adam and Eve
    alleged infrequency in Bible, 51–52
    in Apocrypha, 73–75
    disobedience of, 49, 60–61, 66, 83, 84
    in Gospels, 76–78
    marriage of, 60
    in Old Testament, 54–72
    in Paul, 78–90
Adapa, 157–59
African-American Christians, 89n87
afterlife, 164
Akkadian, 139, 154–57, 158
Alexander, Denis, 125–28
Alexander the Great, 138
Alexandria, 73
Alulim, 158
Ammonites, 139

anachronism, 113–14
ancient Near East, 12, 66, 138
Andreasen, Niels-Erik, 159n57
anti-concordism, 107
Anu, 157
Apocrypha, 52, 73
Aristotle, 38, 39, 96, 98, 153
Assur, 155, 157
Assyrians, 139
Athanasius, 84n74
Atrahasis Epic, 141, 143, 147, 151–53, 159
Augustine, 84–85
Averbeck, Richard, 146–47

Babylonians, 139
Barr, James, 46–47, 52–53, 56–59, 161–66
Barrett, C. K., 80, 90n89
Barth, Karl, 39, 40, 130
Baxter, Richard, 13
Beale, Gregory, 44n50, 69
Bechtel, Lyn M., 66n41
Beethoven, Ludwig von, 21
Ben Sira, 74
Berossus, 138, 153, 156, 157
Bible, records public events, 111
Biblical authority, 134–35
Biblical story, 13, 41–49
Biblical Theology movement, 162

Big Bang cosmology, 110n6
Biologos, 14
biology, recent advances in, 12
blessing, 55, 68
Blocher, Henri, 37, 117, 130n52
Bloom, John, 117–18, 119, 122n33
body-soul dualism, 95, 162
Brandon, S. G. F., 31n20
Bruce, F. F., 89–90, 100
Buccelati, Giorgio, 159

Canaanites, 139, 150
Cartesianism, 95
Cassuto, Umberto, 59, 115, 149, 151
chaos, 155, 157
Chesterton, G. K., 103
Childs, Brevard, 147n24
chimpanzees, 118–19
Chomsky, Noam, 98
Christian story, 133–34
Chrysostom, John, 84–85
clean-unclean distinction, 114
Collins, Francis, 12, 14, 26n4, 52n1,
    96–97n6, 118, 128
comfort (in biblical account of Adam and
    Eve), 136
communities, 96
complementarity (science and faith),
    107–8
concordism, 105–7, 116
corruption, 100, 127
covenant representative, 79
crafts, 113, 114, 150
Cranfield, C. E. B., 85, 88
Creation, The (Haydn), 21, 53
creation accounts, 52–66
critical thinking, 15, 20
Crocodile Dundee (film), 151
curse, 41, 55, 64, 92
Cyprian, 84n74

Darwin, Charles, 28n10, 87
Darwinism, 98
Dead Sea Scrolls, 72
death, 62, 83, 136

before the fall, 115–16
    as "natural," 126–27, 162–63
Delitzsch, Franz, 164
deSilva, David A., 73n51
developmentalism, 28, 29n14
discernment, 65
discourse grammar, 25
disobedience, of Adam and Eve, 60–61, 66
DNA, 12, 105, 130
Driver, S. R., 38, 46
Dunn, James, 86, 88

Ea, 157, 158
"eat dust," 64
Ecclesiasticus, 74
Eden, 44, 46, 57, 59, 60, 66, 69, 92, 150
Egyptians, 138, 139, 150
embodiment, and image of God, 96
Emmrich, Martin, 35n30, 60n22
Enlightenment, 40
Enns, Peter, 28–29, 170n4
Enoch, 75, 90
Enuma Elish, 154–57
Ephraem the Syrian, 84n74
Epictetus, 153
Eridu Genesis, 141
etiology, 63
Eusebius, 84n74
Eve. See also Adam and Eve
    name, 62, 125
    as "serpent goddess," 165
evil, 44, 48
evolution, 22, 126
evolutionary creationism, 34
existentialism, 40
exodus, 108–9
expiation, 134

fall, 13, 15–16, 45–47, 51, 61, 67, 69–71, 104,
    120–21, 126, 134
    Barr on, 163
    Lewis on, 130
farming, 113, 123, 125
Fee, Gordon, 80
firstfruits, 80

Fitzmyer, Joseph, 86–87, 88
flood, 123, 143–46
folklore, 62–63, 66
fossils, 116–17
fruitfulness, 69

genealogies, 57, 66, 115
Genesis
    as alternative worldview story, 149
    date of, 167–70
    lack of technical language, 110
    as "mythical," 12
    as "mythic history," 86
    as polemic, 148–49
genetic diversity, 118–19
geological ages, 106
Gilgamesh Epic, 143, 144, 159–60
glorification, 48
Gnosticism, 111n7
God, generosity of, 71
Goheen, Michael, 27
gospel, 30–31
Gospels, 76–78
grammar, 97–98
grieving, 135–36
Gunkel, Hermann, 63–64

Hallo, William, 57
Harlow, Daniel, 36n34, 52n1, 61n27, 107n3,
    170n4
Haydn, Franz Joseph, 21, 53
Hebrews, 90–91
Heidel, Alexander, 46, 145–46, 155n43,
    164
Hendel, Ronald S., 169n3
Herodotus, 138
historical criticism, 17
historical verisimilitude, 60
historicity, 33–34, 66, 80, 90–91, 113
history, 28–41, 49
    Genesis as, 16–17
    and myth, 31–32
Hittites, 138, 139
Hodge, Charles, 106n2
Holocaust, 59n21

Homer, 114
hominids, pre-Adamic, 122, 123
human dignity, 134
human DNA, 12, 105, 130
human fossils, 117
human freedom, 47
human genome, 118–19
Human Genome Project, 12
humans and chimpanzees, common
    ancestry of, 118–19

illegitimate totality transfer, 163n2
image of God, 53, 56, 93–100, 120, 150
imaginary history, 16
imagination, 20
"in Adam," 62, 79–80, 124, 127, 129, 130
"in Christ," 79–80, 127, 129
innocence, 65
interracial marriage, 99
Irenaeus, 45, 65, 82n72, 84

Jacobs, Alan, 39–40
Jesus
    as new Adam, 43
    resurrection of, 48, 78–79, 81, 106, 108
Josephus, 55n10, 72, 73, 75–76
judgment, 90
junk DNA, 118

Kass, Leon, 39–40, 103
Kelly, Douglas, 33
Kidner, Derek, 46, 96, 124–25, 127, 130
Kiel, Yehudah, 70
Kitchen, Kenneth A., 32–33, 57, 140–42,
    145, 147, 149, 155n43, 169–70n3

Ladd, George E., 40
Lambert, W. G., 147–48, 156
Lamoureux, Denis, 34, 115n21
language, 25, 97–99
Layton, Scott, 165
legends, 144, 146
Lemaître, Georges, 110n6
Lessing, Gotthold, 39
Lewis, C. S., 13–14, 17–18, 20, 28, 29n14,

30, 66n40, 79n63, 91, 96n6,
128–30
lexical semantics, 25
life spans, of pre-flood patriarchs, 151
likeness to God, 154
linguistics, 25
literalism, 33–34, 35, 58, 66, 107n3, 115n21
literary genres, 35
literary reading of Scripture, 23–24,
168–69
literary techniques, in Genesis, 16–17
liturgical, creation accounts as, 54
Longacre, Robert, 25
Lucian of Samosata, 100

Macbeth, 29
magic, 62–64, 66
Marduk, 155
marriage, 60
maturation, 65
Maynard Smith, John, 97
McGrath, Gavin Basil, 123
"mere Christianity," 13
"mere historical Adam-and-Eve-ism,"
13–14, 122n31
Mesopotamia, 31, 138, 140–42
Mesopotamian flood tradition, 145
Mesopotamian prehistories, 35, 57–58,
68, 150
Millard, Alan, 58n19, 138n1, 147–48, 153–
54, 155n43, 156
Moabites, 138, 139
moral renovation, 43
moral sense, 120
Mosaic covenant, 66
Mosaic law, 100
Moses, and authorship of Genesis, 167–70
myth, 28–32, 87, 146–47
    Lewis on, 128–29
"mythic history," 86

narratival argument, of Paul, 81, 82, 83,
86, 88
narratives, 24
Nelson, Paul, 111n8
Neolithic age, 113, 123, 125, 127

new Adam, 60, 68
Noah, 57, 68, 75, 90, 114, 123, 159, 163, 164
nostalgia, Kass on, 103

offspring, 68
ordinary human experience, 19, 20–21
Origen, 84n74
original sin, 15–16, 44, 84
Oswalt, John, 31n19

pain, 47–48, 127–28, 135–36
paleoanthropology, 14
Papageorgiou, Panayiotis, 84n74
Pascal, Blaise, 102–3
Paton, John, 101n14
Paul, 48, 78–90
Pentateuch, sources of, 167–68
perishable, 126–127
permanent truths, 103
Pharisees, 72
Philo, 75, 76
Phoenicians, 138, 139
physical death, 62
Pinker, Steven, 97–98
Plantinga, Cornelius, 42, 48–49
Plato, 128
poetry, Aristotle on, 38
polemic, Genesis as, 148–49
polygenesis, 87, 99–100, 121
"population size approaches," 130
prehistory, 57–59, 68, 146
procreation, and image of God, 99
Promised Land, 60
propitiation, 134
prose, 34
protohistory, 57–59, 68, 146, 147
Purtill, Richard, 20, 30–31, 146

Qumran community, 72, 73

racial justice, 89
Raikes, R. L., 144
Rana, Fazale, 122–23
Reasons to Believe, 122–23
redemption, 49, 66, 134

relational view (image of God), 94
representative view (image of God), 94
resemblance view (image of God), 94
restoration, 136
resurrection, 79, 90, 92, 126, 162
Revelation (book of), 91–92
rhetorical and literary techniques, 16–17
Ross, Marcus, 111n8

sacrament, tree as, 65–66
sanctuary, 69, 92
science-faith complementarity, 107–8
scientific theories, changing of, 106
scriptural imagery, 18
Second Temple Judaism, 52, 72–76, 78,
        85, 87, 88
seed, 68
serpent, 64
Shakespeare, William, 29
shalom, 49
Shea, William H., 158n55
showing, vs. telling, 24, 61, 85
Silva, Moisés, 161n1
Simpson, Gaylord, 29
sin, 42, 48–49, 61–62, 100, 134, 135, 165
slavery, 89n87
sociolinguistics, 25
solidarity, 79, 130
        vs. heredity, 124–25
soul
        and image of God, 95
        immortality of, 162
source criticism, 23, 168
special creation, 122, 124
speech act theory, 25
spiritual death, 62, 115, 126, 166
Stek, John, 36n33
Stoics, 89
story
        Aristotle on, 38
        and worldview, 19, 26–27
Stott, John, 88n82, 123–24
"straight" history, 16
suffering, 47–48, 135–36
Sumerian Flood Tale, 141
Sumerian King List, 140–41, 142, 143,
        144, 151

Sumerian language, 138–39, 158
symbolism, of book of Revelation, 92

tabernacle, 60, 69, 92
temple, 60, 69
temptation, 65
Tertullian, 84n74
Theodore of Mopsuestia, 84n74
theology, and everyday life, 21
Thirty-nine Articles, 14n3
Thiselton, Anthony, 80
Tiamat, 155, 157
"timeless truths," 36–37, 38, 39
Tobit, 73
Tolkien, J. R. R., 112
Towner, W. Sibley, 44–47, 61n27
tree of life, 64–65, 72, 91, 92
tree of the knowledge of good and evil,
        64–65
typology, in Paul, 82

Uan, 157
Ugaritians, 138, 139
unity, of human race in Adam, 51, 89,
        124, 150
universal human experiences, 100–104,
        120
Ur of the Chaldeans, 140
Utnapishtim, 143, 159–60

Vasholz, Robert I., 71
Vawter, Bruce, 45
violence, 61

Waltke, Bruce K., 97n6, 121n30
Walton, John, 31n20, 58n20, 108n5, 139n4
Ward, Keith, 47
Weinfeld, Moshe, 54n7
Wenham, Gordon, 36n33, 43n47, 127, 151,
        164, , 169n2, 170n6
Westermann, Claus, 61n28, 67
Westminster Confession of Faith, 14n3
wisdom, and story, 27n8
Wisdom of Solomon, 73
Wise, Kurt, 34n27

Wolters, Albert, 27
Woolley, Leonard, 143
work, 150
world picture, vs. worldview, 134
worldview
    in Bible, 111n8
    and biblical story, 13
    and story, 19, 26–27, 28, 33, 37
    vs. world picture, 134

Wright, Christopher, 26n6, 43, 60n23
Wright, N. T., 26n6, 32n22, 79, 81–82,
    87–88, 111n7, 127

young earth creationism, 17, 33, 111n8, 122

Zechariah, 77
Ziusudra, 141, 143, 159

SCRIPTURE AND APOCRYPHA INDEX

Old Testament

Genesis

1	4n28, 54, 55, 75, 76, 93, 110, 148, 155
1–2	13, 52, 77, 95, 141
1–3	65, 71, 78, 112
1–4	104, 112
1–5	55, 66, 67, 68, 69, 90, 112, 168
1–11	32, 33, 36, 57, 58, 59, 68, 108, 109, 113, 114, 140, 141, 142, 149, 154, 168, 169, 170
1:1	156
1:1–2:3	52, 53, 54, 55, 149, 168, 169
1:1–2:4	168
1:2	155, 157
1:2–2:3	156
1:3	156
1:16	148
1:24–31	54
1:26	56, 94
1:26–27	93–94, 154
1:26–31	55
1:27	53, 76, 94, 124
1:28	54, 55, 68, 124
1:28–29	61
1:31	54
2	54, 55, 65, 75, 76, 82, 100
2–3	35n30, 37, 55, 59, 62, 69
2–4	55, 123, 125, 168
2–5	55
2:2–3	67
2:4	168
2:4–7	53, 54
2:4–25	52, 53, 54, 56
2:4–4:26	56
2:5	56
2:7	53, 56, 56n11, 75, 82, 152, 154
2:8–9	61
2:15–17	95
2:16–17	71
2:17	62, 63, 115, 165
2:18	56, 57
2:18–25	61
2:19	54n8
2:20	55, 56n11
2:20–28	82
2:21–23	60
2:23–25	60
2:24	60, 67, 76
2:25	55
2:35–41	82
3	25, 44, 46, 53n2, 55, 61, 64, 68, 69, 70, 74, 83, 85, 85n76, 86, 110, 115, 116, 127, 141, 160, 162, 163, 164, 165, 166
3–5	105, 111
3:1	64n36
3:4	63
3:8	60
3:8–13	62
3:10–13	60
3:11	61, 165
3:14	64
3:14–19	55, 60, 64
3:15	68, 85n76
3:16	55, 128
3:16–19	127n46
3:17	56n11, 71
3:17–19	85n76
3:18	128

3:19	70, 115	12:2–3	68	24	170
3:20	56, 62, 62n30,	12:3	79n62	24:1–4	76
	125	12:7	68	34:7	151
3:22	65	13:10	69		
4	55, 57, 60, 61,	13:15–16	68	**Joshua**	
	85n76, 111, 112,	15:3	68	3:16	71
	113, 114, 120,	15:5	68	24:29	151
	124, 125, 127	17:7–9	68		
4–5	91, 99, 115, 141	17:19	68	**Judges**	
4:1	56	17:20	68	11:24	137
4:3–4	114n18	18:18	79n62		
4:8	77	22:17–18	68	**1 Samuel**	
4:11	55, 69	22:18	79n62	13:19–22	150
4:14	111, 112n12,	24:60	68	17	38
	124	25:7	151	17:4	38
4:15	112	26:3–4	68	17:8–10	38
4:17	112, 113, 124	26:4	79n62	**1 Kings**	
4:17–22	113	26:24	68	6:1	109
4:17–24	150	28:3	68	8:41–43	100
4:20–22	114	28:14	68	8:46	70
4:25	55, 56n11, 68	37:20	112n12		
5	55, 57, 68, 113,	37:33	112n12	**1 Chronicles**	
	168	41:57	152	1:1	66
5:1–2	56	48:4	68		
5:1–3	55, 99	50:26	151	**2 Chronicles**	
5:1–5	56			24:20–22	77n57
5:4	113	**Exodus**			
5:32	57	1:11	169	**Job**	
6–9	123, 141, 168	4:3	64n36	31:33	71
6:5	152	7:10–12	64, 64n36		
6:11	152	20:11	67	**Psalms**	
6:18–19	68			8	67
7:2	114	**Leviticus**		33:9	157
7:3	152	1:4	42	50:7–15	152
7:8	114	4:20	42	72	68
7:11	144	5:16	42	72:9	64
8:9	152	11	114	72:17	68
8:20	114	19:9–18	150	87	100
9:1	68	20:24–26	114	90:10	151
9:6	95, 99			104	67
9:8–17	68	**Numbers**		105:26–38	34n29
9:29	151	22	63		
10–11	168	22:28	63	**Proverbs**	
11	68	35:9–34	112	3:18	65, 72
11:1–9	168			11:30	65, 72
11:10–26	57, 151	**Deuteronomy**		13:12	65, 72
11:27–31	140	1:28	150	15:4	65, 72
12–50	60n24, 106	1:39	65	20:9	70
12:1–3	43, 55, 59	4:5–8	100	31:1–9	44n49
		6:14	137	**Ecclesiastes**	
		17:14	137	3:20	70
				7:20	70

7:29	70	**Mark**		15:49	43
12:7	70	7:19	114	15:50	126, 127
		10:2–9	76	15:56	48
Isaiah		10:6	77n55		
2:1–5	100	10:45	47	**2 Corinthians**	
49:23	64	12:18–34	72	7:2	127
51:3	69			11:3	78
		Luke			
Ezekiel		2:22	84n74	**Galatians**	
14:14	114n17	3:38	66	3:28	89, 90
14:20	114n17	11:51	77	6:8	127
28:11–19	69, 70n46				
28:13	69	**John**		**Ephesians**	
28:16	69	1:1	78	4:22	127
31:8–9	69	8:44	63, 77	4:24	43, 95
31:16	69	11:25–26	135		
31:18	69			**Colossians**	
36:35	69	**Acts**		1:15	43
		10:9–29	114	3:10	43, 95
Daniel		17:18	89	3:11	89, 90
6:24	138	17:25	88		
		17:26	78, 88, 100	**1 Timothy**	
Hosea		17:30–31	90	2:13	123
2:8–13	71	23:6–9	72	2:13–14	78
5:7	71	26:26	111	4:4	80
6:7	70, 71n49				
6:10	71	**Romans**		**Hebrews**	
7:15	71	1:1–6	78	11	90, 91
11:1–4	71	4:25	84	11:2	91
13:4–6	71	5:12	83n73, 85, 89	11:4–7	90
		5:12–19	78, 82	11:40	91
Joel		8:18–25	127n46		
2:3	69	8:29	43	**James**	
		15:5–7	100	3:9	95
Micah					
7:17	64	**1 Corinthians**		**1 Peter**	
		11:7–12	78	1:19	42
Habakkuk		15	78, 127		
1:12–13	48	15:2–23	79	**1 John**	
		15:3–8	78	3:8	78
Malachi		15:6	106		
2:15	67	15:12–58	81	**Revelation**	
		15:14–17	135	2:7	65, 72, 91
New Testament		15:17	83	7:9	100
		15:20–23	78, 79	12:9	63, 91
Matthew		15:21	79	20:2	63, 91
12:11	72	15:21–22	48	20:14	92
19:3–9	76	15:22	79	21–22	69
19:4	76, 77n55	15:23	48	21:1–4	91
19:4–5	76	15:26	48	21:1–8	44, 48
19:5	76	15:42–49	78, 81, 82	21:3	92
19:7	76	15:45	82	21:4	92
19:8	76			22:1–5	91–92
23:35	77			22:2	65, 72, 91
				22:14	65, 72, 91

22:14–15   92
22:19   65, 72, 91

Apocrypha

2 Esdras
3:4–11   75n53
3:21–22   75n53

Sanhedrin
4:5   101

Sirach
14:17   74
15:14   74

17:1   74
25:16–26   74
25:24   74
26:1–4   74
26:13–18   74
33:10   74
40:1   74
44–49   75
44:1   75
49:13   75
49:14–15   75
49:16   75

Tobit
8:6   73

Wisdom
1:13   63
1:13–14   74
2:23–24   74
2:24   63, 77, 83n73
7:1   74
10:1   74